What's Your I.Q.?*

*Involvement Quotient

Y0-CIC-524

1. When standing and delivering a 45-minute sermon to my high school students I know they are learning because :

   A. My golden-throated oratory keeps them on the edge of their seats.

   B. Their glassy-eyed stares are only a thin disguise to hide the fact that my message is causing deep inner conviction.

   C. They say "amen" in their sleep.

   D. My class is shrinking (probably due to the Holy Spirit weeding out those who aren't really serious about their faith).

2. My students would rather not be involved in heavy Bible study because:

   A. It's more fun to see me perform.

   B. They prefer reconstituted spiritual food to fresh.

   C. They might have to put themselves in a vulnerable position.

   D. You can't daydream and be involved in learning at the same time.

   E. They might actually *enjoy* the class.

3. Bible learning activities are best for:

   A. Time-killers.

   B. Four to six year olds.

   C. "Professional" educators.

   D. "Unprofessional" educators.

As you have probably guessed, the teaching materials in this book emphasize involvement learning. Based on studies of people's retention of information, we at the Light Force believe that students will learn more about God's Word and remember it longer if they explore it and discover what it means themselves—with the guidance of a teacher. Therefore this book is full of ideas that will help you help your students explore the Bible and have their hearts and lives affected by what they find.

Please feel free to pick and choose. Use the ideas that work best with your particular group of students; substitute ideas of your own where our suggestions are not as appropriate in your situation. It is our prayer that the learning experiences suggested in this book, coupled with the power of God's Word, will challenge and motivate your students—and maybe even stir up those who have grown complacent in their spiritual lives.

You may find that doing the best job with meaningful Bible study will mean that some less essential activities need to be reduced, shifted to another time, or even eliminated. For example, announcements can be printed in advance and handed out to students or posted in the room. You might consider singing fewer songs to allow more time for the study of God's Word. In some churches, Sunday School students are encouraged to contribute their offering during the worship service. Or offering plates may be placed at the classroom door for students to use without taking extra time during the Bible study session. Such ideas may be unfamiliar to some, but most would agree that the purpose of the Bible study time is to grow in God's Word and to accomplish that, we must make Bible study a priority.

Keep in mind that some students may feel uncomfortable being participants rather than spectators, especially if the idea is new to them. But ultimately participants have more enjoyment and reap more benefits than those who are merely waiting to be entertained. The difference will show up in lives that have become equipped to live God's Word.

How to Get the Most from This Course

Nobody knows your students as you do. No one has the grasp of their interest level, needs, maturity, and spiritual awareness that you have as their leader. Your students are unique. They are different from the young people in the church down the street. Because of this you need to be able to create lessons that meet the real needs of your students by introducing them in a fresh new way to the timeless truths of God.

The Light Force Living Word Curriculum is designed to help you do just that. The book you are holding is a tool which you can use to build a learning experience that will influence your students for eternity.

The book itself consists of two parts: the Teacher's Manual section, which gives you directions for the thirteen sessions of the course; and the Student Guide section, which provides reproducible worksheets and other materials for use with your group both in class and out. Let's take a closer look at these tools and how they may be used.

Teacher's Manual Section: Contains complete instructions and Bible resource material for thirteen sessions. Each session contains the Key Verse, Biblical Basis, Focus, Aims, Teacher's Bible Study and session teaching plan. The Teacher's Bible Study provides you with the background information you need for presenting the session material. Each Session Plan gives you two options for the **Approach** (to catch students' interest), the **Bible Exploration** (to examine the Scripture and its meaning for life today), and the **Conclusion and Decision** (to guide students in making personal application of the Bible truths of the session).

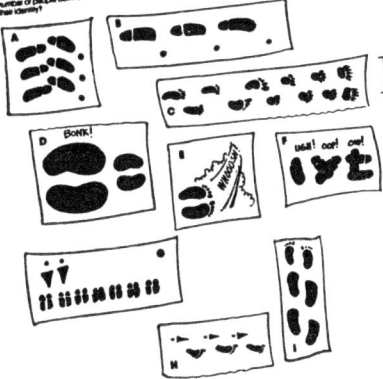

Walking in God's Light

Walking as Jesus Did
Winter #3

Footsteps

Study the footprints below. These footprints belong to a number of people both real and fictional. Can you guess their identity?

A

B

C

D BONK!

E WHOOOSH!

F ouch! oof! ow!

G

H

The Scripture listed below contain examples of characteristic the verse(s) describe.

Matthew 15:32 and Luke 7:13

Mark 10:43-45

Mark 12:28-31

John 13:14,15

John 15:12

Romans 6:2

Ephesians 4:32 and Colossians 3:13

Student Guide Section: This is the feature that allows you to customize this course. It is a reproducible tool you can use any way you like. You can use it as-is or you can cut it up. (See more detailed instructions in the paragraphs that follow.) Its basic intent is to involve your students in searching the Scripture, thinking about it, interpreting it and applying it to their personal lives. Think of the **Student Guide Section** as a resource to make your job easier and more effective.

Here are some ways it can be used:

Use It As-Is: The **Student Guide** pages are designed so you can simply pop them out of the book (they are perforated) and make the necessary number of copies on a copy machine. Prepare enough for your students and a few for visitors.

You can save time by preparing in advance all of the **Student Guide** copies you will need for the course. If limited time is a problem for you, many quick-print shops will copy the pages for a modest price while you are at work or shopping.

You can vary the look of the pages a little by using colored paper—perhaps a different color for each session.

If you use a copy machine at church, or if the office staff makes the **Student Guide** copies for you, you may wish to coordinate your plans with those of other teachers using this course, thereby avoiding a duplication of effort.

Cut It Up: The **Student Guide** design allows you to cut it up and customize it any way you wish. Note that the pages are printed on one side only to allow for this. The material is copyrighted, but permission is hereby given for you to use and copy the **Student Guide** pages as you wish. (**This does not apply to the Teacher's Manual section.**) Be creative! Use the material selectively. Zero in on what works with *your* students. Keep them guessing as to what will come their way at each session—not expecting a "canned" lesson. (See "How to Customize the Student Guide" for helpful ideas on cutting and pasting for reproduction.)

Something Extra: In the **Student Guide** section you will find a number of pages that have absolutely nothing to do with the lessons in the Teacher's Manual section. These are for fun. You may use them in your mailouts to your youth group, in church bulletins, on flyers, etc. Use some of the design elements to create stationery or postcards for your group. Use the cartoons to liven up your **Student Guide** pages.

In some courses in the Light Force Living Word Curriculum series you will find questionnaires and surveys designed to help you get to know and understand your students. You can modify these to fit your own tastes and needs. In other courses you will find special mailouts and flyers to help you communicate with parents and students.

Make Something of It: The people at the Light Force want to encourage you to make the time with your students the most profitable time they spend all week. Use the material in this manual to give you ideas, input and guidance—to spark your thinking. We pray that your ministry to your students may be effective for eternity through your use of the tools within this book.

How to Customize the Student Guide Sheets

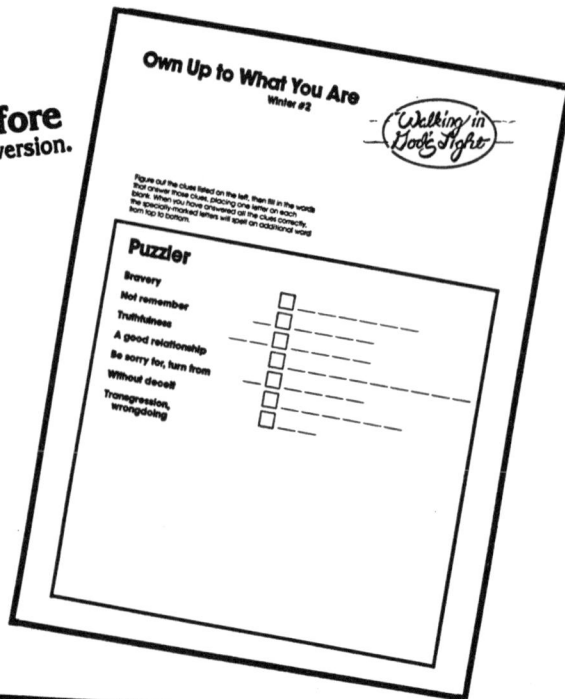

The **Student Guide** pages in this book are there for you to use any way you wish. You can use them as-is, as described in the article "How to Get the Most from This Course." Or you can cut them up and make them your own.

Most students appreciate change. If you have a generous mix of printed **Student Guide** pages, illustrations of your choice, and activities revised and rewritten in your own handwriting, you can make your **Student Guide** always fresh and customized to meet the particular needs of your students.

Cutting and pasting is very easy. All you need is paper, a pair of scissors and a glue stick or a bottle of rubber cement. Decide what activities you want to use from the **Student Guide** section. Pull the appropriate pages out of this book at the perforations. Cut out the part of the page that you wish to use and glue it to a blank sheet of paper. Take the resulting page(s) to a copy machine and make the number of copies you need.

If you want to produce **Student Guide** pages with a more professional look, you will need some of the following simple tools:

- Blank white paper
- Rubber cement
- Scissors or a sharp utility knife (such as an X-Acto knife)
- Correction fluid or white artists' tape
- A small T-square
- Several black felt-tip pens (different point sizes for different thicknesses of lettering).

Start by deciding what activities you want to use from the **Student Guide** section. Pull the appropriate pages out of this book. Use the scissors or utility knife to cut out the part of the page that you wish to use.

Using a small amount of rubber cement, glue the **Student Guide** section to the blank paper. Use the T-square to make sure the lettering is straight: Place the "T" part of the square at the side edge of the paper and use the ruler portion as a guide. Do this before the rubber cement has a chance to dry. Of course, you may wish to place sections of the **Student Guide** at an angle for variety in your design.

After getting the **Student Guide** segment placed correctly, lightly rub off any excess rubber cement with your fingers or with an eraser.

Add any questions or comments you wish to include in the **Student Guide** section, using a black felt-tip pen. For headlines and instructions, a thicker pen will produce heavier letters.

When all the desired wording is in place, add cartoons or illustrations. Use those in this book or others to which you have access.

After
Yours might look like this.

Take your completed original to a copy machine and make as many copies as you will need for the class session. You may wish to use colored paper for added interest.

Note: Some copy machines are so sensitive that they may pick up a "cut line" on things you have pasted up. To avoid this, use correction fluid or white artists' tape around the edges of your pasted-down segments.

To add further interest to your **Student Guide** sheets, try using various paper sizes. Many copiers take paper in several

sizes. Experiment with different sizes in order to maximize your writing space. Or use one side for the **Student Guide** material and the other side for announcements of things to come. (Written instead of verbal announcements save much valuable time for study of the lesson.) Most copiers enable you to print on both sides of the paper.

Keep your eyes open for newer copiers that print in color. You can use felt pens, wrapping paper or other sources to make borders, colorful headlines or other special effects.

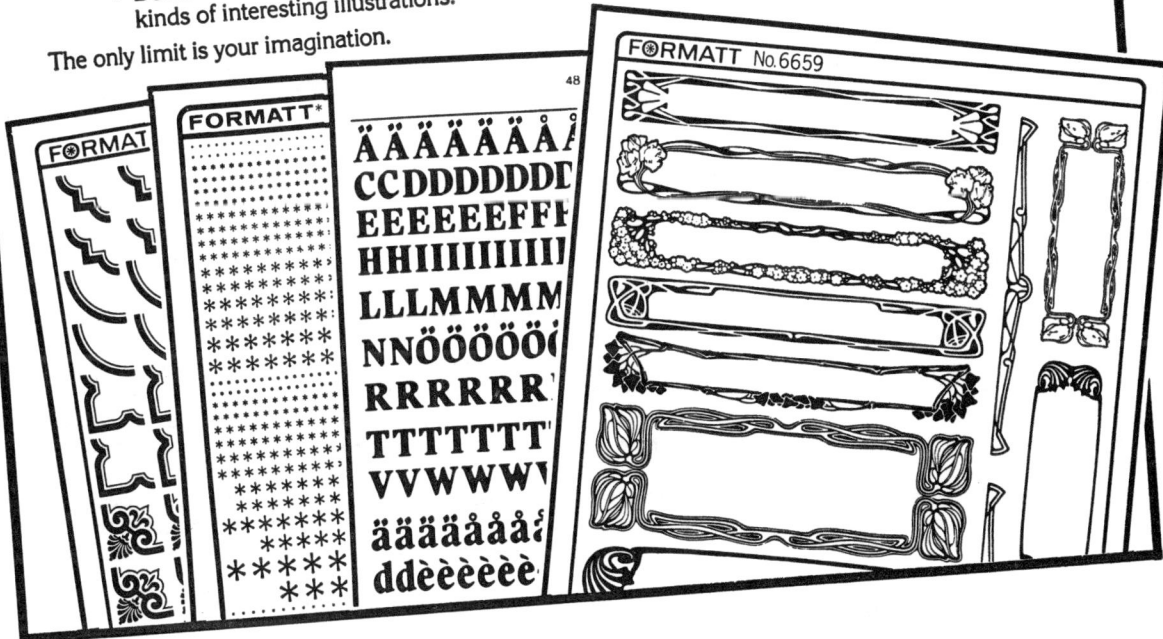

For added "class," see your local art store for some of the following helps:
- Rub-on and stick-on letters, borders and symbols to use for added fun and interest on the Student Guide sheets
- Clip-art libraries (be careful to copy only things that are copyright-free or intended for copying)
- Dover Books publishes many reproducible books with all kinds of interesting illustrations.

The only limit is your imagination.

Presenting Christ to High School Students

How do you present Christ to high school students? Here are some suggestions.

1. Pray. Ask God to prepare each young person to receive the message of salvation and to prepare you to present it.

2. Lay the foundation. High school students are evaluating you and the Lord you serve by everything you do and say. They are looking for people who show a living, growing relationship with God. They are looking for people in whose lives knowing God makes a noticeable difference. And they are looking for people who love them and listen to them as God loves them and listens to them.

Learn to listen with your full attention. Learn to share openly both the joys and the struggles you encounter as a Christian. Be honest about your own questions and about your personal concern for students. Learn to accept teenagers as they are. Christ died for them while they were yet sinners. You are called to love them as they are.

3. Be aware of opportunities. Students *might* come forward after a lesson that deals with salvation, or ask for an appointment to talk after class. However, it is more likely that they will wait for *you* to suggest getting together. Try inviting a student out for a soft drink; you will then have some time alone together in which you can share what Jesus means to you.

4. Don't buttonhole students. Don't lecture them or force the issue. Here are some tips to keep in mind:

a. Put the student at ease. Be perceptive of his or her feelings. Remember that the student is probably nervous. Be relaxed, natural and casual in your conversation; don't be critical or judgmental.

b. Get the student to talk while you listen carefully. Young people will sometimes throw out superficial or shocking statements just to get your reaction. Don't begin lecturing or problem-solving. Instead encourage the person to keep talking.

c. Be gently direct. Do not overpower the student with demands from the gospel. But make no apologies either. God does not need to be defended and neither does His truth. Remember that students may have trouble bringing up spiritual matters. If you sense this, a simple question like, "How are you and God getting along?" can unlock a life-changing conversation.

d. Using a booklet that outlines the plan of salvation can be helpful. Move through the points slowly enough to allow time for the student to think and comprehend. But do not drag out the presentation unnecessarily.

e. Make sure the student understands how to accept Christ. If you feel that he or she understands, ask if he or she would like to accept Christ now. If the answer is affirmative, ask the student to pray with you. Explain that praying is simply talking to God. We can be natural with Him and simply tell Him our needs and our thoughts. In this case the student may tell God of his or her need for Christ and desire to have Him as Lord and Saviour.

Suggest that the new Christian begin growing in the faith. You may wish to suggest some Scripture in an easy-to-read translation of the Bible or a study manual suited to the age and maturity level of the student. (You may want to visit your local Christian supplier to see what is available.)

If the student is not ready to make a decision to accept Christ, suggest some passages of Scripture to read, such as John 14—16; Romans 3—8; or the brief Gospel of Mark. Make sure the student has a Bible or New Testament in an easy-to-read translation. (If he or she does not, you might want to lend or give an appropriate copy.) Remember to pray for the student as he or she gives further consideration to the gospel message.

5. Remember: Your responsibility is simply to present the gospel and to be able to explain the hope that is within you. It is the Holy Spirit who makes the heart ready for a relationship with God.

How to Use the Paperback

Walking in God's Light is the Regal paperback book that accompanies this course. It was written by Jim Larson, Ph.D., a former youth director and pastor who is now working as a marriage and family counselor. The book will give your students added insight into the meaning of 1 John and how to apply its teachings.

Here are several ways you and your students may want to use this text:

• At-home study resource to prepare students for the weekly class session,

• At-home study resource to reinforce material studied in class,

• Midweek Bible study sessions—additional study material following weekly class session theme,

• Valuable and economical addition to each student's personal library.

As a teacher, you will find the paperback text an essential part of your preparation for teaching this course. Material in the book provides readable, nontechnical resources for your study of 1 John. Thought-provoking and discussion-prompting questions follow each chapter, providing you and your students with tools to pursue a deeper knowledge of God's Word. The writings of John come alive with clear and practical applications for twentieth-century living.

Your students may be more likely to obtain and use the book if you make it available in class. You may wish to purchase copies and give them or resell them to students; or arrange with a Christian supplier to give you the books on consignment so you can return unused copies.

The objective of the Light Force Living Word Curriculum is to help the teacher and the student "in all things grow up into . . . Christ" (Eph. 4:15). Encourage each of your students to use the paperback text. It is one of the practical tools designed to help them accomplish this goal.

Discipleship I

This all-new course provides a 6-week adventure in the disciplines in Christian living. Leaders looking for a course that is geared to today's youth while providing a challenge to their more motivated students will find this study fits their needs.

Discipleship I is just the first of a series on this subject. Soon to follow will be two more discipleship courses—each leading students to greater heights of Christian maturity as their understanding of this important subject expands.

Great for growth groups, camps or retreats.

Course materials:

☐ *Leader's Workbook* contains leader's copy of student workbook as well as complete session plans and helpful background articles. Order one for each teacher.

☐ *Student Workbook* gives kids the perfect opportunity to record their spiritual odyssey toward greater Christian discipline and maturity. This book will then become a permanent, personalized reference tool. Order one for each student.

INTERNATIONAL CENTER FOR LEARNING

The Youth Worker's

CLIP ART BOOK

A truly helpful addition to your church office!

The Youth Worker's Clip Art Book gives you hundreds of drawings, charts, forms, and stories that a youth worker can clip out and glue together into a nearly infinite array of attractive and exciting mail outs, posters, greeting cards, and the like. Most of all, it's time saving, and it's fun!

Features:

• Tons of illustrations by four talented Christian artists. You'll find appropriate illustrations to advertise at least a year's worth of your group's activities, special events, and regular meetings.

• Page after page of stationery, greeting cards, and ideas designed particularly for today's youth worker.

• "Spiritual Vitamins." Twelve short stories and object lessons to include in your mail outs.

• Medical release forms, comment cards, attendance cards, prayer charts, Bible study charts, and many more very useful forms.

• Clear and concise instructions for use, and a special section that tells you how to deal with your local printer.

All this and more!

Fill out and return this order blank to your local church supply store, or mail to:

GOSPEL LIGHT PUBLICATIONS
P.O. Box 6309
Oxnard, CA 93031

Your Name _____

Your Title _____

Church Name _____

Church Address _____

_____

_____

Church Phone _____

ORDER BLANK

QTY.	ITEM	CODE	PRICE	AMOUNT
	Discipleship I Leader's Workbook Available September 1984	EL115	6.99	
	Discipleship I Student Workbook Available September 1984	EL111	4.99	
	Youth Worker's Clip Art Book Available October 1984	T5077	12.95	

Living in the Light

UNIT FOCUS

This study of 1 John begins with a unit which examines some of the basic characteristics and benefits of a Christian life-style.

Session 1

Get with It, Gang
Biblical Basis: 1 John 1:1-4
Focus: Fellowship and joy are important parts of the experience God has for His children. Christianity should be characterized by the joy that comes from knowing Christ.

Session 2

Own Up to What You Are
Biblical Basis: 1 John 1:5-10
Focus: Repentence, confession, and forgiveness are important to our relationship with the Lord. Our confession allows God to forgive and cleanse us of our sin.

Session 3

Walking as Jesus Did
Biblical Basis: 1 John 2:1-14
Focus: Christians are called to walk in obedience to God's Word. We can do this by adopting the traits and life-style of Jesus Christ.

Session 4

Get Your Priorities Together
Biblical Basis: 1 John 2:15-17
Focus: Christians are to be transformed by God, not molded by the world. We must examine our lives in the light of Scripture in order to be sure that those things which are important to us are from God and not the world.

Unit Aims

You and your students will have accomplished the purpose of this unit if you can:
- DESCRIBE characteristics and benefits of a Christian life-style.
- IDENTIFY ways Christian characteristics may be demonstrated in believers' lives today.
- CONSIDER areas of your lives where you need to grow in Christian characteristics.

Get with It, Gang

KEY VERSE
"We proclaim to you what we have seen and heard, so that you also may have fellowship with us. And our fellowship is with the Father and with his Son, Jesus Christ. We write this to make our joy complete." 1 John 1:3,4

BIBLICAL BASIS
1 John 1:1-4

FOCUS OF THE SESSION
Fellowship with God through Jesus Christ leads to joy.

AIMS OF THIS SESSION
You and your students will have accomplished the purpose of this Bible study session if you can:
- DEFINE fellowship and joy and EXAMINE in the Bible the relationship between them;
- COMPARE AND CONTRAST attitudes and actions that foster or prohibit fellowship and joy.
- DETERMINE some steps you will take to further build your relationship with Christ.

TEACHER'S BIBLE STUDY

John, the Author

The first Epistle of John is a beautiful letter conveying a message of love and concern from a pastor (or "shepherd") to a group of believers he knew and cared about. The letter does not begin with greetings to the recipients and an identification of the sender as do many other Epistles in the New Testament. It is most commonly agreed that the apostle John, the son of Zebedee, wrote this letter along with 2 and 3 John, the Gospel of John, and Revelation.

The writer of the Epistle clearly claimed that he was an eyewitness of Christ. He supported his message by presenting evidence of his personal experience: "That which was from the beginning, which we have heard, which we have seen with our eyes, which we have looked at and our hands have touched—this we proclaim concerning the Word of life" (1 John 1:1). He verified the truth of his words by describing the involvement of his senses. This statement makes it clear that the author knew Jesus Christ personally. When he wrote of our Lord, he was not relying on hearsay evidence but on his own experiences.

Consider some of the distinctive features of John's writings. He expressed his intense love for Christ and his intolerance of heresy. Several key words and thoughts in particular are unique to John's writing. The use of the term **logos** (the Word) as applied to our Lord occurs in his writings alone (see John 1:1,14; 1 John 1:1; Rev. 19:13). Another expression common to John is **"have no sin."** Other parts of Scripture speak of committing sin but not of having it (see John 9:41; 15:22,24; 19:11, *KJV*). John implied that sin is inherent in us and is a part of us. In comparison, he wrote of Christ, "in Him is no sin" (1 John 3:5). In numerous other instances the author of the Gospel and the Epistle used **opposites** extensively: light and darkness, life and death, love and hate, truth and falsehood, people who know God and people who do not know God.

John, the Pastor

The emphasis within 1 John seems to indicate that through the years John's character had mellowed and deepened, allowing him to speak with sincere conviction about the Christian experience. John addressed his loving exhortations to his "little children" (2:12, *KJV*) and exhibited tender, compassionate care for his readers. The Epistle can be a guide and resource for our own teaching of those we love and are concerned about.

The Epistle was probably written about 90 A.D. in Ephesus, where John spent the closing years of his life. It was most likely written to be circulated among several churches in order to address the situations John observed. At the beginning of the second century, Ephesus was like many of our cities today. It was a port city and a crossroads for trade. It was a cosmopolitan city, with people of many different cultures passing through or living in it. There were Jews, with their worship of the one God. There were Christians. There were people who worshiped many different pagan gods. In some ways it must have been an exciting place, bubbling with the different ideas and languages of the varied people who were passing through or who called it home.

But along with the excitement there were problems. As the various religions bumped up against one another, there was a tendency to merge them, to say, "I'll add your god to my collection of gods, and you add mine to yours." But the Jewish and Christian faiths would have none of this, and so they became the targets of hostility.

As the years went by, living in such a culture took its toll on the Christians. John identified negative characteristics he saw in these early followers of Christ. As you examine these characteristics you will find some marked similarities between believers then and believers today.

• **The newness of Christianity had worn off.** John observed second and third generation Christians who were without the spark and excitement of those who had received Christ as their Saviour during His earthly ministry. The thrill of the first days had, at least to some extent, faded. Christ knew human nature, and had said, "the love of most will grow cold" (Matt. 24:12). Christianity had become a tradition, observed half-heartedly and at times only out of habit. It was treated with easy familiarity and often without enthusiasm.

• **Christians were no longer adhering to God's standards for their lives.** They were compromising on their ethics in order to remain comfortable. They had little regard for the high standards of Christ that were established to set His followers apart from the world (see John 15:19). This description characterizes our society today: a definite decline in ethics and morals taught in God's Word, leading to a point where people establish their own standards.

• **Gnosticism (a cult claiming a superior knowledge) threatened the church from within.** John wasn't concerned with persecution from outside, but rather the subtle seduction from self-appointed innovators inside the church. The Gnostics talked of being born of God, of walking in the light, of having no sin, of dwelling in God, and of knowing God. John used the same language to instruct the Christian believers in the "truth" (see 1 John 1:6-8). The Gnostics did not intend to destroy the church, they intended to make Christianity an intellectually respectable philosophy. Through their own methods, they wanted to purge the church. They were attempting to change Christianity in order to improve it.

The Gnostics believed that all matter was evil and only spirit was good. They therefore denied the incarnation—the biblical teaching that God the Son became a man. Jesus was truly God and truly human—God in the flesh. This doctrine is central to the Christian faith, so the Gnostic denial of it was particularly dangerous. John devoted a good bit of his letter to affirming the truths of the gospel. He was not teaching new truths but instead was reminding his readers of what they already knew. It was the Gnostics who were attempting to initiate teachings that opposed the biblical message. John's desire and purpose as a pastor was to protect the dear ones he loved and to establish them in their Christian faith.

John, the Eyewitness

People are often not interested in others' opinions, since they are satisfied with their own. John earned his right to speak by sharing from personal experience. He had been an involved participant in what he wanted to share about Jesus. In case his readers doubted that the body of Jesus was real, he could assure them of His reality. John was telling the first century Gnostics—and people today—that he was not sharing a theory. He was talking about a Person he knew, whose life was brought out into the open where people could see it (see 1 John 1:2).

John's eyewitness account involved knowing Christ through his senses. He had opportunity to hear and see Him. From the Greek verbs John used we learn that although the action was in the past tense it had continuing results. An expanded translation of 1 John 1:1 reads, "that which we have heard with the present result that it is ringing in our ears, that which we have discerningly seen with our eyes with the present result that it is in our mind's eye . . . " (Wuest). John had experienced the man Jesus.

John continued by emphasizing the ways he looked at Jesus. It was no mere gaze. The Greek root for the word John used is the same as for the word "theater." It is the kind of intent gaze that involves steady, deliberate concentration. **John was saying that for three years the apostles gazed upon Christ intently in order to study and investigate Him.**

In addition, John didn't gaze from a distance; he was up close, he actually touched Jesus Christ. The opportunity to physically touch Jesus impressed on his mind beyond a doubt that this was a real man.

Jesus wants us to believe in Him even though we don't have His physical body here to convince us. He told Thomas, often referred to as the doubting disciple, "Blessed are those who have not seen and yet have believed" (John 20:29). We can neither see or touch Him today, but we need to allow Jesus to be real in our lives so that His reality is apparent to those we influence.

Yet, we need to do more than just hear and see. Our hearing needs to be for the purpose of truly listening to our Lord. Our seeing must be a concentrated gaze at our Saviour and an intense investigation of a world in need of Him. Young people are searching for answers—often in the wrong places. They want evidence and proof that Christ is everything we say He is. As teachers and leaders we have the opportunity to present a Jesus we have seen, heard, and experienced by faith. High schoolers can respond favorably to a Jesus they have seen proven real before them through teachers, leaders, and parents. You can demonstrate Christ's reality

in the way you relate to your students. Try to make time this week to accomplish one or more of the following:

• Send notes and cards acknowledging visitors or absent members, or encouraging regular attendees.

• Spend time at an activity one or more of your students is involved in such as a football game, skating or a school play or concert.

• Plan an outing or party for your students.

A good way to develop an ongoing relationship is to develop an appointment calendar and schedule a time to meet with each student, either alone or in twos or threes.

Fellowship Leads to Joy

John felt compelled to make his experience with Christ available to everyone (see 1 John 1:3). He wanted his readers to share in the fellowship he knew. Fellowship involves a sharing between two or more people who have something in common. **Christian fellowship is a partnership with Christ and therefore is available to those who have united with God through faith in His Son (see John 17:21-23).** God wants us as partners and companions. When we become His children, He invites us to share in all that He is.

Fellowship with Christ implies that we jointly participate with Him. It is a process of getting to know Jesus Christ better and better. Christ is a Person we should want to learn about and spend time with, one worthy of our quality communication.

It may be difficult for some high schoolers to understand how to have a relationship with someone they cannot see, hear, or touch. Guide them in understanding that **they can get to know Christ better through reading the Bible**—a tangible object that might be considered His love letter to us. **They can get to know Him better by talking to Him in prayer.** Prayer can be sharing their hearts, rejoicing in the beautiful world God has made, adoring Him for His very nature. It can also take the form of specific requests. As students see what God does (or does not do) in response to requests, they get to know Him better. They begin to learn what is important to Him and what is less important to Him. For example, many Christians have found that He responded promptly to a need when a family was without food. But He may not choose to indulge our wants and desires for things that are not really needs.

In addition to time spent privately with our Lord, time spent with other Christians will help us develop our relationship with our Lord. As we get together and share our insights about God, we help each other get to know Him better. And, of course, we also build our relationships with one another. Fellowship among Christians means that we are united in love because of our common partnership with Christ. As it is used among Christians today, fellowship usually means sharing friendly social conversation, food, and maybe some singing. But John's use of the word implies sharing the things of Christ, using opportunities together to talk about God and His Word. It is a unique way for Christians to participate in each other's lives.

In addition, although fellowship with God and with one another is basically spiritual, it extends into practical applications as well. The Greek word *koinonia* that is translated to mean fellowship in 1 John can also mean communicating, sharing, contributing, and distributing. It involves sharing with others what we are and what we have.

In 1 John 1:3,4, John explains that fellowship between God, His Son, and His children ultimately leads the way to joy. And not just a little joy, but the fullness of joy, overflowing and abundant (see Rom. 15:13). Peter describes this joy as glorious and inexpressible (see 1 Pet. 1:8).

True Christianity is to be characterized by joy. Let's take a moment to define the word, since it is so important. **Joy means delight and exultation. In the Christian context it is not merely an emotion, such as happiness, but a character quality produced by the Holy Spirit. It is not affected by circumstances; in fact, joy may exist in spite of or even as a result of suffering.** Although we experience joy caused by circumstances or conditions, we need to seek a more permanent possession of it. We can be joyful no matter what our circumstances are, because those circumstances cannot change the fact that we are born again, that we know we are God's children, that He loves us, that our Lord Jesus is preparing a place for us in the Father's house. Joy is a quality, not merely an emotion, and consequently needs to be developed and cultivated. Our fellowship with God contributes to this process.

Your students may progress through several conflicting emotions in short lengths of time. They need to recognize the need for qualities that endure. It will be important for them to distinguish the difference between happiness and joy. Happiness is an emotion. It can be caused by pleasant circumstances, good health, a beautiful day. It can be destroyed by unpleasant circumstances, poor health, a gloomy day. Christian joy is based on our relationship with God and Christ. As we build our relationship with God He can develop honest inner joy in us. It can be an exciting adventure to watch God produce this effervescent fruit of His Spirit in our lives and in the lives of those around us (see Gal. 5:22,23).

Joy can be threatened by disunity and by negative influences (see Phil. 4:1-4; James 1:2). But we can retain our joy because it is comes from God and is maintained as we maintain our fellowship with Him. Our joy is made possible through the empowering of the Holy Spirit no matter what circumstances or conditions prevail. Jesus Himself promised us joy (see John 15:11; 16:22,24; 17:13).

The challenge to seek fellowship and to find joy is for all Christians—students and teachers alike. John considered the acquisition of these worthy of a special letter; we need to acknowledge their importance for us personally.

THIS WEEK'S TEACHING PLAN

APPROACH TO THE WORD

APPROACH (5-7 minutes)

Materials needed: A copy of Student Guide section "Scrambled Definitions" for each group of three learners.

Preparation: Before class, make copies of the "Scrambled Definitions" sheet and cut the definitions apart on the lines provided. (Save one copy of the sheet intact for future

reference.) Put each set of scrambled definitions into an envelope. You will need an envelope for every three students. Note that you have mixed together the definitions for two different words.

As class begins, guide students in forming groups of three. Give each group an envelope. Explain, **"In the envelope you will find the definitions for two words. Assemble the cut-apart words and phrases into two statements that make sense. Then determine what word is defined by each definition."**

Allow time for students to work. Be available to help any who do not understand the instructions, but don't help them with the answers.

Regain students' attention and ask for their responses. If needed, read the correct definitions from the Student Guide sheet you retained. The words defined are "fellowship" and "joy."

Make a transition to the Exploration by saying something like this: **"In case you haven't already guessed, our session today is going to deal with these two ideas of fellowship and joy, and what they have to do with one another."**

ALTERNATE APPROACH (3-5 minutes)

Materials needed: Chalkboard, overhead transparency or flip chart on which you have written the statements for the activity below.

Guide students in forming small groups of two or three. Indicate the chalkboard or other surface on which you have written these statements:

1. Fellowship can take place only between people who think alike.

2. There is a difference between happiness and joy.

Scrambled Definitions

| This word means |
| sharing between two or more people |
who have something	in common.	It involves
joint participation.	Christians have in common
with each other	their relationship to Christ,
the Holy Spirit,	and God	the Father,
with all the spiritual resources	that God provides.

This word means	delight and exultation.
In the Christian context	it is
not merely an emotion	but a character quality
produced by the Holy Spirit.	It is not
affected by circumstances;	in fact, it may exist
in spite of	or even as a result of suffering.

Explain, **"Discuss your responses to the statements on the chalkboard. Make sure everyone gets a chance to answer each one."**

After students have had a few minutes to talk, regain their attention and ask for a few volunteers to report their responses to the whole class.

Make a transition to the Exploration by saying something like this: **"It's interesting to see what ideas we all have about fellowship and joy. Today we're going to have an opportunity to explore the meaning of these words and what they have to do with one another."**

BIBLE EXPLORATION

EXPLORATION (30-35 minutes)

Materials needed: Copy of Student Guide section "How It Works" for each group of three or four students, pens or pencils, extra Bibles, butcher paper and felt pens or chalkboard and chalk.

Step 1 (5-7 minutes): Give a brief introduction to the book of 1 John, describing the author and the situation that existed in the Ephesian church as explained in the Teacher's Bible study. Point out that false teachings had arisen in the church and were leading believers astray or confusing and upsetting them. John wrote his letter to reaffirm the truth about Jesus Christ and how people can become God's children through Him. Explain that fellowship and joy are key themes of John's letter and that these are the ideas you will be exploring together in this session.

Step 2 (8-9 minutes): Have a series of questions as indicated here written on butcher paper or chalkboard. Display the questions to students and ask them to listen for the answers as the Scripture is read. Ask a student who reads well to read aloud 1 John 1:1-4. (If you are not well acquainted with your class, read the Scripture yourself or have students read individually. You will need to find out who the good readers are before asking people to read aloud.)

Ask students for their responses to the questions on the butcher paper or chalkboard:

• What did John explain that gave him the right to say what he said? (He was an eyewitness of Christ, someone who heard, saw, and even touched Him.)

• Why does John say he is writing this Epistle? ("To make our joy complete"—v. 4.)

• Who is the fellowship with? (With the Father and with His Son, Jesus Christ, and with other believers.)

• What kind of joy is he speaking of? (The joy that comes from fellowship with God.)

Include any question you think is relevant and helpful. Make sure the basic facts from the passage are adequately covered. Stress the main point of this session: that fellowship leads to joy. Our fellowship with God and our fellowship with other believers both contribute to our joy.

Step 3 (5-7 minutes): Ask students to suggest how people today would understand the words "fellowship" and "joy." Then provide the following definitions. (If you used the original Approach, simply review the definitions.)

Fellowship means a sharing between two or more people who have something in common. It involves joint participation. Christians have in common with each other their relationship to Christ, the Holy Spirit, and God the Father, with all the spiritual resources that God provides.

Joy means delight and exultation. In the Christian context it is not merely an emotion but a character quality produced by the Holy Spirit. It is not affected by circumstances; in fact, joy may exist in spite of or even result from suffering.

Step 4 (10-12 minutes): Guide students in forming groups of three or four. Give each group a copy of the Student Guide

---

section "How It Works." Indicate to each group which assignment from the sheet they should work on, or let groups choose. Explain, **"John says that if we have fellowship, then we will have joy. This Student Guide sheet will guide you as you explore some additional Scripture that will give you further light on this topic. Then you will apply what you learn to some situations that might happen in people's lives today."**

After allowing time for students to work, regain their attention and ask each group to report. Discuss how fellowship can lead to joy in the situations described in the assignments and in the responses suggested by learners.

Conclude this step by summarizing the main points of the Scriptures just studied:

We have **fellowship** when we walk in the light of Christ; our fellowship should be a unity like the unity of God the Father and God the Son, so that people will look at us and know that God has sent us and that He loves us; fellowship involves sharing together in the ministry of the gospel. **Joy** comes from God as we trust Him and as we love Him, obey His commands and experience His love; it is part of the fruit of the Spirit; it "grows" in our lives as we yield to Him; it comes not only when we are experiencing positive things but even when we are facing trials. We can be joyful even in the midst of a difficult time, because our joy is based on our fellowship with God, and our relationship with God is not damaged by our trials. In fact, sometimes we get closer to Him in the midst of difficulties.

Make a transition to the Conclusion by saying something like this: **"We have talked today about fellowship and joy, and how our fellowship with God through Christ and our fellowship with other Christians can contribute to our joy. Let's take a few moments to consider our response."**

ALTERNATE EXPLORATION (35-50 minutes)

Materials needed: Long piece of butcher paper, felt pens, masking tape, extra Bibles, pens or pencils, chalkboard and chalk or overhead projector with transparencies and pens or flip chart and felt pens.

Step 1 (5-7 minutes): Follow Step 1 in the original Exploration.

Step 2 (3-4 minutes): Ask students to suggest how people today would understand the words "fellowship" and "joy." Then provide the following definitions. (If you used the original Approach, simply review the definitions.)

Fellowship means a sharing between two or more people who have something in common. It involves joint participation. Christians have in common with each other their relationship to Christ, the Holy Spirit, and God the Father, with all the spiritual resources that God provides.

Joy means delight and exultation. In the Christian context it is not merely an emotion but a character quality produced by the Holy Spirit. It is not affected by circumstances; in fact, joy may exist in spite of or even result from suffering.

Step 3 (10-15 minutes): Provide paper and pencils. Guide students in forming groups of four to six. Explain, **"Please read 1 John 1:1-4. Then work together to create a paraphrase of these verses. Express the same ideas in your own words. And write your paraphrase as if it were going to be read by a person who has been a Christian only a short time. Use the definitions of fellowship and joy that we just talked about."**

After allowing time for students to work, regain their attention and ask them to read their paraphrases. Summarize students' ideas about the passage, and add any insights they may have missed, using information from your own study of the Word and from the Teacher's Bible Study.

Step 4 (10-15 minutes): Write the words "fellowship" and "joy" on an overhead transparency, flip chart or chalkboard. Write the following Scripture references on the board under the appropriate heading, leaving space to write additional information later: Fellowship: 1 John 1:7; John 17:20,21,23; Philippians 1:3-6; Joy: John 15:9-11; Romans 15:13; Galatians 5:22,23; James 1:2-4. Assign each verse to a student to read aloud.

Say something like this: **"As you read your verse or listen to the others read, think about what the verse says about fellowship or joy. Then we'll record this information."**

Have a student read the first verse. Ask learners to restate what it says about fellowship or joy. Record their ideas on the chalkboard or other surface. Continue with the remaining verses.

Step 5 (7-10 minutes): Have students remain in their groups. To half the groups assign "fellowship" and to half assign "joy." Provide butcher paper and felt pens. Explain, **"We need to make sure we can take the truths of Scripture, such as those we have just studied, and apply them to life today. So let's imagine a typical Christian high school student. You will write a story or draw a cartoon strip about the person. Give this person a name, and put him or her into a situation that might come up at home or at school. The 'fellowship' groups should show their person experiencing true Christian fellowship in some way. In your story or cartoon include the results of that fellowship for the main characters and its effects on other people who see it happening. The 'joy' groups are to write or draw a story that shows the Christian experiencing true joy. Show what produces joy in a believer."**

You may wish to give students an example to help them get started. Read one of the assignments from the "How It Works" sheet and provide your own ending to the story.

Allow time for students to work. Then reassemble the class and have the groups share their stories or cartoon strips.

Make a transition to the Conclusion by saying something like this: **"Fellowship and joy are key themes in John's letter because they are important parts of the experience God has for His children. Let's take a few moments to look at our personal response to what we have studied today."**

CONCLUSION AND DECISION

CONCLUSION (5-7 minutes)

Materials needed: Copy of Student Guide section "Time Will Tell" for each learner, pens or pencils.

Explain, **"We saw in our study of the Scripture that our fellowship and joy as Christians are derived from our love relationship with Christ and with His people. It takes time to build a relationship. Let's use the 'Time Will Tell' sheet as a guide to help us think about how we will**

Time Will Tell

If joy in our lives is dependent upon the quality of our fellowship with Christ and others, then it is worth our time and effort. What things can you do this week to get to know Christ better? How can you be a better Christian friend?

Use this space to identify ways you can help strengthen and improve fellowship with God and what you can do to make yourself a better friend.

I want to be joyful so . . .

use our time this week."

Allow a few minutes for students to read the directions and fill in their responses. Then close with prayer.

ALTERNATE CONCLUSION (10-15 minutes)

Materials needed: Refreshments, balloons, ribbon, masking tape, push pins, colorful paper plates, cups and napkins, plastic utensils, large sheet of butcher paper, felt pens in various colors; optional—record player and records or tape recorder and tapes of joyful music.

Explain, **"We've been talking about fellowship and joy. These are words with some really deep meaning. However, as we conclude our time together I want to focus on the lighter aspects by having a good time together. In fact, we're going to have an instant party!"**

Quickly assign different students to do the following tasks:
1. Using felt pens, write reasons for joy on uninflated balloons. Blow up balloons, tie them with ribbon and tape or pin to walls;
2. Place plates, cups, utensils and napkins on tables;
3. Set out the refreshments you have provided;
4. Start the music.

Meanwhile, tape the butcher paper to a wall. Across the top write, "Joy!" Give felt pens to students who do not have tasks and tell them to write on the paper a few words describing something that gives them joy or expressing their gratitude for the joy God provides. As other students complete their tasks give them the same instructions.

Gather students around the table(s). Briefly give thanks for the refreshments and for the fellowship and joy that God provides. Then join students in enjoying the party.

Own Up to What You Are

KEY VERSE
"If we confess our sins, he is faithful and just and will forgive us our sins and purify us from all unrighteousness." 1 John 1:9

BIBLICAL BASIS
1 John 1:5-10

FOCUS OF THE SESSION
God forgives and cleanses us when we confess our sins.

AIMS OF THIS SESSION
You and your students will have accomplished the purpose of this Bible study session if you can:
- DEFINE the words sin, confession, and forgiveness;
- DISCUSS the benefits of confessing sin and the problems that result from denying it;
- IDENTIFY specific sin in your lives and seek forgiveness.

TEACHER'S BIBLE STUDY

As John's Epistle develops, it is evident that he was serious about exposing the danger of doctrines that challenge the foundations of Christian ethics. He was concerned about the influence of the Gnostics who believed that all conduct was morally indifferent. John insisted that we recognize that God asks His people to adhere to moral and ethical standards. We must consider this problem: How can an unholy human being have a partnership with a holy God? John considered the problem and presented not only humanity's attempts to solve it, but God's perfect solution as well.

God Is Light
In 1 John 1:5 God is described as light. By using that word, John revealed many facets of the character and person of God. Throughout the Bible, light is referred to in the following ways:

• It implies glory, splendor, and radiance. It is a representation of God that causes us to be in awe of His majesty (see Isa. 60:1,19).

• It is symbolic of God's perfect purity and divine holiness (see 1 Tim. 6:16). It is even considered a cleansing agent: clothes are sometimes put in the sunlight to clean and refresh them (see 1 John 1:7).

• It guides us. It shows the way and identifies the path (see Ps. 119:105,130). It is more than just the opposite of darkness,

it is in direct conflict with darkness (see John 3:19-21).

• It reveals everything. It illuminates darkness. It exposes flaws, impurity, and any imperfection in our life. In addition, light reveals truth (see John 3:19-21).

In contrast, darkness is used to represent a Christless life (see 1 Thess. 5:4,5), an enemy of light (see Col. 1:13), immorality (see Rom. 13:12), and life lacking direction and order (see John 12:35). In darkness, life is filled with everything that seeks the shadows because it cannot stand the light. Our regeneration in Christ transferred us out of Satan's darkness and into God's light.

Before we can teach students about fellowship, we need to understand that some students may not have the light of God in their lives. Our first responsibility is to introduce them to Him.

When John writes about light in 1 John 1:6,7, he is establishing God as the absolute perfection. He is everything light ascribes to Him and more— without any particle of darkness. John is explaining that this is the problem. How can people who are in darkness approach and have fellowship with God, who is light? We devise ways to relate to Him but they don't work because they are not *His* ways.

John shows us how we can have fellowship with a perfect and holy God. This fellowship is not available on easy terms.

We must deal with the obstacles that are part of our fallen, sinful human condition.

Obstacles to Fellowship with God
John's nitty-gritty sharing about a Christian's fellowship with God and how sin affects it begins in 1 John 1:6. Although he has come to be called "the apostle of love" because of his teachings, John was called the "son of thunder" by Christ. He was a big, tough, rugged fisherman and he didn't mince words. In verse 6 he says that if you are claiming to have fellowship with God but are still walking in darkness, you lie. Calling someone a liar is certainly not a compliment, but John is obligated to identify that which is opposite to God's truth. He implies that people are deliberately and knowingly misrepresenting themselves. They are acting as hypocrites who say one thing but do another. Their words and life-style are inconsistent with each other.

We have a choice between having fellowship with God or walking in darkness. We can't do both, and there is no other alternative. If we choose to say one thing and do another, our hypocrisy will be exposed (see 1 Cor. 4:5).

John completes his thought by saying that in addition to lying, these people "do not live by the truth" (1 John 1:6). Their whole life is a lie. The Christian life is not merely knowing, understanding, or even speaking the truth; we must be "doing" the truth. This is a challenge that should keep us continually seeking God's help as we attempt to do our part through getting to know Him better and following His instructions as found in the Bible.

In his Gospel, John explains that our actions will be exposed to God's light. "Whoever lives by the truth comes into the light, so that it may be seen plainly that what he has done has been done through God" (John 3:21). When we walk in the light, the light shines on us so that those around us can see the light reflecting from us.

John's descriptions intensify as he progresses through chapter 1 of his Epistle. If living inconsistently is lying (see verse 6), leading ourselves astray is deceit (see verse 8), and denying sin makes God out to be a liar (see verse 10). Each accusation has its own tragedy, but they all lead to the same position apart from God. All of them illustrate humanity's attempt to bridge the gap between God and ourselves in our own way. But these efforts are doomed to failure. The space becomes wider instead of narrower with each attempt.

Having dealt with the issue of people who lie about their way of life, John turns to those who deny the fact of sin (see 1 John 1:8). These people are not deliberate liars but rather are self-deceived. A surprising number of people actually believe that they have not sinned, for they associate sin with doing things that are morally wrong and evil. They resent being called sinners. They don't realize that sin is falling short of God's standard of perfection, and that no human being can meet that standard. Their denial of their sinfulness is a serious matter, because it keeps them from realizing their need for God.

In order to understand a discussion of sin and our individual part in it, we need a correct understanding of the word "sin." In verse 8, "sin" is singular and refers to the fact that we are members of a fallen race. Sin is a part of us because we are human beings (see Rom. 5:18,19). By nature we are incapable of meeting God's standards. This is an inescapable fact, and we need to acknowledge it. It is interesting to note that we deceive neither God nor our friends, only ourselves, when we claim to be without sin. How sad it is to be the only one fooled in a matter involving our own destiny.

In addition to the definition of "sin" as our inherited fallen nature, we also need to understand that there are individual acts of sin. We sin—commit individual acts of disobedience to God—because we have that sinful nature. But some people deny that they have ever sinned (see 1 John 1:10). Again, these people fool no one but themselves.

Others disclaim responsibility for their sins. They blame heredity, environment, temperament, physical conditions, or another person's actions. It is characteristic of all of us to avoid the responsibility for sin. But no excuse is relevant. No one who really understands what God's law requires can ever think of himself or herself as sinless. In its essence, sin is the contradiction of God. It is not merely selfishness, although self-centeredness is involved. Sin is a violation of God's perfect holiness.

The result of refusing to acknowledge sin is to make God out to be a liar. What an awesome accusation! The slightest insinuation that God lies is the ultimate in rejection of everything He is. John makes an appropriate observation: anyone who could call God a liar is without His Word (see 1 John 1:10). People who can say that they have no sin in their lives probably have never let the Word of God penetrate their hearts at all. Certainly they haven't let it influence them.

A goal of our Christian experience is to be so saturated with and involved in the Scriptures that we are constantly aware of our position as children of God. This will do two things: (1) It will make us less likely to sin, because we will be growing in Christlikeness (see Rom. 8:29; 2 Cor. 3:18); and (2) It will make us more sensitive to sin and more willing to confess our sins and to ask God to deal with them.

Consider David: although God had placed him in a position of power and honor as king, he committed adultery and murder (see 2 Sam. 11:1-27). After the prophet confronted him with his sin, David sought forgiveness and restoration from God (see 2 Sam. 12:1-13; Ps. 51). He described the dreadful effects of unconfessed sin and the joy that followed confession and forgiveness (see Ps. 32). Like David, we need to acknowledge that sin is not simply a surface problem. It affects our whole being—it is serious.

Fellowship with God and Others

As he refuted the errors that prompted him to write, John dealt with a complementary truth. While inconsistent living, refusing to acknowledge our sinful state, and denying sins are disgraceful, the opposite is glorious. When we "walk in the light, as he is in the light" (1 John 1:7), we are able to experience fellowship with one another and we are purified from all sin by Jesus' blood. Wow! Super!

What does "walking in the light" mean? Think about the literal meaning of the term. When you are outside at noon on a clear day, the sunlight illuminates everything around you. You can see buildings, trees, fences. You can walk confidently because you can see the ground and you know you aren't about to step on a rock or run into a wall. But if you are in the same location at midnight on a moonless, cloudy night (and there is a power failure), the lack of light means that you can't see what is around you. You have to shuffle along slowly and carefully, for you don't know when you might turn your ankle by stepping on a stone, or you might bump into a wall or a tree.

When we walk in God's light, we can see where we are going in terms of morals, ethics, life-style. We don't have to stumble into sin, because the light shows what it is.

How do we get into God's light? Our journey begins when we acknowledge that we can't measure up to God's standards of perfection; that we need a Saviour, and that Saviour is Jesus Christ. Once we receive Him, our walk continues as we attempt to live for Him with the help of the Holy Spirit. Our walk should be a steady progress toward living out the revealed will of God. It is a process accomplished day by day, little by little, throughout our lives.

As we walk with Him, God offers us cleansing for those times when we do sin. Your students may be able to recite 1 John 1:9—but do they understand it? It is the statement of God's solution to the problem of maintaining our fellowship with a holy God. Our confession and His forgiveness produce a restoration of our relationship. Despite the seriousness of sin and lying and deception, the Bible is not without hope and optimism. In fact, the heart of the Bible is its presentation of God's creative answer to human sin. Our hope and encouragement are founded on the fact that through the work of Christ, God has a way of dealing with our sin.

Confession and Forgiveness

When we confess our sins we acknowledge to God that we are sinners, not only by nature but also by practice. The proper attitude for our confession includes admitting that we have deviated from God's standards. Common biblical word pictures of sin depict the ideas of missing a target or taking the wrong road. We have missed the bull's-eye of God's perfection. We have traveled on a route of our own choice rather than the one God had planned for us.

As Christians it is important that sin matters to us; the nearer we are to God, the closer the fellowship, the more terrible sin will be to us. Admitting the sin is our first step. It is accompanied by repentance, which means turning away from the sin.

We all sin, but we don't have to let this fact keep us from having fellowship with God. If we confess our sin we will receive forgiveness which enables us to continue in that fellowship (see Prov. 28:13).

A study of the word "confess" is helpful to our understanding of how God can pursue a partnership with us. To confess means to say the same thing as, to agree with God concerning our sin. When God, through His Word, says that what we have done is sin, we need to look at our action from His perspective. Not only do we agree about our sin, we must turn from it. Real repentance includes an intention to give up the sin. Naturally, sometimes we struggle and struggle with something we know is wrong. God does not turn His back on us simply because we commit the same sin over and over. In fact, He works with us so closely that He actually helps us *want* to do what He wants (see Phil. 2:13).

Our confession is to our God. The one who is light is the only one who is truly faithful and just. It is God's nature and character to be completely faithful to His promises, and He has promised to forgive (see 1 John 1:9; Heb. 10:23). Indeed, He will not only forgive, but forget (see Jer. 31:34).

Besides being perfectly faithful, He is perfectly just. We could expect a righteous God to condemn rather than forgive, yet our God does forgive. When Christ died on Calvary, He paid the penalty that we rightly deserve for our sin. Christ satisfied God's need for justice. He died once for all sin (see Heb. 9:26). That is the basis of the valuable gift offered us by God. If we acknowledge the sacrifice of Christ and incorporate Him into our lives, we join ourselves with God and become part of His family. One of our privileges is the opportunity to go directly to God the Father and humbly confess our sins. Then, because He promised to forgive and cleanse us, He always will. What a unique and often unappreciated privilege!

In His forgiving, God does some additional wonderful things for us:

• God sends our sins away. Psalm 103:12 even guarantees that He removes our sin from us "as far as the east is from the west."

• God accepts Christ's payment for the debt we owe for sin. He is also generous in His forgiving. There will never be a reason for God to refuse mercy to one who honestly repents. When we are personal and particular concerning our sin, God completely and graciously pardons (see Prov. 28:13).

• God purifies or cleanses us (see 1 John 1:9). He does more than forgiving—He erases the stain of sin. The verb that John used suggests that the blood of Jesus Christ should be cleansing and purifying continually and consistently. It is another one of those processes in the Christian's life that is to go on constantly. As we sin, we repent and confess; then God pardons and cleanses. While we will sin again, and He will forgive again, the process of confession and repentance enables God's Spirit to work in us, changing us to become more like Him. While we will never in this life be completely free of the possibility of sin, we can experience true growth in becoming more like Him and less like our former selves.

John shows us that fellowship with God is always available. Our responsibility is to acknowledge our sin and then go to God for the forgiveness that will cleanse us and allow us a fresh start. As members of God's family we enjoy a relationship which can be broken but also restored. If we walk in the light we have fellowship . . . and if we confess our sins He is faithful and just to forgive us.

THIS WEEK'S TEACHING PLAN

APPROACH TO THE WORD

APPROACH (8-10 minutes)

Materials needed: Copies of Student Guide section "Puzzler," pens or pencils.

Give each student a copy of Student Guide section "Puzzler" and make sure everyone has a pen or pencil. Explain, **"Take**

about three minutes to figure out the clues and fill in the horizontal words. Then the specially-marked letters will spell an additional word vertically. This word is part of our session topic for today."

If students seem to be having difficulty, give them additional clues to help them figure out the horizontal words.

After students have worked for three minutes—or when most seem to have completed the puzzle—take them through it word by word. For example, you might say, **"What is a seven-letter word that means bravery? . . . Yes, the word is 'Courage.'"** Continue in this fashion until you have gone through all the words written horizontally. Then ask for the key word for the lesson ("Confess"). Then go back through the clue words and ask, **"Why might 'courage' be an appropriate clue word for 'confess'?"** Clue words and reasons for their appropriateness are as follows: *Courage*—It often takes courage to confess our sins; *Forget*—God not only forgives, He forgets our sins when we repent and confess them; *Honesty*—It takes honesty to confess; *Fellowship*—Confession restores our fellowship with God; *Repent*—Repentance is a necessary part of dealing with our sins; *Sincere*—Our confession and repentance must be sincere; *Sin*—Our wrongdoings are what we must confess.

Move to the Bible Exploration by saying something like this: **"This puzzle has given us a little preview of the material we'll be covering in this session. Let's see what John has to say about sin, fellowship, confession and forgiveness."**

ALTERNATE APPROACH (5-7 minutes)

Materials needed: Copies of Student Guide sheet "Stranger Than Fiction."

Distribute Student Guide sheet "Stranger Than Fiction" and tell students, **"Take a few moments to read the examples of ways other people seek forgiveness or approval from their gods and think about the questions that go with the examples. Then we'll talk about it."**

Own Up to What You Are
Winter #2

Walking in God's Light

Figure out the clues listed on the left, then fill in the words that answer those clues, placing one letter on each blank. When you have answered all the clues correctly, the specially-marked letters will spell an additional word from top to bottom.

Puzzler

Clue	Answer
Bravery	[C] O U R A G E
Not remember	F [O] R G E T
Truthfulness	H O [N] E S T Y
A good relationship	[F] E L L O W S H I P
Be sorry for, turn from	R [E] P E N T
Without deceit	S [I] N C E R E
Transgression, wrongdoing	S [I] N

Stranger Than Fiction

The paragraphs below describe how people of other cultures and religions seek forgiveness and approval. Read the paragraphs and answer the questions.

The sacrifice of a black llama and subsequent drinking of its blood mixed with cornmeal is a ritual performed even today by Peruvian Indians. This is a part of a week-long tribute to the sun god in which the Indians seek forgiveness and blessing.

The English word "thug" comes from the name for a group of devotees of Shakti, a Hindu sect, called Thugi. Thugi ravaged the countryside of India in the 1800s, strangling human victims to satisfy Shakti's desire for blood. The Thugi believed that by satisfying Shakti, they would be granted her favor.

In the Buddhist system a person is looked upon as being holy or unholy based upon the pluses or minuses accumulated in life through good or bad deeds. People are "destined" to either paradise or purgatory.

Shiite Muslims believe the death of Mohammed's grandson Husein in battle several hundred years ago atoned for their sins.

During the Middle Ages some Christians believed forgiveness could be purchased by giving money to profiteering monks and priests.

Which of the above statements seems the strangest to you? Why?

Allow time for students to read. Then regain their attention and ask for their responses to the discussion questions. Then make a transition to the Bible Exploration by saying something like this: **"People have many ways of trying to be forgiven. Sometimes when we've been involved in a Christian church for a long time we don't realize how remarkable the biblical teaching about forgiveness is. Today we're going to take some time to look at this teaching."**

BIBLE EXPLORATION

EXPLORATION (30-35 minutes)

Materials needed: Copies of Student Guide sheets "Confession and Forgiveness" and "Forgiveness in Action" for each student, extra Bibles, pens or pencils.

Note: Before copying the "Confession and Forgiveness" sheet, notice that Scripture references are given with the clues. This makes the puzzle easier for students to complete. If your students are especially sharp, or if you have extra time for your class session, you may wish to white out these references before copying the Student Guide sheet. That will make the puzzle more of a challenge.

Step 1 (10-15 minutes): Guide students in forming pairs. Give each student a copy of the "Confession and Forgiveness"

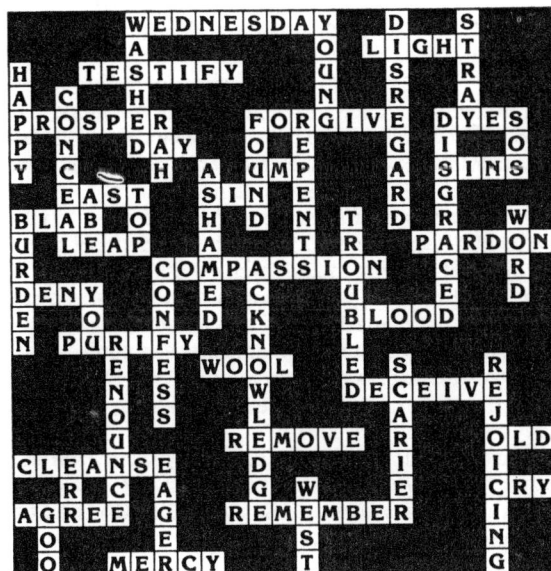

Student Guide section. Make sure everyone has a pen or pencil. Explain that students are to read the Scripture listed on the sheet and then work on the crossword puzzle. You may wish to explain that completing the puzzle will provide a way to introduce them to some of the key ideas about forgiveness in the Scriptures. Note that the puzzle is based on the *New International Version* of Scripture. If students do not have this version, make sure they realize that the puzzle may use words that mean the same as those used in their Bibles.

After allowing time for the students to work, regain their attention. Ask if students have any blanks that they have not been able to fill in, and provide any needed answers. (See answers on this page.) Ask each pair to take one minute to select the most significant idea they encountered in doing the puzzle. When the minute is up, ask students to share the ideas they selected. Take some time to discuss the concepts found in the puzzle. Use the following outline, adapting it to meet the needs of your particular students. (For example, if they are highly aware of their own sinfulness, you can spend more time on the availability of forgiveness. If you have students who are new to the idea of people being sinners, you may need to spend more time on that idea.) Here's the outline:

1. Sin means that we do not measure up to God's standards of perfection. Every human being is sinful by nature, and we all commit individual acts of sin (acts which disobey God or fall short of His perfection).

2. God has provided through Jesus Christ the means to be forgiven of our sin. When we receive Christ as our Saviour we receive forgiveness. Then, as believers, when we commit individual sins we can repent and confess and experience His forgiveness and cleansing.

3. Repentance means that we turn away from the sin to God with the intention and desire of not committing the sin again. Confession means that we agree with God that a specific action is sinful.

4. Once we confess and experience God's forgiveness, God forgets our sin and puts it as far away as the east is from the west.

Use material from your own study of God's Word and from the Teacher's Bible Study to guide your discussion.

Step 2 (17-20 minutes): Give each student a copy of the Student Guide sheet "Forgiveness in Action." Explain, **"Remain**

Forgiveness in Action

Create a short contemporary situation about a high school student who sins and needs forgiveness.

For example: Debbie Smith was barely passing math, so when a friend offered her the answers for an upcoming quiz she was thankful. Now she doesn't feel right about it.

Share what the student in your story could ask of God. Use Psalms 32 and 51 as examples and guides.

in your pairs and work together to create a story about a young person who sins and needs forgiveness. Use Psalms 51 and 32 as instructed on the page. Be prepared to share your stories." Allow time for students to work. Then regain their attention and ask them to share their stories. Summarize the use they have made of Psalms 32 and 51 as they portrayed the process of sin, repentance, confession, forgiveness and cleansing. *Note:* Psalm 51:11

might give some students the impression that sin can cause God to turn away from a person and remove His Holy Spirit from that person's life. You may wish to point out that when David wrote the Psalm the relationship of people with the Spirit was different than it is now. Believers have the Spirit permanently in their lives, though their actions may grieve Him (see Eph. 4:30).

Make a transition to the Conclusion by saying something like this: **"We've discovered what sin, confession, and forgiveness are. We have seen how David, the second king of Israel, incorporated confession into his life. Even as a king, he recognized his need to be forgiven by God. Let's consider our need for forgiveness."**

ALTERNATE EXPLORATION (30-40 minutes)

Materials needed: Extra Bibles; pens or pencils; two index cards for each learner; chalkboard and chalk, overhead projector with transparencies and pens, or flip chart with felt pens, on which you have written the lists for Step 2 below (keep the lists out of sight until you are ready to use them: tape blank paper over the chalkboard, keep the overhead transparency in a folder, or turn the flip chart to a sheet of blank paper); large sheets of paper, scissors, sheets of blank paper, felt pens, glue.

Step 1 (3-5 minutes): Read 1 John 1:5-10 aloud, or have a student who reads well do it. Then go back to verse 5 and ask for a volunteer to paraphrase the verse (restate it in his or her own words). Ask another student to paraphrase verse 6, and so on through verse 10. Paraphrasing will help students concentrate on the meaning of the verses and state that meaning in their own language.

Step 2 (10-15 minutes): Display the chalkboard or other surface on which you have written the following lists:

FORGIVENESS	CONFESSION
Isaiah 55:7	Proverbs 28:13
Jeremiah 31:34	Luke 15:7
Psalm 103:12	Isaiah 59:12

Give each student two index cards and guide students in forming pairs. Tell students, **"Write the word Confession at the top of one card and the word Forgiveness at the top of the other. Work with your partner to create a recipe or formula for each word, using 1 John 1:5-10 and the Scripture listed on the chalkboard to guide you. In your recipes or formulas, describe the importance of confession and of forgiveness and tell what each word means. Then add details that you pick up from the Scriptures."**

You may wish to give students an example of a recipe based on another scriptural concept, such as this: "Recipe for Love: 1 cup caring, 1 cup selflessness, 1 cup trust and loyalty, 1 teaspoon each of the spices of fun and humor; mix together thoroughly and bake in the heat of daily life. This mixture is essential to a healthy and fulfilled life."

Option: If your time is limited or your students need more time to accomplish an activity, have each pair work on one word, assigning "confession" to half the pairs and "forgiveness" to the other half. Any who finish early can work on the word not assigned to them.

After about 7-10 minutes, regain students' attention and ask for volunteers to share their recipes or formulas. Guide them in a discussion of the meaning and importance of confession—acknowledging sin—and God's forgiveness—releasing us from the penalty, cleansing us of the impurity. Use material from the Teacher's Bible Study and your own study of God's Word to help you guide the discussion.

Step 3 (7-12 minutes): Explain to students that the class is going to create a magazine called "True Confessions of Forgiven Believers." The first step is for each student to write an **anonymous** true story of an incident in which he or she

sinned, then confessed and received God's forgiveness. These stories should not describe sins that are too recent or too deeply personal. Students may be more comfortable relating an incident from their childhood. *Be careful to make this a "safe" activity so you don't cause students to have negative feelings about your class.*

Before students begin writing, share an example of your own, describing an incident in which you sinned, then confessed and experienced God's cleansing and forgiveness.

Provide papers and pens or pencils and let students write. Be sure to remind students to include the part about confession and forgiveness. Warn students when they have three minutes left for writing.

Step 4 (7-10 minutes): Collect the students' stories and shuffle them thoroughly. Then guide students in putting them together into magazine format. Assign different students to different tasks as indicated below.

Create a cover with the title "True Confessions of Forgiven Believers" (or the class may wish to come up with a title of their own).

Create inside pages by gluing students' stories to large sheets of paper.

Somewhere in the magazine include this statement (or a paraphrase in your own words): "This is the only place these confessions are recorded. Because they have been confessed and forgiven, these incidents have been wiped out of the heavenly computer banks."

Somewhere in the magazine include the text of 1 John 1:9.

See illustration for an idea of how the magazine might look.

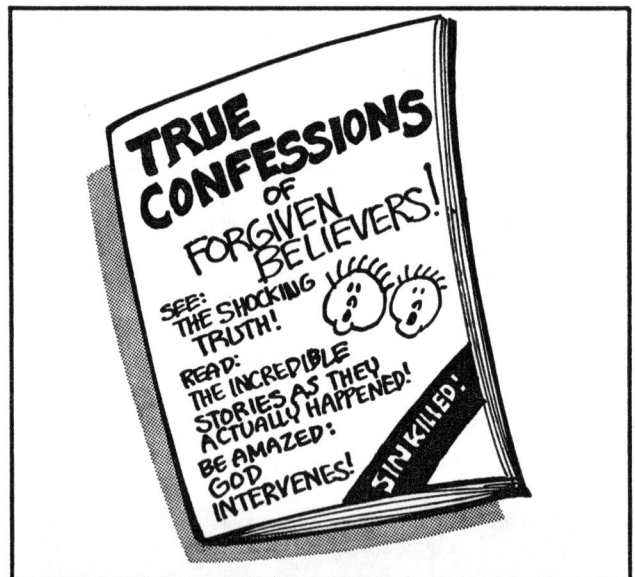

As students work, remind them that the magazine is a reminder that we all sin and fall short of God's standards—but He has provided a way to take care of the problem so that our fellowship with Him may be maintained.

When work on the magazine is complete, post it in the room so that it may continue to remind students of the importance of confession and forgiveness.

Options: You may wish to conclude the session by burning or shredding the magazine as a dramatic demonstration of the fact that God forgets our sins that have been confessed. Another option would be simply to collect the stories without making the magazine. Put the stories in a large envelope and destroy them without even reading them.

Make a transition to the Conclusion by saying something like this: **"We have talked about the importance of confession and forgiveness in our walk with the Lord. Let's take a few moments to consider our personal need for forgiveness."**

18

CONCLUSION AND DECISION

CONCLUSION (5-7 minutes)

Materials needed: Paper and pens or pencils.

Provide paper and tell students, **"It's great to have the possibility of being forgiven and cleansed and having our sins completely forgotten by God. Let's take a few moments to write a thank-you note to God or a prayer of thanksgiving expressing our response for His gift."**

Let students have a few minutes to write. Then close with a prayer of thanksgiving.

ALTERNATE CONCLUSION (3-5 minutes)

Materials needed: Paper and pen or pencil for each learner.

Write the following sentence on the chalkboard or overhead:

"You're right, Lord, I agree with you concerning my sin, I . . . "

Distribute paper and encourage students to complete the sentence prayerfully. Allow time to write, then say something like this: **"If you have any questions please feel free to come share them with me. Maybe you would like to offer this as a prayer to God right now. We'll have one or two minutes of silent prayer to give you an opportunity to do that. Then I will close in prayer."**

After praying encourage those who asked forgiveness to throw their papers away, helping them to realize that once sin is forgiven by God, it is forgotten.

Option: To make a more dramatic object lesson, you may wish to burn students' papers. You will need matches, a metal wastebasket or small portable barbecue grill or a fireplace, and a fire extinguisher or bucket of water. Use this option only if you are confident that you can do it safely.

Special Note

For some students this discussion of confession and forgiveness may be too elementary. Others may have a number of questions about the topic that are not dealt with in the session plan. You may wish to give such students a challenge assignment. The "Sticky Questions" Student Guide sheet proposes a number of questions and suggests Scripture passages to search for the answers. You may wish to provide additional resources such as a Bible dictionary, a topical Bible and a Bible concordance. These tools will direct students to biblical teachings on the topic of forgiveness. They may also, by the sheer volume of Scripture devoted to the topic, reveal the importance God attaches to it.

Sticky Questions

The subject of forgiveness can raise some sticky questions. There are principles in Scripture that answer these questions, but it takes some work to dig them out and apply them correctly. Challenge your brain by taking at least one of the questions on this sheet and seeing if you can find the biblical answer in the Scriptures listed

Matthew 6:12,14,15; 12:31,32; 18:2-5; 18:21,22;   Mark 3:29; 4:12; 11:25;   Luke 7:47; 17:4;   Acts 2:38;
Romans 2:1-4; 2:12-16;   Ephesians 1:7-10;   Colossians 3:13;   Hebrews 8:12;   1 John 1:9

Can you sin with the intent of asking for forgiveness later?

What about the person who has never heard of Christ?

What is the unforgivable sin?

If Hitler repented on his deathbed would he be forgiven?

What happens to small children who die?

Will God hold it against me if I do something that I do not know is a sin?

Will God forgive you if you carry a grudge?

Will God forgive you if you do the same thing over and over again?

Walking as Jesus Did

KEY VERSE
"Whoever claims to live in him must walk as Jesus did."
1 John 2:6.

BIBLICAL BASIS
1 John 2:1-14

FOCUS OF THE SESSION
Christians should adopt the character traits and life-style of Jesus Christ.

AIMS OF THIS SESSION
You and your students will have accomplished the purpose of this Bible study session if you can:
- EXPLORE some of the character traits and actions of Christ;
- DISCUSS ways believers today can adopt these character traits and actions;
- DECIDE on specific traits or actions to concentrate on in the coming week.

TEACHER'S BIBLE STUDY

Just as it is important to have an honest appraisal of ourselves in relation to the sin in our life, 1 John chapter 2 begins by explaining that simply acknowledging sin is not enough. John wanted to share with his readers the fact that sinning is not consistent with Christ's commands for those who follow Him. The subject of sin is prominent for a reason. John, because of his love for his readers, wanted them to know precisely the meaning of sin and its dangerous results.

A Message in Love
As John proceeded to share his warning about sin, a tender note came into his writing. He used a Greek word that literally means "my little born ones" or even "my little born-again ones" (see 1 John 2:1) and is commonly translated "My dear little children." As John reminded his readers about the seriousness of sin he did not scold them. Rather he tried to love them into obeying. Ann Kiemel Anderson has become known for her gentle and sincere way of "loving people to Jesus." Similarly, John knew these spiritual children and their weaknesses, yet he wanted to love them to goodness.

John explained that God's provision for the sinning Christian is found in His Son. Christ possesses a three-part qualification as described in 1 John 2:1,2. These qualifications are interrelated and depend on one another.

Jesus Christ the Advocate
First, John describes Christ as being our defender or advocate. He uses the Greek word *paracletos* to describe Christ. This word and its related forms express several valuable thoughts in Scripture. A verb form is used to mean "comfort," as in the Septuagint version of Genesis 37:35 and Isaiah 61:2, and in Matthew 5:4. The noun *paracletos* has also been defined as "one who lends his presence to friends." Jesus is our friend; Paul wrote that Christ is at the right hand of God interceding for us (see Rom. 8:34). The writer of Hebrews also presented that idea and emphasized Christ as our High Priest who is even now appearing in God's presence on our behalf (see Heb. 7:25; 9:24).

The most common usage of *paracletos* is "someone called to one's side" in order to be a helper and counselor. The word itself has come to mean a helper, supporter, and above all, a witness in someone's favor, an advocate in someone's defense. The Greek word was used so much that it became a part of other languages as well. The Jews in particular adopted the word and used it as a legal term denoting an advocate to plead one's cause, one who would intercede on behalf of another; the opposite of an accuser. It was used to describe the counsel for the defense, whose job is to plead the defendant's case and convince the court of his or her innocence.

It may be helpful to suggest that your students visualize Christ as a participant in a heavenly courtroom situation. The dramatic effect created is a sobering reminder of Christ's active ministry in our daily lives. In Revelation 12:10 we are told that Satan accuses us "before our God day and night." Yet God the Son, Jesus Christ, died for us and consequently can step in as our advocate or defender. It is significant that John described no stipulations for Christ's availability as our defender. Of course, John was addressing believers, but aside from that, Christ's action is not dependent on anything we do. He does not wait until we repent, nor until we confess our sin. The moment we sin, Jesus Christ is available to defend us, just as Satan is ready to accuse us. At that point, it is our responsibility to request and make use of the defense that He offers.

Jesus Christ the Righteous One
John's second statement about our Lord is "Jesus Christ, the Righteous

One"—a description of Christ's character. As a member of the Godhead, He has the attributes of God including righteousness and holiness. As our defender, He does not try to excuse our sins. He asks for no leniency, no setting aside of His own divine law. He acknowledges our guilt but presents His own sacrifice as the grounds for our acquittal. As God, He planned to become the means by which His holy and just nature can be satisfied. He offered Himself as the sacrifice required for our sins (see 1 Pet. 3:18). Even as His death on earth was for us, His work now in heaven is also for us. As the Holy Spirit convicts us of our sins, we repent and confess them to the Father. Then, as a righteous judge, God can pardon our sins and cleanse us because the punishment has been satisfied by Christ. It is only through a righteous Saviour that we can be cleansed from all our unrighteousness.

Jesus Christ the Atoning Sacrifice

John explains that Christ is our atoning sacrifice. The thought is not that He has provided it, nor offered it, but that He Himself *is* the sacrifice. He is high priest, altar, and sacrifice all in one (see Gen. 22:8; 2 Cor. 5:10). He made atonement for sin—"not only for ours but also for the sins of the whole world" (1 John 2:2). Christ is complete for everyone (see John 3:16). Through Him, our fellowship with God is restored and maintained.

The Believer's Responsibility

This session presents your students with the challenge of overcoming sin. In order to do that, they will need to have a clear understanding of what God expects of them. John stated his purpose for writing in 1 John 2:1: "so that you will not sin." This is the Christian ideal. John didn't want those dear to him to sin. Yet he followed that admonition with the statement that Christ has satisfied God's penalty for our sin and for the world's sin. John wanted his readers to walk in obedience to God's word. He wanted them to realize that sinning is not a necessity in a Christian's experience, but he realistically acknowledged that it will at times be an ingredient.

Those who are continually living in fellowship with God will not continually keep on sinning (see 1 John 3:6). John did not say that a Christian never commits an act of sin, but that a Christian is not to sin habitually. The practice of sin excludes any true knowledge of Christ (see Matt. 7:21). When anything in our life is done consistently it becomes a habit. John warned against any sin being repeated often enough to become a habit.

In 1 John 2:3-6, John seems to be repeating himself when expressing the need for us to be obedient to God. This repetition lends emphasis to what he said and

shows how important he considered his subject to be. We are to obey God's Word (see v. 5). Keeping God's commandments requires a watchful attitude to discover where we fall short of His expectations. Then we must attempt to follow His instructions as closely as possible, with the help of the Holy Spirit. Peter sheds further light on the issue by saying that since Christ has died for our sins we should die to them as well, and live for righteousness (see 1 Pet. 2:24).

Just as we sin by doing things God commands us not to do, we also sin by not doing what God has commanded. "Anyone, then, who knows the good he ought to do and doesn't do it, sins" (Jas. 4:17). Your students may find obeying God's positive commands more of a challenge than obeying the negative ones. Remind them that Jesus Christ is our example. We are to walk as He walked (see 1 John 2:6). And He will help us to do so (see Phil. 4:13).

If we are to walk constantly in God's light, than everything we do and don't do is exposed. Every sin, no matter how small or seemingly insignificant, causes an interruption in our ability to let God's light shine through us because it breaks our fellowship with Him. John contended that we do not have a personal relationship with Christ unless we live in practical conformity to His will. Keeping God's commandments is what is meant by walking in the light.

Although God's commands are a part of His Word, God's Word is much more than simply His commands. It is important that your students realize that the Bible is God's revelation of Himself to us and that it tells us His will for our lives. High schoolers often find themselves being confronted with authorities who differ with one another, such as parents, teachers, church leaders. They need a clear realization that the Bible is a totally reliable guide to God's truth, His wishes, His viewpoint regarding human life and relationships. God's Word describes God's personality and character. Obeying God's Word is more than a matter of doing specific deeds that God commands; it also means conforming to everything God has revealed Himself to be. Since He is just, we must be just. Since He is loving, we must be loving. We must "walk as Jesus did" (1 John 2:6).

What does it mean to walk as He did? It means to walk in the Spirit as He walked in the Spirit, depending on and communicating with the Father rather than relying on our own will power. It means that we accept His priorities as our priorities; we love God above everything else, and our neighbor as ourselves. When our priorities follow His, then our attitudes and actions toward others will follow His example as well.

Love's Challenge

Walking and living as Jesus did was not a new concept to John's readers. Thus John explained, "I am not writing you a new command but an old one, which you have had since the beginning. This old command is the message you have heard" (v. 7). Commentators generally agree that John was talking here about the command to love. This command went back to Old Testament times (see Lev. 19:18). Yet it was a "new command" (1 John 2:8) because it was raised to a new level in the life and teachings of Jesus Christ (see John 13:34,35; 15:10,12; 1 John 3:16). Love had new meaning after being lived out in Christ. His self-sacrifice demonstrated a new standard of love, one we are to imitate.

In this session you and your students will be looking at some Scriptures that describe specific characteristics of Christ. These are traits that believers today can and should emulate with the help of the Holy Spirit. Christ expressed His love through humility (see Phil. 5:2-8; John 13:14,15); kindness (see Eph. 4:32); forgiveness (see Col. 3:13); compassion (see Matt. 15:32 and Luke 7:13); patience (see 1 Tim. 1:15,16); obedience (see Heb. 5:8; John 15:10); and mercy (see 1 Tim. 1:15,16). When we follow in Christ's footsteps, these characteristics are the evidence of our love for God and for other people.

Jesus taught that our entire obligation can be expressed in the one word—love (see Mark 12:28-31). He said that all the commandments could be boiled down to love moving in two directions: first toward God, then toward other people. As our love is expressed toward those we are in contact with each day, it will have an effect not only on them, but on ourselves as well.

Since loving is a specific command from God, obeying it allows us closer fellowship with Him. In contrast, John pointed out that hatred separates us from each other and from God. According to John, relationships are absolute: we either love or hate. John accepts no neutrality in human relationships (see 1 John 2:9-11).

The Christian's challenge goes beyond the question of whether something is right or wrong. Instead it asks if it will please God. Our actions are considered in light of our motives; the question is whether we are acting on the basis of love. If we are in fellowship with God and walking with Him, then we will want what we do to be examined and evaluated by Him. A good example is the psalmist who expressed a wish to be searched, known, and tested (see Ps. 139:23,24).

John's letter should remind us of who we belong to and what He has done for us. When we realize we are forgiven, we can begin to see God's love illustrated before our eyes. Although sin is a temptation to us as well as to the "dear children" to whom John wrote, we have a defender—Christ Himself. Our ability to "keep the Word of God" is not a result of our own strength or ability; it is possible only with the help of God. We are dependent upon Him for the strength and help we need to avoid sinning. And when we do sin and need pardon, we depend upon Him to for-give our sins "on account of [Christ's] name" (1 John 2:12).

What's in a Name?

The Jewish people and people of other ancient cultures used names in a very special way. A name was not simply what someone was called, it stood for the whole character of the person. The statement that our sins have been forgiven "on ac-count of his name" (1 John 2:12) implies that we are forgiven because of the whole character of Christ.

Although names themselves don't carry as much meaning today, it is vital that you know your students' names. Make an effort to learn a little about their fami-lies as well. It is possible that by meeting or learning about their parents and fami-lies you will discover something important about them that will be helpful in teaching them and meeting real needs in their lives.

THIS WEEK'S TEACHING PLAN

APPROACH TO THE WORD

APPROACH (5-10 minutes)

Materials needed: Paper, pencils.

Guide students in forming two teams. (Have them count off "one, two, one, two" or use another simple method.) Give each team paper and a pencil; select (or have each team select) one person to be the recorder for the team. Tell the teams, **"Each team is to think of a person who will be known to the other team. You might choose someone on the church staff or some other person that we all know about. Keep your voices down as you discuss your choice, so the other team can't hear you. After deciding on a person, list characteristics of the person. For example, you might say, 'Thoughtful, forgetful, loves to eat'—that sort of thing. Keep your lists positive or at least lighthearted; no negative traits. List as many things as you can think of. Then I'll get your attention and let each team try to figure out the identity of the other team's person."**

Allow 2-5 minutes for students to decide and list; warn them when one minute remains. Then reassemble the class and let one team name characteristics while the other team tries to guess the person's identity. Then reverse the process.

Make a transition to the Bible Exploration by saying something like this: **"It's interesting how we can readily identify a person if we know enough of his or her characteristics. In today's session we are going to look at some characteristics that are supposed to identify us as Christians. Let's see what we can find out."**

ALTERNATE APPROACH (3-5 minutes)

Materials needed: Student Guide sheet "Footsteps."

Give each student a copy of the Student Guide sheet "Footsteps." Or, if you prefer, you may reproduce the drawings on the chalkboard or flip chart, or make an overhead transparency from the sheet.

Explain to students that the "footsteps" on the Student Guide sheet represent a number of well-known individuals, both fictional and real. Ask students to guess the identity of the various people. (Answers: a. Charlie Chaplin, b. Peg-Leg Pete or Captain Ahab, c. Wolfman, d. David and Goliath, e. Enoch, f. the Three Stooges, g. Snow White and the Seven Dwarves, h. Cinderella, i. Moses at the burning bush.)

Make a transition to the Exploration by saying something like this: **"It's interesting to see how we can identify certain people by the way their footprints look. In the Scripture we are going to examine today we are told to walk as Jesus walked. Let's see what kind of footprints we should leave if we are going to be like our Lord."**

Walking in God's light

Walking as Jesus Did
Winter #3

Footsteps

Study the footprints below. These footprints belong to a number of people both real and fictional. Can you guess their identity?

BIBLE EXPLORATION

EXPLORATION (30-40 minutes)

Materials needed: Bibles; paper; pens or pencils; chalkboard and chalk or overhead projector with transparencies and pens or flip chart with felt pens; shoe boxes or other boxes, each containing a shoe or a picture of a shoe (each shoe should be of a different type, such as a child's shoe, a man's work shoe; one box with a shoe or picture for each group of four to six students).

Step 1 (10-12 minutes): Guide students in forming groups of four to six. Have them read 1 John 2:1-14 and underline everything in the passage that tells believers what to do or what not to do—for example, "I write this to you so that you will not sin" (v. 1). Allow 5-7 minutes for this task. Warn students when one minute remains. When time is up, regain students' attention and ask them to report their results. Spend a few minutes talking about John's desire that Christians not sin, his realistic understanding that Christians will still sin sometimes, and his description of Christ as the advocate and the atoning sacrifice for our sins. Use materials from the Teacher's Bible Study and your own study of God's Word.

Step 2 (10-12 minutes): Direct students' attention to verse 6: "Whoever claims to live in him must walk as Jesus did." Explain that believers need to be developing personal traits that are like those of Christ and a life-style that is like Christ's. The next part of the session will give students an opportunity to examine some traits and actions that believers need to emulate.

Have students continue to work in their groups. Give each group one or more of the following Scriptures: Matthew 3:13-15; Matthew 11:29; Matthew 14:23; Luke 23:34; John 5:30; John 15:10; Philippians 2:5-8; 1 Timothy 1:15,16; Hebrews 5:7; Hebrews 5:8; Hebrews 7:26; 1 John 3:5. Tell them to look up and read their assigned Scriptures and write a description of the character qualities described (or implied by Christ's actions). Allow 5-7 minutes for this activity, warning students when one minute remains.

Regain students' attention and ask each group for a report on its findings. List character qualities on the chalkboard, overhead transparency or flip chart as students report them. Summarize what the students have learned by saying something like this: **"What a wonderful world it would be if we all really followed Christ's example! We would be surrounded by loving people who were sympathetic to our needs. Selfishness would be replaced by the desire to help others. Bragging and showing off would be obsolete as we all tried to act in a way that was pleasing to God. While this sort of perfection may not happen in our lifetimes, we can do our part, with God's help. We can try our best to be evidence of Christ's love in the world today."**

Step 3 (10-12 minutes): Give each group a shoe box (or other box) containing a shoe or a picture of a shoe. Make sure the types of shoes are varied—a child's shoe, a running shoe, a man's work shoe, a "little old lady's" shoe and so on. Explain, **"We've been talking about walking as Jesus walked. And we've listed some character traits of Christ. Now you are to figure out what kind of person would wear the shoe given to your group. And then you are to figure out what you as high school students could do for that person— some action that would be Christlike and would model the characteristics we discovered and discussed earlier in this session. You can also use the list we made of Christ's characteristics to guide you."**

Allow 5-7 minutes for students to work together, warning them when one minute remains. When time is up, regain their attention and ask them to share their ideas. List their suggestions on the chalkboard, overhead transparency or flip chart.

Option: To make this activity move more quickly, put a blank index card in each shoe box. Distribute boxes. Allow one minute for group to write their ideas on the card, then have groups pass their boxes to the next group. Each group should add a new idea to each card as it comes by.

Make a transition to the Conclusion by saying something like this: **"We've taken a look at some of the characteristics believers need to develop if they are to walk as Jesus walked. And we have listed some things teenagers can do for various kinds of people. Now let's get personal and think about what we will actually do."**

ALTERNATE EXPLORATION (40-50 minutes)

Materials needed: Bibles, extra paper, extra pens or pencils, chalkboard and chalk or overhead projector with transparencies and pens or flip chart and felt pens, copies of Student Guide sheet "Track a Trait."

Step 1 (10-12 minutes): Follow Step 1 in the original Exploration.

Step 2 (12-15 minutes): Direct students' attention to verse 6: "Whoever claims to live in him must walk as Jesus did." Explain that believers need to be developing personal traits that are like those of Christ and a life-style that is like Christ's. The next part of the session will give students an opportunity to examine some traits and actions that believers need to emulate.

Have students continue to work in their groups. Give each student a copy of the Student Guide sheet "Track a Trait."

Track a Trait

The Scriptures listed below contain examples of characteristics of Christ. In the space provided write the characteristic the verse(s) describe.

Matthew 15:32 and Luke 7:13

Mark 10:43-45

Mark 12:28-31

John 13:14,15

John 15:12

Galatians 6:2

Ephesians 4:32 and Colossians 3:13

1 Peter 1:15

1 John 3:16

Explain, **"Work together in your group to read the Scriptures listed on your sheet. Then list the character traits or actions that the Scriptures indicate were part of Jesus' life."** Allow 5-7 minutes for this activity, warning students when one minute remains.

Regain students' attention and ask each group for a report on its findings. List character qualities on the chalkboard, overhead transparency or flip chart as students report them. Review what your students have discovered by saying something like this: **"These Scriptures give us a good picture of how Jesus wanted us to live, reflecting His loving, compassionate, humble, forgiving and holy nature. Let's examine ways these traits can be demonstrated in life today."**

Step 3 (15-20 minutes): Have each group select one of the character traits the class has listed. Tell class, **"Prepare a brief drama that would show how this characteristic would help in a situation that you witnessed recently or one that is common at your school or neighborhood. For example, you might portray what would happen if a high school football player put the needs of other people ahead of his or her own selfish desires. How would this help improve team spirit at the next football practice? Work together to write a script and then decide who will play each role. Take a couple of minutes to rehearse your drama before I call time. Be prepared to share your dramas with the rest of us."**

Allow 7-8 minutes for students to write and rehearse,

warning them when three minutes and then one minute remain. When time is up, reassemble the class and ask groups to present their dramas. Summarize the ideas students have shared through their dramas by saying something like this: **"There is one underlying trait that is the basis of all the others. Jesus taught in Mark 12:28-31 that this trait is love—first the love of God, and flowing from that the love of other people. The other characteristics are ways of demonstrating our love for God and others."**

Make a transition to the Conclusion by saying something like this: **"We have seen how we are to become more like Jesus, and we have seen some of the specific traits that are involved. Let's take a few moments to think about our personal response to what we have studied today."**

CONCLUSION AND DECISION

CONCLUSION (3-5 minutes)

Materials needed: Paper, felt pens.

This Conclusion is appropriate for use with the original Exploration.

Give each student a piece of paper and a felt pen. Explain, **"Since we've been talking so much about shoes, I want you to draw a shoe. It can be any kind of shoe you want. Then write on it one thing you will try to do this week to be Christlike. You might want to select one of the ideas we talked about earlier in the session, or you might have an idea all your own."**

After students have had time to work, ask for volunteers to display their shoes and describe the action they have chosen. (Do this only if you're sure students will be comfortable sharing.)

Option: Provide a huge piece of butcher paper and have your students work together to draw one giant shoe. They may wish to indulge in some humor and creativity by including a hairy leg or by writing an appropriate motto on the sock coming out of the shoe, such as "Live Christ's way." Have each student select a Christlike action to try this week and write that action on the shoe. Attach the paper to the wall as a visual reminder.

Close in prayer.

ALTERNATE CONCLUSION (3-5 minutes)

Materials needed: Copies of Student Guide sheet "Walking Along," pencils.

Give each student a copy of the Student Guide sheet "Walking Along." Explain that it provides an opportunity to plan some steps of growth. As students prayerfully consider

Walking Along

Think of some steps you need to take to follow Jesus more closely. Write your ideas on the signposts below.

character qualities and actions that they have studied today, they may realize that they have some growing to do to live up to Christ's kind of life. No one becomes perfect overnight. Planning a step-by-step program allows for the natural growth patterns of human beings. You might suggest that students place a fairly easy step at the beginning of their path, and then add more difficult steps as they go along. For example, if a student is already doing fairly well at praying regularly, he or she might want to choose a first step that would improve the frequency or the amount of time spent praying.

It would be helpful if you would share with students your own personal step-by-step plan for growth. The value of this course will be enhanced if you participate in the spiritual growth opportunities offered to students throughout the quarter.

Allow a few minutes for students to think, pray and write. Then close in prayer.

Get Your Priorities Together

KEY VERSE

"Do not love the world or anything in the world. If anyone loves the world, the love of the Father is not in him."
1 John 2:15

BIBLICAL BASIS

1 John 2:15-17

FOCUS OF THE SESSION

Christians are to love God, not the "world."

AIMS OF THIS SESSION

You and your class will have accomplished the purpose of this session if you can:

- DISCUSS John's instruction not to love the world;
- IDENTIFY attitudes that demonstrate love of the world;
- CHOOSE a response to the biblical injunction against loving the world.

TEACHER'S BIBLE STUDY

John started his letter by talking about the Word of life and walking in the light. Then he came to the challenge of refusing to "love the world or anything in the world" (1 John 2:15). He presented this concept without compromise. Like many of his previous statements, this one allows no grey areas. John associated those who love the world with those who do not have God's love. According to John, we either do or do not love the world and consequently have or do not have the Father's love in us.

Loving the World

This is the first use of the word "world" in this letter, but the subject comes up repeatedly later on in the Epistle. It is important to determine what John meant by loving the world. Let's begin by discovering what he did *not* mean. He did not mean that we are not to love the world of nature. God's creation is beautiful and we are blessed to be able to enjoy it. The psalmists lead us in praising God for a glorious world (see Ps. 19:1-6, for example).

John was also not saying that we are not to love our fellow human beings. God loves all people so much that He sent Christ to die for us (see John 3:16).

What we are not to love is the world that leaves God out and is in opposition to Him. The world can take things that are neutral or even good and blow them out of

proportion, inducing us to put those things first in our lives rather than putting God first. This world is "under the control of the evil one" (1 John 5:19). The principles of Satan, rather than the principles of God, prevail. Any time people put selfish pleasures or material possessions or power or anything else above God, they are loving the world and following Satan's principles, whether they know it or not.

Loving the world is not necessarily a conscious decision. It can involve a subtle process of considering anything or anyone as being the most important thing there is. It means allowing something to become more and more precious until it is more important than loving God and living for Him. It can involve taking on the value systems of the world rather than holding to the value system of God.

J. B. Phillips' translation of Romans 12:2 offers this helpful warning: "Don't let the world around you squeeze you into its own mold." Children enjoy playing with clay or dough, pushing it into molds and then taking out shapes that are reproductions of the mold. Or they may simply press an object into the clay to make a likeness of the object. The apostle Paul insisted that we Christians should not allow ourselves to be shaped by anyone but God. We should not allow ourselves to be made into a likeness of the world. At times, even though we avoid the mold, we

allow the world to make impressions on us.

Worldliness

Each Christian is presented with a choice, as John described it, to love God or to love the world. Loving the world is referred to as "worldliness"—being like the world, being squeezed into its mold. The world's mold may change from society to society, from culture to culture. In some places the world may exert pressure on us to put money and material things first in our lives. In other places the center of attention may be physical pleasure, or political power, or gaining a good reputation. None of these things is bad in itself. They are things that God has put into the world for us to use. But when we pay more attention to the gift than we do to the God who gives it, we have moved into worldliness.

As we seek to find the balance point where we make proper use of the things God gives us, without making them the center of our lives, Paul's words can give us an ideal to strive for. He stated that through Christ "the world has been crucified to me, and I to the world" (Gal. 6:14). A dead person does not respond to people, activities or other stimuli. If we are crucified we are dead so far as the world is concerned. We do not respond to its enticements. Of course, this is a statement of the ideal. It is true as God sees it. We may, however, find that we need to grow into that truth. Our everyday experience may need some time to catch up with God's reality. Bit by bit the world's attractiveness to us should diminish.

Yet high schoolers are pressured from all directions to conform to an accepted life-style that usually excludes God and the standard of life He requires. Your students will feel particularly influenced by their peers and by the daily bombardment from television, radio, and magazine ads that make promises about things the world can offer them. They are presented with the lure of popularity, romance, beauty, pleasure and happiness. People may put these things first in their lives in order to satisfy inner needs which ultimately can be satisfied only by a close personal relationship with God. Only through the Holy Spirit's work in our lives will we be willing and able to escape being squeezed into the world's mold; only with His help can we learn to put God first.

God wants and expects us to grow and change as we learn about Him. He has called us to be holy and obedient (see 1 Pet. 1:14,15). The good news is that God has made a provision so that we can resist the world's pressure. We can "clothe" ourselves with the Lord Jesus Christ and "live by the Spirit"; then we will not "gratify the desires of the sinful nature" (see Rom. 13:14; Gal. 5:16). We can make Christ so much a part of our life that the world's temptations no longer seem so tempting. We will learn to keep things in perspective, to use money or enjoy friendships or other pleasures without making them the center of our lives. As we grow in close fellowship with God, as John described, we become more and more sensitive to His will for us.

Characteristics of Our World

The worldly temptations that we are to avoid are characterized by three descriptions in 1 John 2:16: "the cravings of sinful man, the lust of his eyes and the boasting of what he has and does." Each describes a passionate desire, not merely an interest. These are the world's temptations for us—and have been from the beginning. They were part of Satan's tactics when tempting Eve (see Gen. 3:1-6) and our Lord Jesus (see Matt. 4:1-11).

The expression **"The cravings of sinful man"** (or "lust of the flesh"—*NKJV*) describes a situation in which our senses lead us to desire what we cannot or should not have. Or we may take something that is a gift of God, such as food or sex, and give it top priority in our lives instead of giving God the top priority.

Many people identify "the cravings of sinful man" with sexual sin. While this is part of the picture, these cravings also include our selfish ambitions and our tendency to measure everything by material standards. It includes our demand to satisfy our own desires even at another's expense. It may involve gluttony, selfish extravagance in material possessions, lack of discipline in the use of time, an unrestrained seeking after pleasures, and waste or excess in any area of life.

To understand your students, you need to be aware of the form the "cravings of sinful man" take in their lives. Different facets of media and society will grab and captivate them, from fashionable jeans to sexual freedom. John described the world as a place characterized by the temptation to become a servant to all of the desires of our flesh.

This category of cravings may be described as the *desire to have*. Rather than loving God, we make our own ambition and comfort our god (see Rom. 8:7,8).

It is important for Christians to realize, though, that the pleasures or possessions are not necessarily wrong in themselves. They become dangerous when they draw our attention away from God (see 1 Cor. 6:12). Thus one person may be able to enjoy an activity such as running, making it one part of a balanced life that is centered on God; but another may find running to be so addicting that a relationship with God is neglected. The latter person has fallen into the sin of "loving the world" by leaving God out, but the former has not. This distinction will be refreshing for some students who may have an inaccurate understanding of God's commands for us in the Bible. It will be a challenge for them to consider the difference their attitudes and motives make in considering traditional "do's and don'ts" (see 1 Cor. 10:23,24).

The **"lust of his eyes"** is the temptation to exploit those things that can be seen. Satan is eager to lead us astray from our devotion to Christ (see 2 Cor. 11:3). He will tempt us with the attractive things the world offers—all of its glitter and outward show. The "lust of the eyes" invites us to be happy through the things we can buy and display and look at with pride. It places ultimate value on material possessions. It promotes a spirit that wishes to have everything it sees, and then flaunts what it has. It is a *desire to see,* yet it can never be satisfied; even acquiring what is desired will not be enough. "Death and Destruction are never satisfied, and neither are the eyes of man" (Prov. 27:20). When we turn away from the Lord and seek our satisfaction elsewhere, we put ourselves in a no-win position in which we will never find true satisfaction and fulfillment.

The **"boasting of what he has and does"** is a particular pride of life, an attempt to feel superior to someone else. It is a self-centered *desire to be.* It is an attitude which prides itself on wealth, talent, education, and any other area in which one is capable of excelling or pretending to excel. It is not simply taking pleasure in a possession or ability as a gift from God; it's assuming, "I'm better than other people because I have this possession or this skill." This human pride is not acknowledged by God; in fact, it is described as foolishness (see Prov. 26:12; 1 Cor. 3:18,19).

The original rebellion of the angel Lucifer was characterized by his opposition to God's authority. Because of pride, he made five selfish "I will" statements summarized by "I will make myself like the Most High" (see Isa. 14:12-14). His boastful sin resulted in God casting him out of heaven (see Ezek. 28:16; Rev. 12:9). Now known as Satan, he has power in our world (see Eph. 2:2) but will eventually be cast into hell (see Rev. 20:10). Pride in our life is no small matter. It is of great concern to God, for it causes us to leave Him out of our lives (see Ps. 10:4). This is a loss to Him, for He deserves the allegiance of all His creatures. And it is a loss to us, for we close ourselves off from the love, joy and fullness of life He offers (see John 15:9-11; 10:10).

Eternity's View

John's warning to avoid loving the world and the things in it is for our own good. John wanted his readers to realize why a Christian's devotion cannot be divided between God and the world. Loving the world demonstrates that we do not actually belong to God (see 1 John 2:15). In addition, loving the world is a waste of our time. If we attach ourselves to the world's aims and ways, we are giving ourselves to something that has no future. Nothing in the world has any permanency: "this world in its present form is passing away" (1 Cor. 7:31).

On the other hand, when we make God the center of life, we give ourselves to something that is permanent. We are investing in our own eternity. The person "who does the will of God lives forever" (1 John 2:17).

Some high school students allow their circumstances or friends to make their life decisions for them. It is easier and more popular to conform to the world. However, it is important to learn to follow God's principles rather than simply responding to the world's pressure. Your students need help in learning and applying biblical standards to make their alternatives and the consequences more clear. The Scripture can become a valuable resource for their decision-making.

THIS WEEK'S TEACHING PLAN

APPROACH TO THE WORD

APPROACH (3-5 minutes)

Materials needed: Student Guide Sheet "List Your Likes" for each learner, pens or pencils.

Ask students to look over their "List Your Likes" Student Guide Sheet. Tell them, **"Number the listed items in order**

Get Your Priorities Together — *Walking in God's Light*

Winter #4

List Your Likes

Number the items listed below in order of your preference, with number one being the item you like best. (This is not to say that you necessarily like everything on the list. The higher numbers may represent things you don't like at all.)

Eating this food: _____	Bubonic plague
Sleeping in	The flu
Math class	Pizza
Writing letters	Sand in your hot dog
A sunny day	Sand in your shorts
Spearmint chewing gum	Going to the dentist
Reading a mystery novel	Getting a flu shot
Watching reruns	A runny nose and no Kleenex
Playing _____ (sport)	Cats
	Dogs

---

of your preference, with number one being the item you like best."

After the students have had a few moments to number their lists, have them share their answers. Make a transition to the Exploration by saying something like this: **"Different things in the world are important to each of us. Today we are going to look at some statements John made about the world and the things in the world. We'll see what he said and what it means for us today."**

ALTERNATE APPROACH (5-7 minutes)

Materials needed: Chalkboard and chalk or overhead projector with transparencies and pens or flip chart with felt pens.

Have the following statements written on the chalkboard or other surface when students come into class. Read the statements one at a time. Ask the students who agree with the statement to raise their hands, then students who disagree. Move through the statements quickly.

- God made the world.
- We should love and care for the things God made.
- Therefore we should love the world.

Now you're ready to present a challenge to students. Ask

this question, which should *not* appear on the chalkboard: **"But 1 John chapter 2 says we are not to love the world. Does that mean that there's a contradiction here?"**

Let students cope with the issue for a minute or two. Then make a transition to the Bible Exploration by saying something like this: **"There is no real contradiction; it's just a matter of understanding what is meant by the word 'world' in different contexts. Today we're going to explore what John said about not loving the world, and see what he meant by that."**

BIBLE EXPLORATION

EXPLORATION (30-40 minutes)

Materials needed: Copies of Student Guide sheets "The World According to John" and "Everything in the World" for each learner, extra Bibles, pens or pencils.

Step 1 (7-8 minutes): Guide students in forming pairs and tell them, **"Read 1 John 2:15-17, then look at your Student Guide sheet 'The World According to John.'**

The World According to John

Read 1 John 2:15-17.

Now summarize the main truth of that Scripture in 20 words or less:

Definition:

When John said that we are not to love the world, he did not mean that we are not to enjoy and care for the world of nature, nor did he mean that we are not to love human beings. Rather he was saying that we should not put anything in the world before God in our lives. The world around us opposes God or ignores Him. We are to love Him totally and give Him top priority.

First note that it gives you a definition of the meaning of loving the world. Read that definition. Then work together to determine the main ideas in John 2:15-17 and to summarize these ideas in 20 words or less. This activity will help you clarify the meaning of the passage as you work to express it in a brief statement."

Allow time for the students to work. Then regain their attention and ask them to share their summaries with the class.

Step 2 (5-6 minutes): Review with students the definition of loving the world from the student sheet. Loving the world means putting things in the world before God. It may mean opposing God or ignoring Him. It means having our priorities out of balance. John was not talking about the world of nature, which God created, nor the world of humanity, which God created and which He loves. It's important that students clearly understand this point, since many people become confused about this definition. Enjoying a beautiful sunset or a good meal, listening to music, loving family members and friends are definitely *not* the kinds of things John meant when he said we are not to love the world.

Step 3 (20-25 minutes): Briefly go through the three phrases in 1 John 2:16; these describe what John *did* mean by loving the world. Use the explanations from the Teacher's Bible Study to explain "the cravings of sinful man, the lust of his eyes and the boasting of what he has and does." Point out that these phrases are defined on the Student Guide sheet you are about to distribute.

Have each pair of students join with another pair to form small groups of 4-5 students. Give each student a copy of the Student Guide sheet "Everything In the World" and additional paper. Assign to each group one of the three categories from

---

Everything in the World

Think of some typical situations at school, in your neighborhood or at home that might fit into one of these categories from 1 John 2:15-17. Use extra paper, if necessary, to write a story or draw a cartoon strip showing one of these situations.

"The cravings of sinful man." _____

Definition: This description involves the desires of that part of our nature which is ours because we belong to the human race. These cravings may involve sexual sin, selfish ambition, and our tendency to measure everything by material standards. This category includes our demand to satisfy our own desires at another's expense.

"The lust of his eyes." _____

Definition: This category involves the temptation to exploit those things that can be seen. The world offers all sorts of pageantry, glory and outward show. It tempts us to think we can find happiness in the things we can buy and display. It places ultimate value on material possessions.

"The boasting of what he has and does." _____

Definition: This phrase has to do with the attempt to feel superior to someone else. It is a self-centered desire to be somebody special by putting others down. It is pride in wealth, talent, education or any other area of achievement. This pride is not simply a realistic recognition that God has given us gifts and abilities, it is thinking that these gifts and abilities make us better and more important than other people.

---

verse 16 (these are listed on the sheet). Tell students, **"Think of some typical situations at school, in your neighborhood or at home that fit into this category. Then use your extra paper to write a story or draw a cartoon strip about one of these situations. For example, under 'lust of his eyes' you might write a story or draw a cartoon about someone who sees a stack of money on his parents' dresser and takes some of it, even though he knows he's not supposed to do so."** You might wish to explain that the categories may overlap, so that a single action might seem to fit more than one description. There are no hard and fast rules about this, so students should simply come up with a story that seems to fit pretty well into their assigned category.

Let students work, warning them when one minute remains. When time is up, regain their attention and ask groups to share what they have written or drawn. Ask a few questions such as these: **"Why might a person be attracted to this sort of thing? What makes the difference between a legitimate use and enjoyment of some things and an involvement that becomes 'loving the world' in the way that we are not supposed to? How can believers figure out that difference? How can we avoid crossing the line from the legitimate to the forbidden?"** Use ideas from the Teacher's Bible Study and your own study of God's Word to help you guide students in this discussion.

Make a transition to the Conclusion by saying something like this: **"We have talked about avoiding a love of the world and the things in the world. We have talked about some of the world's attractions. Now let's consider what we should do about this information."**

ALTERNATE EXPLORATION (40-45 minutes)

Materials needed: Extra Bibles, copies of Student Guide sheet "The World According to John," extra paper, pens or pencils, a sheet of poster board for each group of 4-5 students, glue or tape, scissors, felt pens, a variety of old magazines, catalogs, and newspapers; optional—copies of Student Guide sheet "Everything in the World."

Steps 1 and 2 (12-14 minutes): Follow Steps 1 and 2 in the original Exploration.

Step 3 (25-30 minutes): Briefly go through the three categories in 1 John 2:16, using the descriptions from the Teacher's Bible Study to explain "the cravings of sinful man, the lust of his eyes and the boasting of what he has and does."

You may wish to distribute the Student Guide sheet "Everything in the World," which gives these definitions.

Have each pair of students join with another pair to form small groups of 4-5 students. Indicate the magazines, glue and other supplies. Explain, **"Look through the magazines, catalogs and newspapers to find pictures and words which depict some of the things the world offers. Look for two kinds of things—ads and other presentations which simply present information about a product or service that is available, and those that make unreasonable promises about what the product can do for us, or which use an exploitive approach to sell a product. An example of the latter category would be using the sex appeal of attractive young women to sell automobiles. An example of unreasonable promises would be implying that using this product will solve all your major problems. After you have found a number of things for both categories, put it all together into a montage on a piece of poster board. Place the basic informational type of materials on one side, and the exploitive ones on the other side of your poster board. Be prepared to share your montage with the rest of us and to explain how the elements you have included fit in with the Scripture we have studied today."**

Let students work for 10 to 15 minutes, warning them when three minutes and then one minute remain. Then regain their attention. Have each group post their montage on the wall and share its message with the rest of the class.

Ask a few questions such as these: **"Why might a person be attracted to the things you have included on your montages? What makes the difference between a legitimate ad and an exploitive one? How can we tell the difference between a proper use and enjoyment of some things and an involvement that becomes 'loving the world' in the way that we are not supposed to? How can we avoid crossing the line from the legitimate to the forbidden?"** Use ideas from the Teacher's Bible Study and your own study of God's Word to help you guide students in this discussion. Stress the point that it's the person's attitude that makes the difference. Two different people can be involved in the same activity. One person keeps God first in his or her life, so there's no problem. The other person puts the activity first, and therefore is loving the world instead of God.

Make a transition to the Conclusion by saying something like this: **"We have discussed the importance of Christians guarding against loving the world, and we have attempted to define what that means in the context of John's letter. We have explored some of the things in our world that we may need to be careful about as we arrange our priorities. Now let's consider our personal response."**

CONCLUSION AND DECISION

CONCLUSION (3-5 minutes)

Materials needed: Extra Bibles, copies of Student Guide sheet "Reminder Card" (try to make the copies on card stock or heavy paper; then cut out each credit-card shape), felt pens.

Give each student a credit-card shaped piece of card stock. (If you are unable to copy the shapes onto card stock, copy them onto regular paper; provide sheets of card stock, scissors, and glue. Let each student glue a credit-card shape to a piece of card stock and cut it out.)

Explain, **"On your 'credit card' draw a little picture or symbol representing something that really tempts you to 'love the world.' Nobody else needs to know what this is all about, so you can be honest about this. Then write the words of Matthew 22:37 on the card. You can carry**

Reminder Card

[blank card template with 8 card-sized boxes arranged in 4 rows of 2]

this card in your pocket or your wallet as a reminder of the importance of putting God first."

You might want to look into the possibility of laminating the cards for students, or encouraging them to have it done. Libraries often have machines that will laminate small things at a low cost.

Close the session with prayer, asking God to help all of you love Him and put Him first.

ALTERNATE CONCLUSION (5-7 minutes)

Materials needed: Copies of Student Guide sheet "Balance the Books," pens or pencils.

Explain to students that the world sometimes looks good to us because its attractions seem immediate and readily apparent, whereas the benefits of loving and obeying God may not seem so obvious. In order to take a more objective look at the contrast between what the world offers and what God offers, students will complete a "ledger sheet" such as a bookkeeper might use to keep track of the financial records of a company. Distribute the "Balance the Books" sheet and ask students to

Balance the Books

List some of the attractions the world offers and some of the benefits that God offers. (Remember that "world" here means the world system that leaves God out and is opposed to Him.)

If you need some reminders about what God offers, check out some of these verses: **John 3:16-18; 4:13,14; 10:10; 11:25,26; 14:2,3,16,17; 15:11**

The World	God

complete it by filling in some of the things offered by the world and some of the things offered by God. (The sheet includes some Scripture references to help students remember some of God's benefits.) Then students are to fill out the "Bottom Line" portion of the sheet indicating which side of the ledger has more to offer.

After allowing time for students to work, close in prayer.

Major on the Majors

UNIT FOCUS

This unit examines John's discussion of several important issues: the matter of antichrists who teach false doctrine; the importance of standing firm in the faith despite the pressure of these antichrists; the joy of being children of a loving heavenly Father; and the necessity of demonstrating to others the love that He has lavished on us.

Session 5

Pick up on Today's Antichrists
Biblical Basis: 1 John 2:18-23; 4:2,3
Focus: The biblical way to measure a religious teaching is to determine what it says about the identity of Jesus Christ. John offers two important truths that form the "bottom line": Jesus is the Christ (which means that He is God); and Jesus Christ came in the flesh. He is God in a human body.

Session 6

Dealing with False Teaching
Biblical Basis: 1 John 2:24-27; John 4:1-26; 16:12-15; Acts 17:11; 2 Timothy 3:16,17; Hebrews 4:12; 10:24,25
Focus: In dealing with false teaching and people who are involved with it, believers need to think defensively and act lovingly. We should protect ourselves against the infiltration of unbiblical doctrines, but we should be gracious to the people who believe in and teach such doctrines.

Session 7

R Is for Relationship
Biblical Basis: 1 John 2:28—3:10
Focus: God wants to have a close, Father-child relationship with each of us. He is neither a tyrant nor an indulgent softy. He loves us lavishly; He makes demands of us; He helps us meet His demands.

Session 8

Put God's Love to Work in You
Biblical Basis: 1 John 3:11-18
Focus: Godly love involves forfeiting something that one values in order to help someone in need. Such love is evidence of the life of God within a person. People without this sort of love do not have God's life within them.

Unit Aims

You and your students will have accomplished the purpose of this unit of study if you can:
- NAME criteria for determining whether religious teachings about Christ are correct;
- DESCRIBE the relationship God wants to have with His children;
- EXPLAIN how believers can demonstrate that they have the love of God within them by sharing that love in practical, caring actions;
- DETERMINE ways they will respond to the important issues raised in this unit.

Pick up on Today's Antichrists

KEY VERSE
"Who is the liar? It is the man who denies that Jesus is the Christ. Such a man is the antichrist—he denies the Father and the Son." 1 John 2:22

BIBLICAL BASIS
1 John 2:18-23; 4:2,3

FOCUS OF THE SESSION
The biblical way to measure a religious teaching is to determine what it says about the deity of the Lord Jesus Christ.

AIMS OF THIS SESSION
You and your students will have accomplished the purpose of this Bible study session if you can:
- EXAMINE John's statement about the importance of stating that Jesus is the Christ;
- DISCUSS the meaning of the word "Christ";
- EVALUATE several teachings, using the biblical standards;
- MEMORIZE 1 John 2:22 so that it will be available to you when you need to use it.

TEACHER'S BIBLE STUDY

As he wrote to his "dear children," John moved from the importance of avoiding a love for the world to the importance of resisting false teaching. Evidently there were people among the believers who were trying to lead them astray from the truth about Jesus Christ. The situation was not to be taken lightly. John could not remain silent while watching this deception happen to those he considered extra-special. He wrote, "this is the last hour; and as you have heard that the antichrist is coming, even now many antichrists have come. This is how we know it is the last hour" (1 John 2:18). It has been the "last hour" for nearly 2,000 years. It is the hour when Christ is building His church. And it is important that His people have a correct understanding of who He is.

Antichrists and Deceivers
When John said that many antichrists had come, he was describing those who were against Christ. The word "antichrists" can refer either to opponents of Christ (those who are "anti" Christ) or to those

who put themselves in the place of Christ, claiming to be Christ. One idea suggests open opposition and the other subtle infiltration. In either case, antichrists battle against the true Christ. Those who are against God employ any number of methods to oppose Him.

John explained that these antichrists had left the church to which they never actually belonged. They had appeared to be one thing but were in reality something quite different (see 1 John 2:19). Acts 20:30,31 offers an appropriate description and warning: "Even from your own number men will arise and distort the truth in order to draw away disciples after them. So be on your guard!" Jesus Himself warned, "False Christs and false prophets will appear and perform signs and miracles to deceive the elect—if that were possible. So be on your guard; I have told you everything ahead of time" (Mark 13:22,23). John added his own warning about those who would attempt to lead Christians astray. He explained that they came not as open enemies but professing

to be friends. They were misleading and deluding Christians.

Jesus Is The Christ
In the face of so many who oppose Christ, 1 John 2:22,23 offers us a standard by which to measure their message. The truth is that "Jesus is the Christ" and that by acknowledging Christ the Son we acknowledge God the Father.

What did John mean when he said that it was a mark of the antichrist to deny that Jesus is the Christ? Today we are so accustomed to thinking of Him as "Jesus Christ" that we do not really think about the meaning of the title. The word "Christ" is a Greek word meaning "anointed." It is the equivalent of the Hebrew word "Messiah," which also means "anointed." In order to understand the significance of this word we need to look back into history.

To "anoint" means to rub or smear with oil. In ancient times people used oil for its cosmetic and medicinal values. It was their hand lotion, their cologne, their hair conditioner. In addition, oil was used for anointing in religious practices, such as the anointing of the objects pertaining to worship (see Exod. 30:12-29). Priests and kings were anointed as a sign that they were set apart for their special tasks.

The idea of anointing may be considered as one strand in the complex tapestry of the Old Testament. Another strand is the thought of the coming Redeemer. The promises of this coming One began immediately after the Fall (see Gen. 3:15) and are interspersed throughout the Old Testament (see, for example, Isa. 9:6; 53:1-12).

The "Anointed One" strand and the "coming Redeemer" strand came together as people understood more and more about the promises God was making to them. They saw that this One who was to be sent by God would be set apart for a special task and that He would have attributes of priests and kings. Thus He came to be known as the Messiah (in Hebrew) or the Christ (in Greek). The Jewish people may or may not have realized that their coming Messiah was to be God Himself in a human body. But they certainly knew that He was to be someone special.

When the angel Gabriel gave Mary the news that she was the woman chosen to be the mother of the long-awaited Redeemer, he referred to the coming One as "the Son of the Most High" and "the Son of God" (Luke 1:32,35). Later, when Jesus asked His disciples to express their understanding of His identity, Peter said, "You are the Christ, the Son of the living God" (Matt. 16:16). Jesus accepted this description and responded affirmatively: "Blessed are you, Simon son of Jonah, for this was not revealed to you by man, but by my Father in heaven" (v. 17).

Near the end of Jesus' ministry on earth, some Jewish people asked Him, "How long will you keep us in suspense? If you are the Christ, tell us plainly" (John 10:24). Jesus' reply included the statement, "I and the Father are one" (v. 30). While this statement may seem innocuous to us, the Jews knew the great significance of it. Jesus was, in fact, claiming to be God (see vv. 31-33).

Thus, when the apostle John wrote that the measuring stick for correct belief is the statement, "Jesus is the Christ," he was saying that the standard is the deity of Christ. Those who deny that Jesus is God are teaching false doctrine. It's as simple as that.

(For more study regarding the deity of Christ, you may wish to examine John 1:1 with Revelation 19:11-16; John 14:11; Matthew 11:27; Acts 2:36; Hebrews 1:1-3.)

John explained that not everyone who professes to be a Christian actually is one (see 1 John 2:19). A liar is one who simply does not tell the truth. The antichrists lie because they pretend to be part of the Christian community but in reality deny that Jesus is the Christ (see v. 22).

Later in his Epistle, John added another test: "Every spirit that acknowledges that Jesus Christ has come in the flesh is from God, but every spirit that does not acknowledge Jesus is not from God" (1 John 4:2,3).

In John's day it was the Gnostics who denied the union of divine and human in one person. They refused the truth of the Incarnation. Instead they said that Jesus was a human man who for a brief period of time was given divine powers (or even temporarily adopted into the Godhead). They denied that the man Jesus and the eternal Son of God were the same person possessing two perfect natures.

The Gnostic heresy is repeated in our day, with all sorts of variations and changes. At its core is always the denial of Christ's deity. Since it is not possible to deny the Son without also denying the Father (see 1 John 2:22,23), groups that deny Christ's deity are in fact denying the true nature of God Himself. And they are denying the "good news" that human beings can be restored to a right relationship to God through Christ. The deity of Jesus Christ is basic to salvation. If He is not God, He cannot be our Saviour. God had to become a man in order to provide redemption for us.

The Christian's Opposition

For those who believe that God's Word is authoritative, there is no choice but to accept the test that it presents. Many in the world come with the message that all roads leading to God are good, or that all religions are freeways that bring us to the same place. Jesus said that He is the only way to God and that it is a narrow road that leads to eternal life (see John 14:6; Matt. 7:13,14).

There is a trend today toward worldwide unity for religions. Unity is desirable for churches with orthodox Christian beliefs, but sometimes this movement exerts pressure on us to overlook or at least minimize the things that divide the religions and to emphasize the areas of agreement. This practice may lead to confusion about essential doctrines of the Bible. We must never lose sight of the fact that Jesus is the Christ, and that this statement means that He is God.

Another area of confusion has to do with human nature. Many believe that people are naturally good. Yet throughout the Bible we are reminded of our sinful and rebellious nature (see Jer. 17:9; Rom. 3:23). The first rebellion in history happened in the garden of Eden where the environment was perfect and there was no heredity to blame actions on (see Gen. 3:1-24).

In John's day the Gnostics boasted of superior knowledge. Today we are exposed to a similar gnosticism by people professing to have special knowledge or extraordinary experiences. No matter what claims they make, they are subject to the same question: Who do they say Jesus is?

It may be important during this class session to note the difference between intellectually knowing that Jesus is the Christ and knowing Him personally. Even if students know the facts that are God's truth they may not have incorporated these facts—and the Person of Christ—into their lives. James wrote that even the demons believe in God (see Jas. 2:19); Paul said that we must believe by faith in the Person and work of Christ to truly belong to Him (see Gal. 2:16).

Even a religion that talks about Jesus can be a counterfeit, an unbiblical religion. Many imitate Christ and try to replace Him. People seek fulfillment of their deep spiritual needs; some find a substitute satisfaction apart from God's revelation in His Word. It is our challenge to expose high school students to the truth of the gospel of Christ and provide ways by which they can learn to make the gospel meaningful, practical, and usable for their lives. They will have to find for themselves the answer to the question, Who is Jesus? And they will need to be prepared to ask the same question when confronted by any group, religion, or cult claiming to offer new, additional, or contrary information. At the same time, we want our students to be sensitive and courteous to those who adhere to different doctrines. It is possible to stand firmly on the truth of the gospel without demeaning people who adhere to other teachings.

Test Them Yourself

Some religions and groups can be identified quite easily as unbiblical by their obvious denial of Christ's deity. Others are camouflaged and hidden behind familiar language and traditions which mask their true beliefs. Often they offer an imitation of the true gospel which is actually directly opposed to our historical Christianity. The word "cult" is sometimes used to describe a group that adheres to unorthodox teachings. Often a cult gathers around a specific person or someone's individual interpretation of the Bible. Many aggressively prey upon Christians, especially young ones or those who are not well grounded in the Bible. Some leaders even lie in order to protect their mission and their followers.

It may be helpful while examining God's test of those who oppose Him to know something about the view of Jesus held by various groups. Note that each group's view of Scripture also plays an important role. Cults usually either reinterpret the Scripture to suit their particular ideas, or produce additional books without which they consider the Bible incomplete. These are the methods that enable them to deny the true character of our God.

Jehovah's Witnesses are followers of the interpretations of Charles T. Russell and J. F. Rutherford. Russell and his early followers claimed to have the only true interpretation of the Bible, which was based upon their own preconceived ideas. Russell published a series of books titled *Studies in the Scriptures.* He said that no one could properly understand the Bible without them.

Jehovah's Witnesses believe that God transferred life from heaven to Mary and that Jesus' birth on earth was not an incarnation. (That is, Jesus was not God in a human body.) They describe the doctrine of the Trinity as a creation of Satan. They say that Jesus was God's first creation and that the Father is greater than the Son. They say Jesus is "a mighty god" but not "the Almighty God" and did not take His human body to heaven, only a spirit. For them, "the death of Jesus removed the effects of Adam's sin on his offspring and laid the foundation of the New World of righteousness including the Millennium of Christ's reign."[1]

The Church of Jesus Christ of Latter Day Saints (known as the Mormon church) adheres to the teachings of Joseph Smith and Brigham Young, and the "God-breathed" proclamations of their current prophets. "From the very beginning, Mormons said the Bible is unreliable, even though it is used by them and they lay claim to being biblical. The eighth Article of Faith in Mormonism states, 'We believe the Bible to be the word of God as far as it is translated correctly.' Mormonism, in reality, needs an unreliable Bible because the Bible contradicts almost all of Mormonism's doctrines and practices."[2] Three books form the central written authority of the Mormon faith: The *Book of Mormon, The Pearl of Great Price,* and *Doctrine and Covenants.*

Mormon doctrine is polytheistic—that is, it teaches that there are multiple gods. It says that the God of our world was once an ordinary man who has since become exalted, and that ordinary men may become gods. This doctrine says that Adam is our Father and our God, and that Jesus is the son of this Adam-god and Mary. According to some Mormons, Jesus was the one being married at Cana. Mormons reject the fact that Christ is part of the divine Trinity. Rather, they say that the faithful will become gods as Jesus did.

The Mormon doctrine of salvation says that faith is not enough; it must be supplemented by baptism, obedience to the requirements of the Mormon church, a life of good works, and keeping God's commandments. In other words, Christ's work was ineffective for the cleansing of some sin. His death atoned only for the sin of Adam, but people will be punished for their own sin.[3]

Christian Scientists are disciples of Mary Baker Eddy. Her "revelation" is found in her textbook *Science and Health with Key to the Scriptures.* "The Christian Scientists, like the other mind science cults, deny the all-sufficiency and inerrancy of the Bible . . . . Instead the mind science cults hold the writings of their founders/ leaders as a better and more accurate revelation than that found in the Bible. Christian Science considers Mrs. Eddy's textbook and other writings as virtually infallible."[4]

Christian Science denies the Trinity and the deity of Christ. It teaches that Jesus is God's Son, not God; and contends that He never physically died as the disciples thought, nor did He rise from the dead. His ascension was also merely a change from one sphere to another.

The Unity Church follows the teachings of Charles and Myrtle Fillmore. The Fillmores wrote that Jesus Christ was simply a parable of a man passing from a natural to spiritual consciousness. Unity teaches that the difference between Jesus and us is in the demonstration of our inherent spiritual capacities; we have not yet expressed perfection as Christ did. The Fillmores also taught that no miraculous change takes place when a person is "born again," but that it is a process of perfecting our character and form. Unity conveniently redefines biblical terminology to make it fit their teachings.

The Bahai Faith acknowledges Moses, Jesus, Mohammed, Zoroaster, Buddha, Confucius, Krishna, Lao and a prophet named Baha'u'llah. All are considered manifestations of the divine being. Each appeared in his own time to illuminate the people who lived at that time. God revealed Himself through each of them, culminating in Baha'u'llah. This prophet's writings, rather than the Bible, are considered the final authority in matters of religion.

Baha'ism claims that the only important things are unity and brotherhood; they seek to totally unite the world.

Unitarians attempt to exalt reason and rationalism. Unitarians have no official authoritative or representative statement because the theology of each person is the reflection of his or her own personal "religious" experience—and these may vary and change. Thoughts commonly agreed upon include the oneness of man with the Eternal, every form of life being divine, and the essential goodness of human nature. Unitarians apparently claim to be a form of Christianity, yet they deny the historic doctrines of the Christian Church (the trinity, the deity of Christ, His virgin birth, the vicarious atonement, Christ's bodily resurrection, and His return). Unitarians suggest that God's plan of redemption as portrayed in the Bible is offensive and immoral.

For additional help in understanding the basics of Christian doctrine and the teachings of cults, the following books by Walter Martin may be helpful (all are published by Regal Books, Ventura, California): *Essential Christianity, The New Cults, Martin Speaks Out on the Cults.* Dr. Martin also has a number of cassette tapes on the topic of cults. They are available through Gospel Light, P.O. Box 3875, Ventura, California 93006, or at your local Christian supplier.

In this lesson your students will be presented with the truth about Christ in order that they may be better equipped to evaluate the doctrines of other religions and cults. High schoolers who are not aware of the specific standard by which they can measure a group's beliefs will be susceptible to false doctrines. You can help them to become aware of the existence of antichrists and their teachings, and to explore what the Bible really says about God, Jesus Christ, and the way to salvation. Scripture will be their best defense against any who would attempt to draw them away from God (see Ps. 119:9,105).

Note: The topic of false teachings continues in Session 6, which emphasizes how to respond to people who are involved in cults. If you find that your students have a high level of interest in this subject, they may need further study. You might wish to offer a midweek study group using the course *Counterfeits At Your Door,* available from Gospel Light Publications or through your local supplier.

Some of your learners may not know Christ personally. They might be offended by the biblical insistence that those who deny the deity of Jesus Christ are deceivers and antichrists. You will need to exercise caution and tact in the way you present the material, without compromising on the doctrines that are important and essential about Christ.

Footnotes

1. Walter R. Martin, *The Kingdom of the Cults* (Grand Rapids: Zondervan Publishing House, 1966), p. 46.
2. James Bjornstad, *Counterfeits At Your Door* (Ventura, California: Regal Books, 1979), pp. 104, 105.
3. Martin, *Op. cit.,* chapter 6.
4. Dr. Walter Martin, *Martin Speaks Out on the Cults* (Ventura, California: Regal Books, 1983), p. 71.

THIS WEEK'S TEACHING PLAN

Approach to the Word

APPROACH (3-5 minutes)

Materials needed: Student Guide sheet "Which Way to the Game?" for each learner, scissors, extra pens or pencils.

Distribute copies of Student Guide sheet "Which Way to the Game?" Read the instructions aloud. Note that students are to

---

Which Way to the Game?

Hurry! You're almost late for the biggest basketball game of the year. You need to get to the Cedar High gym as quickly as possible.

Instructions: Cut out the traffic signs below. By trial and error, place all signs in the appropriate spots on the maze. Only one combination of signs will correctly complete the maze.

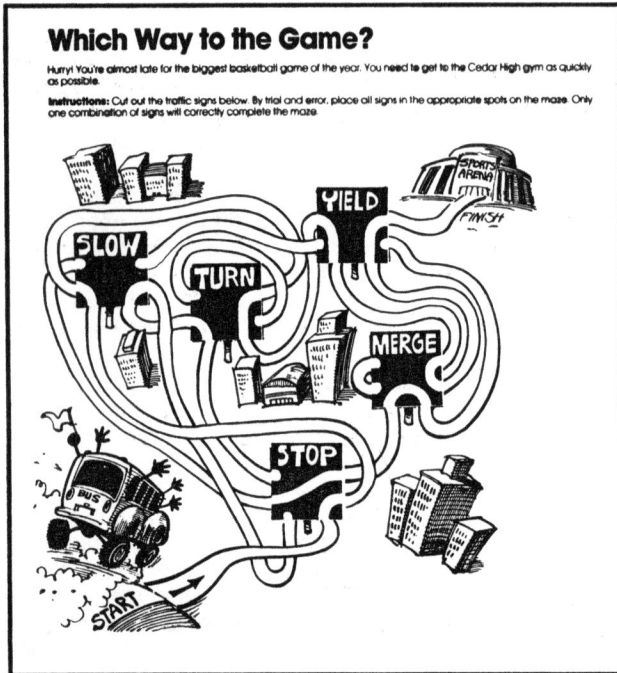

---

cut out the traffic signs provided on the sheet. They must put them in the correct arrangement on the maze in order to create the correct pathway to the Sports Arena.

After allowing a few minutes for learners to work on the Student Guide, make a transition to the Exploration by saying something like this: **"You had to choose the right direction to travel in order to get through the maze correctly. The Bible gives us information that will help us make the right choices when we hear ideas about Jesus. It helps us go in the right direction in our understanding of who God is. Let's take some time to see what some of this information is."**

ALTERNATE APPROACH (3-5 minutes)

Materials needed: Yarn, scissors, ruler or tape measure.

Bring a supply of yarn to class along with several pairs of scissors. Give each student the task of cutting a certain length of yarn, with different students having different lengths to cut. Do not let them use any measuring device.

When all students have cut a piece of yarn they think is the right length, produce a ruler or tape measure and see how close each segment of yarn is to the assigned length.

Make a transition to the Exploration by saying something like this: **"We found that trying to measure our yarn without a ruler was not totally accurate. Similarly, trying to evaluate religious teachings requires a standard by which we can measure. Today we're going to take a look at a couple of standards given to us by John that we can use to evaluate religious teachings."**

Bible Exploration

EXPLORATION (20-30 minutes)

Materials needed: Student Guide sheets "Put Them to the Test," "Can You Spot Flak from the Antichrists?" and "Truth or Consequences" for each learner, extra Bibles, extra pens or pencils.

Step 1 (10-15 minutes): Guide students in forming pairs. Ask them to read 1 John 2:18-23 and then turn to the "Put Them to the Test" Student Guide sheet. Have them study each

---

Put Them to the Test _____

According to the Scriptures listed below, what standard should we use to measure the truth of statements about Christ?

1 John 2:22,23:

1 John 4:2,3:

Scripture and then fill in the blanks as instructed, stating the standards by which believers can measure the truth of statements about Christ.

When students have finished, ask them to share the standards they discovered. Ask a few questions such as these: **"Do you understand what God requires? How does that make you feel? Who can paraphrase the key thoughts for us?"** Emphasize the importance of the two statements: Jesus is the Christ, and Jesus Christ came in the flesh.

Distribute the Student Guide sheet "Can You Spot Flak from the Antichrists?" and go over the information it gives about the

---

Can You Spot Flak from the Antichrists?

Ask just about anyone in your church what the mark of the antichrist is and they will probably tell you that it is the number 666, which might be glued, stapled, pinned, or tattooed to obvious parts of a person's anatomy. Wrong.

---

mark of the antichrists. You may wish to provide additional information from the Teacher's Bible Study. To say "Jesus is the Christ" is to say that He is God. This is the standard given by John for measuring any belief system. Those who deny the deity of Christ also deny the very nature of God. That's why John said that those who deny the deity of Christ deny both the Father and the Son (see 1 John 2:22).

Step 2 (1-2 minutes): Briefly say something like this: **"God's standards apply to everyone. There are many people around us who appear to be very good, even 'religious,' yet they deny that Jesus is God. You are surrounded in your neighborhoods, at school, or at work by people who will offer all kinds of information and opinions about God and Christ. These people may seem to be Christians, but they might not even be close. When presented with people's ideas about Christ, it is important that you remember the standard the Bible gives."**

Step 3 (10-15 minutes): Guide students in forming groups of three to five. Ask them to look at the "Truth or Consequences" Student Guide sheets. Give each group one of

---

Truth or Consequences

Read one or more of the following situations. Then answer the questions that follow the description of the situation. If a Scripture from the "Put Them to the Test" sheet seems appropriate in responding to the situation, jot it down.

---

the assignments from the sheets and say something like this: **"Have someone in your group read the situation aloud to the others. Then work together to evaluate the beliefs represented. Determine whether they pass the test given in 1 John. Complete the evaluation called for on the Student Guide sheets."**

After allowing time for students to work, have the groups report their results. Re-emphasize the importance of measuring every teaching against the biblical standard of the deity of Jesus Christ.

Make a transition to the Conclusion by saying something like this: **"We've learned God's standard for judging unbiblical teaching. If it is going to help us we need to be able to retrieve it from our minds whenever needed. Let's consider how we will include it in our evaluation of other beliefs."**

ALTERNATE EXPLORATION (30-45 minutes)

Materials needed: Bibles, paper, pens or pencils, copies of Student Guide sheet "Can You Spot Flak from the Antichrists?"

Preparation: Well before your class session, talk to three or four people in your church (lay persons or members of the pastoral staff) who have a special interest in studying cults. Ask each person to prepare some information on one particular cult (a different one for each person). Ask these individuals to come to your class prepared to take part in a panel discussion as if they were actually members of the respective groups. Guests may wish to bring some materials documenting the beliefs of the cults they "represent."

Step 1 (10-12 minutes): Provide blank paper. Guide students in forming pairs. Ask them to read 1 John 2:18-23 and 4:1,2. Then explain, **"In these sections John talks about the antichrist—someone who is against Christ or tries to put himself in Christ's place. John gives us two very specific statements about how we can tell who this person is. Go back and look in the passages to find these statements. Then write them out on your paper."**

After a few minutes regain students' attention and ask for their responses. They should have discovered the statements, "Who is the liar? It is the man who denies that Jesus is the Christ. Such a man is the antichrist—he denies the Father and the Son" and "Every spirit that acknowledges that Jesus Christ has come in the flesh is from God, but every spirit that does not acknowledge Jesus is not from God."

In other words, the one who is promoting false doctrine about Jesus is the antichrist, the one who is against Him. The true doctrine about Jesus is that He is the Christ and that He came in the flesh. Because we are so accustomed to thinking of Him as "Jesus Christ" we may miss the significance of the title. Distribute copies of the Student Guide sheet "Can You Spot Flak from the Antichrists?" Go over it with students, providing additional information from the Teacher's Bible Study if you wish.

Step 2 (10-12 minutes): Explain to students that they will have an opportunity to question several guests who will represent several organizations with beliefs that differ from biblical Christianity. (Sometimes these organizations are called "cults.") As preparation, students are to examine some of the Scriptures listed on the "Can You Spot . . . " sheet and then come up with a few questions to ask the guests. (You may wish to assign the Scriptures to different pairs to make sure all are covered.) Sample questions might include, "What is your teaching about Jesus Christ? What is your teaching about the way human beings must relate to God?" and so on.

Step 3 (10-20 minutes): Introduce your guests. Explain that they are actually people in your church fellowship, but that for today's session they are playing the roles of members of different religions. Ask each one to give a brief summary of the teachings of the religion he or she represents. After all have done this, let students ask questions. Guests should remain in

their roles, saying things like, "We teach that Christ is . . . "—not, "They teach . . . . " This may be difficult for guests, but it will maintain a more realistic atmosphere.

When about two minutes remain, call for one or two last questions. Then thank your guests and permit them to leave before you conclude the session. Make a transition to the Conclusion by saying something like this: **"We've learned a good measuring stick for judging religious teachings, and we have had an opportunity to hear what some groups teach about Jesus Christ. If the test—the measuring stick—is going to work for us, we need to have it available to us when we are presented with information about Christ. Let's consider 1 John 2:22 individually and think about how we can refer to it when we come upon various teachings about Jesus."**

CONCLUSION AND DECISION

CONCLUSION (3-5 minutes)

Materials needed: "Handy Dandy Lie Detector" Student Guide sheet, scissors, thumb tacks, completed "Lie Detector."

Remind students of the importance of having the biblical standard of truth available so it can be used whenever they need it. Distribute the "Handy Dandy Lie Detector" Student Guide sheets, scissors, and thumb tacks. Have students follow

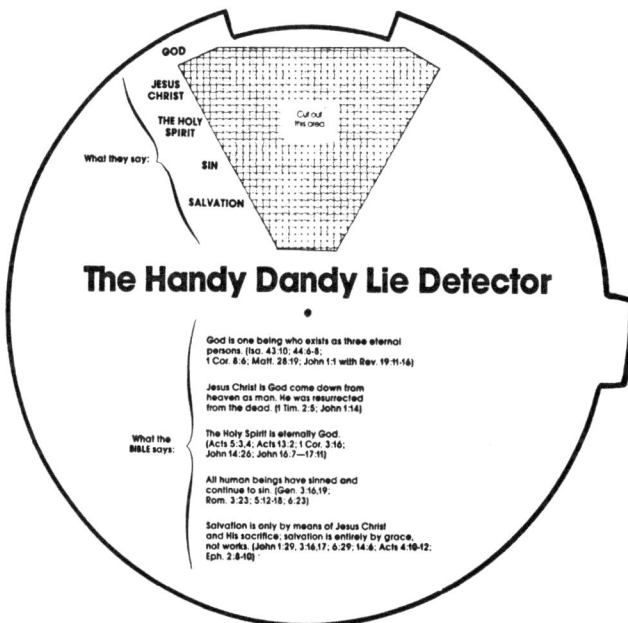

The Handy Dandy Lie Detector

GOD
JESUS CHRIST
THE HOLY SPIRIT
What they say:
SIN
SALVATION
Cut out this area

What the **BIBLE** says:

God is one being who exists as three eternal persons. (Isa. 43:10; 44:6-8; 1 Cor. 8:6; Matt. 28:19; John 1:1 with Rev. 19:11-16)

Jesus Christ is God come down from heaven as man. He was resurrected from the dead. (1 Tim. 2:5; John 1:14)

The Holy Spirit is eternally God. (Acts 5:3,4; Acts 13:2; 1 Cor. 3:16; John 14:26; John 16:7—17:11)

All human beings have sinned and continue to sin. (Gen. 3:16,19; Rom. 3:23; 5:12-18; 6:23)

Salvation is only by means of Jesus Christ and His sacrifice; salvation is entirely by grace, not works. (John 1:29; 3:16,17; 6:29; 14:6; Acts 4:10-12; Eph. 2:8-10)

the directions on the Student Guide sheets to cut out the segments and assemble the "Lie Detector." Show them your completed version as a model. Suggest that they keep the "Lie Detectors" in their Bibles as a reminder of the biblical standard for measuring religious teachings.

Close in prayer.

ALTERNATE CONCLUSION (1-2 minutes)

Explain, **"As Christians, we need to be able to refer to the biblical standard of truth whenever we need it. One good way to guarantee that we can do so is to memorize it. Let's spend a few minutes working on this."** One way to help students memorize the verse is to break it into phrases. Repeat each phrase a number of times with students. Ask students to recite the verse together when they seem to have it learned. Encourage learners to review the verse regularly in the coming week to cement it in their memory.

Close in prayer.

Dealing with False Teaching

KEY VERSE
"Now the Bereans were of more noble character than the Thessalonians, for they received the message with great eagerness and examined the Scriptures every day to see if what Paul said was true." Acts 17:11

BIBLICAL BASIS
1 John 2:24-27; John 4:1-26; 16:12-15; Acts 17:11; 2 Timothy 3:16,17; Hebrews 4:12; 10:24,25

FOCUS OF THE SESSION
In dealing with false teaching and people who are involved with it, believers need to think defensively and act lovingly.

AIMS OF THIS SESSION
You and your students will have accomplished the purpose of this Bible study session if you can:
- DESCRIBE biblical standards for evaluating religious teachings;
- DISCUSS ways to respond to peers who are involved in cults or other forms of false teaching;
- DETERMINE one step you will take to prepare yourself for a potential encounter with someone who is involved in some form of false teaching.

TEACHER'S BIBLE STUDY

In Session 5 you and your students examined John's warning about antichrists—people who deny the deity of Jesus and therefore the very nature of God. In this session you will again discuss false teachings. This time the emphasis will be on the believer's response in two areas: (1) defending his or her own thinking from false doctrines and (2) acting graciously and lovingly toward people who believe false teachings.

Defensive Thinking
In 1 John 2:26 the apostle told his "dear ones" that he had a reminder for them. Because there were people trying to lead them away from God's truth, John instructed them to stand firm in what they had learned. He asked them, in the light of what they had been taught in the past, to "hang in there."

In Session 5 we saw two criteria suggested by John for evaluating a teaching: (1) It must acknowledge that Jesus is the Christ (see 1 John 2:22). We saw that this means the same as saying that Jesus is God. (2) The teaching must acknowledge

that Jesus Christ has come in the flesh (see 1 John 4:2,3). These two statements can be put together in one sentence: Jesus, He is God in a human body. Believers who have studied the Scripture and become convinced of the truth of this statement have made one good step toward protecting themselves from false teaching.

Help for the Christian: The Holy Spirit
John assured his readers—thus assuring us—that believers are equipped to stand against those who would deceive them, because they have God's revealed truth in them. We don't have to accept uncritically every wind of doctrine that blows by us. We can test doctrine against the two bedrock statements examined in 1 John and against the entire revelation of God's Word.

Numerous cults bombard us, attempting to win our allegiance. Some have gained support because they claim to have special revelation. Many people are naive enough to fall for teachings that sound good, without subjecting those

teachings to any kind of test of their authenticity. Christians should not be so gullible.

John's readers had been taught the truth. He urged them to stick to that truth rather than falling for a counterfeit system. And he assured them that the anointing they had received from God remained in them to teach them about all things. Every believer has the Holy Spirit within, to teach and to guide. Jesus Himself promised, "When he, the Spirit of truth, comes, he will guide you into all truth. He will not speak on his own; he will speak only what he hears, and he will tell you what is yet to come. He will bring glory to me by taking from what is mine and making it known to you. All that belongs to the Father is mine. That is why I said the Spirit will take from what is mine and make it known to you" (John 16:12-15). The Spirit can show us the truth or falseness of any doctrine if we will ask Him to do so.

Help from God's Word
God provides another help in our search for the truth: His Word, the Bible.

It's a history book; it's a love letter from our heavenly Father; it contains what we need to know about Him and the life He wants us to live. "All Scripture is God-breathed and is useful for teaching, rebuking, correcting and training in righteousness, so that the man of God may be thoroughly equipped for every good work" (2 Tim. 3:16,17). "The word of God is living and active. Sharper than any double-edged sword, it penetrates even to dividing soul and spirit, joints and marrow; it judges the thoughts and attitudes of the heart" (Heb. 4:12). If we will study God's Word with the help of God's Spirit, we have an unbeatable combination!

This is not to say that human teachers are unnecessary or undesirable. God sets aside certain people with special gifts and skills in the area of Bible study and Bible teaching (see 1 Cor. 12:28). These people can spend their time studying the Bible with the Spirit's help and then share with the rest of us what they have learned. But we should never accept *any* person's teaching without question. We should follow the example of the people of Berea. When they heard the apostle Paul preach in their synagogue, "they received the message with great eagerness and examined the Scriptures every day to see if what Paul said was true" (Acts 17:11). Notice that while they *received* the message eagerly, they did not automatically *accept* it. They checked it out for themselves against God's Word. The result? Many of them believed in Jesus (see v. 12).

Help One Another

Another source of help for the believer confronted with a new teaching is other Christians. The author of Hebrews urged, "Let us consider how we may spur one another on toward love and good deeds. Let us not give up meeting together, as some are in the habit of doing, but let us encourage one another—and all the more as you see the Day approaching" (Heb. 10:24,25).

Christians can encourage one another in the Christian faith. One way we do this is by meeting together regularly for Sunday School, worship, Bible study, youth groups, caring groups and other ministries. High school students can meet informally on their campus, eating lunch together and sharing what they are learning currently from God's Word. If there is a Christian club on campus, that is another source of encouragement.

For specific help in understanding the truths of the Bible and checking out a new doctrine, young people might consult their pastor, youth pastor, volunteer youth leader, parent, or another adult who has a good understanding of God's Word and how to interpret it correctly.

Gracious Actions

It is important to think defensively when confronted with a teaching that may not be biblical. We have seen that we have a number of helps available to us: the Holy Spirit, God's Word, other believers. All can help us defend ourselves against untruth. We need to remember, however, that we need not be defensive toward the *people* who are involved in various forms of false teaching, such as cults. We must follow our Lord's example in treating people graciously even as we stand firm for the truth.

You and your students will examine the encounter between the Lord Jesus and the woman at the well in Samaria. This story provides a model of the way a Christian should treat people when trying to share God's truth with them.

Although it is not the main point of the story, the woman was involved in an unbiblical form of worship, and Jesus talked with her about worshiping the true God. In addition, her personal life demonstrated a lack of morality, and Jesus also addressed this issue kindly but firmly.

The account is found in John 4. Jesus and His disciples were traveling, evidently on foot, through Samaria. Jews and Samaritans did not get along very well, but our Lord was not one to adhere to negative social conventions. It didn't bother Him to travel through an area where His ethnic group was not appreciated.

So the little group came to the city of Sychar. Jesus was tired, so He sat down by the well while His disciples went into town to buy food. A woman came to the well to get some water. Jesus asked her for a drink. Note that He made the first effort at contact, that He did it courteously, and that He started out with a commonplace human experience, the need for a drink of water.

The woman was surprised that a Jew would speak to a Samaritan, so she asked Him about it. He responded, "If you knew the gift of God and who it is that asks you for a drink, you would have asked him and he would have given you living water" (John 4:10). Still treating the woman with courtesy and dignity, He made a tantalizing statement that was just about guaranteed to cause the woman to ask for more information.

And of course she did ask, giving Him the opportunity to tell her more about the living water—water that will permit people never to thirst again, "a spring of water welling up to eternal life" (v.14). The woman, still thinking in everyday, earthly terms, asked Him to tell her more about this water so that she would not have to undergo the daily effort of drawing water from the well.

Jesus responded by asking her to bring her husband. She replied, "I have no husband" (v.17). Jesus pointed out that she was quite right—that she had had five husbands, and was presently involved with a man to whom she was not married. Yet He did this quite politely and without using any condemnatory language: He simply stated the facts. He even gave her a compliment of sorts; He told her, "What you have just said is quite true" (v. 18).

That He knew about her life in such detail was a source of amazement to the woman, as it may be to modern-day readers. It evidently was a manifestation of His divine nature. Naturally believers today do not have the advantage of being God in human flesh, but we do have God the Holy Spirit within us. He may not choose to reveal to us intimate facts about the lives of people we talk to, but He can help us to be sensitive to their needs and to find the right words to say to them.

At this point the woman brought up a theological issue. She may have been uncomfortable with the personal tone the conversation had taken, or she may have been expressing a hunger to know the truth about God. She said, "Sir, I can see that you are a prophet. Our fathers worshiped on this mountain, but you Jews claim that the place where we must worship is in Jerusalem" (v. 19).

The woman was part of a group that adhered to a false teaching. The Samaritans were descendants of mixed marriages between Jews and pagans. They had, over the years, turned away from the worship of the true God, and there was mutual hostility between Samaritans and Jews. Jesus responded to the woman with a clear statement of the truth (see vv. 21-24). He was courteous but He did not soften the truth at all. When the woman referred to the coming Messiah, He straightforwardly declared, "I who speak to you am he" (v. 26).

Your study of the passage will end with verse 26, since the focus is on Jesus' treatment of the woman. You may wish to read verses 27-42 for the conclusion of the story, including the amazement of the disciples and the conversion of many people in the town through the testimony of the woman.

As you guide your students in their study of the Bible in this session, remind them of the two important elements in responding to false teachings: *Think defensively, act graciously.*

THIS WEEK'S TEACHING PLAN

APPROACH TO THE WORD

APPROACH (5-7 minutes)

Materials needed: Copies of Student Guide sheet "What Do You Say?"

Make sure each student has a copy of the Student Guide sheet "What Do You Say?" Guide learners in forming pairs.

Dealing with False Teaching
Winter #6

Walking in God's Light

What Do You Say?

Read the statements below and decide whether you agree or disagree with each one.

1. A false teaching is not the same as a difference in interpretation.

2. If a church is truly a Christian church, it will not have any false teachings.

3. A church can be correct in many of its beliefs and still be false in some.

4. A sincere Christian can have an incorrect understanding of a Bible passage.

Instruct them to look over the Student Guide sheets together and to discuss their responses to the agree-disagree statements. After allowing about three minutes, regain students' attention and ask them to report their responses. You might wish to point out that many sincere believers have different ways of understanding a number of biblical subjects. Just because someone disagrees with one's interpretation does not necessarily mean that that person is following a false doctrine. People can be mistaken in their understanding of what God is saying to us through the Bible—after all, He is an infinite God attempting to communicate with very finite people. But there are criteria for determining that a whole system of teaching is false. Those are the criteria given in 1 John.

Move to the Bible Exploration by saying something like this: **"Last week we talked about a biblical standard for evaluating religious teachings. This week we are going to continue our exploration of the problem of false teaching by determining what we should do when we are faced with such a teaching and how we should respond to friends who may be involved in organizations that support such teachings. These organizations are sometimes called cults. First let's review the Bible's standard for evaluating a doctrine or teaching."**

ALTERNATE APPROACH (5-7 minutes)

Materials needed: Dictionary, chalkboard and chalk, paper, pencils.

Select from the dictionary a word that students are not likely to know. One example is "scrofula"—tuberculosis of lymph glands, especially in the neck. Write the word on the chalkboard. Guide students in forming teams of four or five. Give each team paper and pencil.

Explain, **"Your task is to determine the meaning of the word written on the chalkboard and write down the meaning you decide on. Then we'll compare what the different groups have written."**

Allow one or two minutes for students to think, discuss, and

write. Then regain their attention. Ask the groups to report their ideas. Then read the actual definition from the dictionary.

Make a transition to the Bible Exploration by saying something like this: **"Our little exercise pointed out that we need to check against an authority to make sure that we really understand the meaning of a word. Similarly, we need to check with the authority—the Bible—when we are trying to figure out whether a certain teaching is true or false. Let's take some time today to see how we can be prepared to deal with various teachings we may encounter."**

BIBLE EXPLORATION

EXPLORATION (25-35 minutes)

Materials needed: Bibles, pens or pencils, copies of Student Guide sheets "The Biblical Brilliance Quiz" and "Encounter in Samaria."

Step 1 (3-5 minutes): Ask students to restate the standards for evaluating a religious teaching from Session 5. They should be able to state that a teaching is false if it (1) denies that Jesus is the Christ (which means that He is God) and/or (2) denies that Jesus Christ came in the flesh (see 1 John 2:22; 4:2,3). Such teaching denies the very nature of God and prevents its followers from knowing Him (see 1 John 2:23).

Explain that these two statements are the "bottom line" when it comes to doctrine. Many other scriptural teachings rest on these and therefore must be accepted by people who accept these, but there are other areas that are open to discussion. That's why there can be so many opinions about a number of things by people who adhere firmly to the basics of the gospel of Christ.

Step 2 (10-15 minutes): Make sure each student has a copy of the Student Guide sheet "The Biblical Brilliance Quiz."

The Biblical Brilliance Quiz

Read 1 John 2:24-27; John 16:12-15; Acts 17:11; 2 Timothy 3:16,17; Hebrews 4:12; Hebrews 10:24,25. Then complete the statements below by selecting the correct word(s) to fill in the blanks.

1. The people John wrote to in 1 John had probably "heard from the beginning" that _____
   a. nice people wash their hands before dinner
   b. Jesus was the Son of God
   c. Jesus was one of God's children just as they were

2. The Holy Spirit teaches believers _____
   a. how to get ahead in life
   b. how to "tune-in" to the cosmos
   c. truth

3. The Bereans were more noble than the Thessalonians because _____
   a. they received more blessings from God
   b. they didn't eat meat
   c. they received the gospel eagerly and compared it to Scripture

4. Christians today should _____ like the Bereans.
   a. be suspicious of Paul
   b. study Scripture
   c. be noble

5. Scripture comes from _____
   a. wise teachers
   b. a bunch of guys who died 1,900 years ago
   c. God

6. Scripture is good for _____
   a. impressing others with your good memory
   b. teaching, rebuking and training
   c. recording ancient customs and poetry

7. One way Christians can continue to grow is by _____
   a. giving each other vitamins as gifts
   b. not developing bad habits
   c. sharing with and encouraging one another regularly

8. Based on the Scriptures you have just read and on your own ideas and experiences, list ideas for ways believers can prepare themselves to recognize and deal with false teachings.

Guide students in forming groups of four to six. Explain, **"Read the Scripture indicated on your student sheet and answer the questions you find there. Be prepared to share your findings with the class when we finish."**

After allowing time for students to work through the assignment, regain their attention and ask groups to report their responses to the questions. Emphasize the points that believers must study the Bible, rely on the Holy Spirit to teach them, and encourage one another to stick to the truth of the gospel.

Step 3 (10-12 minutes): Explain, **"Whenever we deal with false teachings there is going to be some tension between the way we respond to the teaching itself and the way we respond to people who are involved in the group that pushes the teaching. We've explored some ways we can protect ourselves against false ideas. Let's explore some Scripture and see if we can come up with some ideas on how to treat the people involved in those ideas."**

Distribute copies of the Student Guide sheet "Encounter in Samaria." Have learners return to their groups and work

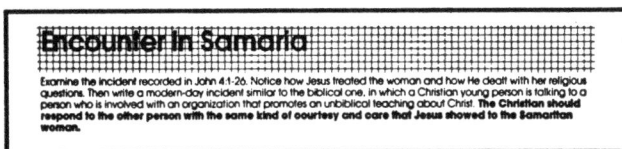

Encounter in Samaria

Examine the incident recorded in John 4:1-26. Notice how Jesus treated the woman and how He dealt with her religious questions. Then write a modern-day incident similar to the biblical one, in which a Christian young person is talking to a person who is involved with an organization that promotes an unbiblical teaching about Christ. **The Christian should respond to the other person with the same kind of courtesy and care that Jesus showed to the Samaritan woman.**

together to read the Scripture and write a story as instructed on the sheet.

After allowing time for students to work on the assignment, regain their attention and ask them to present their work. Emphasize the importance of the courtesy and dignity with which Jesus treated the woman of Samaria, coupled with His straightforward presentation of the truth about God. Explain that it is possible to be **defensive in our thinking**—to protect ourselves against false doctrine— and at the same time to be **loving in our actions** toward people who believe those false doctrines.

Make a transition to the Conclusion by saying something like this: **"We've talked about the importance of recognizing false teachings and protecting ourselves against them, while at the same time maintaining courtesy and love toward people who believe in those teachings. Let's spend some time thinking about how we will apply these ideas personally."**

ALTERNATE EXPLORATION: (40-55 minutes)

Materials needed: Bibles, copies of Student Guide sheet "The Biblical Brilliance Quiz," portable television, video cassette recorder and camera, video cassette tape, note cards with information about the beliefs of several cults (use information from Teacher's Bible Study and resources listed there), other resources giving information about the teachings of cults, paper and pencils, chalkboard and chalk or flip chart and pens.

Steps 1 and 2 (13-20 minutes): Follow Steps 1 and 2 in the original Exploration.

Step 3 (10-15 minutes): Explain to students that they are about to form groups to examine the teachings of several cults. Name the cults for which you have prepared information and let students select the cult in which they are interested or about which they have the most knowledge. Group students according to their selection of cults and give each group the appropriate note card. Indicate any additional resources you have provided.

Explain, **"We're going to video tape some short plays about dealing with people in cults. First you need to read John 4:4-26. Pay special attention to the loving way in which Jesus treated the woman. List some of the things He said that show His courtesy and His caring attitude;**

then list the things He said about religious matters. We'll discuss that briefly before we go on to the video tapes."

Allow 5-10 minutes for students to examine the Scriptures. Then regain their attention and ask for their lists of Jesus' statements. Point out that Jesus was firm about the truth concerning Himself and the Father, yet He was kind and courteous to the woman. (See Teacher's Bible Study for additional ideas.)

Step 4 (15-20 minutes): Tell students, **"Now examine the information about the cult assigned to your group and think about ways Christians could respond kindly and courteously to someone who was part of that cult. Then prepare a script for a three-minute video play showing an encounter between a Christian and cult member. You will write a script, record it with the video equipment, and then show it to the rest of the class."**

Allow time for groups to plan and write. Circulate between groups, making yourself available to answer questions or provide encouragement. Warn students when three minutes remain for completing their scripts.

Have the video equipment ready to use, and let the group that is ready first record its play. Record the other groups in turn. Then play back the tape—students will enjoy seeing their work.

You might wish to consider sharing these video plays with others in your congregation. For example you could have a "high school night" at an evening service, in which you explain what the class has been studying and then show the video tapes.

Option: If you do not have video equipment, you could still do the plays in class, without recording them. You could also present them in a live performance at an evening service.

Move to the Conclusion by saying something like this: **"We have looked at the importance of defensive thinking coupled with loving actions when dealing with false teaching. Let's take a few minutes to think about how we will personally apply what we have discussed today."**

CONCLUSION AND DECISION

CONCLUSION (5-7 minutes)

Materials needed: Poster board or construction paper in various colors, felt pens in various colors, copies of Student Guide sheet "Think Defensively, Act Lovingly."

Think
Defensively,
   Act
   Lovingly

When confronted with a religious teaching you're not sure about, you need to check it out. You need to be prepared to defend yourself against it if it is false. And at the same time you need to be gracious toward the person who is presenting it to you. (Remember, many of the people in cults are unknowingly misled and are desperately trying to find God. They are not necessarily foaming-at-the-mouth mad dog agitators.) The following pointers will help you when you encounter cults.

1. **Know what you believe.**
You need to know what the Bible says. You find out by reading and studying it.

2. **Don't make any quick decisions.**
Situations can be manipulated to make just about anything look right at the moment. Don't make choices based on emotions; make them based on your intellect, which involves your study of the Word with the help of the Holy Spirit.

3. **Seek the wisdom of others.**
Ask for advice and insights from spiritually mature people.

4. **Check out the facts.**
God's truth can stand up to investigation. Check out what you hear with what the Word of God says.

5. **Don't be fooled by those who distort the Bible.**
Anyone can twist the meaning of Scriptures. That's why it's important to have a good grasp of the Word of God.

6. **Remember that God loves the person.**
Jesus died for all of us, even the person who is trying to sell you on a false doctrine. Be kind and

Invite students to create posters with slogans representing the way they should respond to false teachings. They may wish to use variations on the theme, "Think defensively, act lovingly," or they may come up with original slogans. After allowing several minutes for students to work, ask for volunteers to share what they have done. Encourage students to take posters home as reminders of the session. Close in prayer. Distribute copies of Student Guide sheet "Think Defensively, Act Lovingly" for students to take home as added reinforcement of the session focus.

ALTERNATE CONCLUSION (5-7 minutes)

Materials needed: Copies of Student Guide sheets "Plan of Action" and "Think Defensively, Act Lovingly," pens or pencils.

Note: Use this Conclusion if most of your students know someone who is in a cult. Or, if you have only one or two such students, you may wish to use both Conclusions, offering learners the option of doing either one.

Be sure each student has a copy of the Student Guide sheet "Plan of Action." Invite students to use the sheet to prepare a personal plan for a way to approach and talk to a friend or family member who is involved in some form of false teaching.

After allowing time for students to work, close in prayer. Distribute copies of Student Guide sheet "Think Defensively, Act Lovingly" for students to take home as added reinforcement of the session focus.

Plan of Action _____

Use this sheet to plan how you will approach and talk to someone you know who is involved in a cult or other form of false teaching. You might wish to write your plan in dialogue form, supplying the words you think your friend will say. Or you might wish to write only your side of the dialogue, planning what you could say to express clearly the biblical teachings about Christ. Remember to stick to the essentials and not get sidetracked on less important issues.

Cult this person is in:

Scriptures I will use:

What these Scriptures mean:

How I will get together with the person:

R Is for Relationship

KEY VERSE

"How great is the love the Father has lavished on us, that we should be called children of God! And that is what we are!"
1 John 3:1

BIBLICAL BASIS

1 John 2:28—3:10

FOCUS OF THE SESSION

God wants to have a close, Father-child relationship with each of us.

AIMS OF THIS SESSION

You and your class will have accomplished the purpose of this session if you can:

- LOCATE words and phrases in 1 John 2:28—3:10 that portray the relationship God wants to have with people;
- DISCUSS ways a Christian can cultivate a close relationship with God;
- PLAN ways to improve the way you relate to God.

TEACHER'S BIBLE STUDY

Having dealt with the problem of the antichrists—the people who taught false doctrine about Christ—John turned to a discussion of matters within the family of God. In 1 John 2:28—3:10 he discussed the relationship of the heavenly Father with His children. He spoke of God's love, His righteousness, His purity. He spoke of the fact that because we live or abide in God and His seed remains in us, we cannot live in a state of continual sinning. This is God's answer to the problem of sin—a dynamic, living relationship, not a matter of rules and willpower.

Gnostic Views

The Gnostics of the Apostle John's day found the remedy for sin not in being born of God, but in their own philosophical system. Some chose to interpret the Greek philosophy of the separation of body and soul by denying the flesh through asceticism; some interpreted the same idea to mean that they could indulge the body profusely, since the flesh did not matter. Either way, they thought they had no need for Christ's atoning blood or for any other kind of help from God. The idea that God relates to us as an ideal Father, with a tender and self-sacrificing love, and that at the same time He demands our allegiance, contradicts the world's popular views of God.

The fact that our God loves us as a Father and calls us His children is one of the key concepts of Christianity. Understanding that God wants to relate to us as a Father helps us desire to show our allegiance to Him in the face of false teaching, to understand and adopt His kind of love, and to have the courage to discern spiritual things as we grow in the knowledge of His ways.

A Caution

Before we examine the teaching in 1 John about our Father-child relationship with God, it is necessary to point out that many young people have inadequate or abusive fathers, and many have no father in the home at all. When they hear, "God is a Father," they may not visualize the loving, unselfish Person the Bible describes. The father image may, for some, be more of a detriment than a help in understanding who God is. Keep in mind the individual needs of your students as you guide them through this session. You may even wish to say something like this: "When we say that God is a Father, we are not saying that He is like earthly fathers, who may disappoint us with their human flaws. Rather, we are saying that God is the original Father and a model for earthly fathers.

If your own father has shortcomings and flaws, look to your heavenly Father for the perfection and love that you need."

The Loving Father

The idea of a father-child relationship is woven through 1 John 2:28—3:10. Various words and phrases point to the ideal Father-child relationship between God and the Christian. John spoke of Christians being "born of Him" (2:29) and being "born of God" (3:9). He spoke of God as "Father" (3:1) and three times of believers as His children (see 3:1,2,10). John even used reproductive imagery to say that those born of God cannot continue to sin because God's *seed* remains in them (see v.9). God didn't choose us to be His slaves or pawns, but His children (see Gal. 4:7). Notice John's exclamation: "that we should be called the children of God! *And that is what we are!*" (1 John 3:1, emphasis added). Think of the honor and privilege it is to be children of the Creator of the universe, the Lord of glory.

John pointed out that God's children "take after" their Father—they look like Him in that their lives reflect His values. (See 1 John 2:29; 3:3,6,7,9,10). A righteous God produces righteous children.

John's insistence that God's children behave righteously spoke boldly to the

Gnostics, some of whom lived out their belief in the separation of soul and body by indulging in all sorts of physical pleasures. Furthermore, John's affirmation that God is righteous reassures us that we can trust Him to be fair. In the face of all the suffering in this world and the unexplainable trials we ourselves experience (which seem to loom especially large for teenagers), we can know that our righteous God is supplying escape, comfort, and solutions to our dilemmas (see 1 Cor. 10:13; Rom. 8:28).

To further spell out the tone of our relationship with God, John used the one word that high school students will not miss: love. He declared, "How great is the love the Father has lavished on us . . . " (1 John 3:1). The context describes a Father who gives freely, even giving His own Son, yet demands accountability.

John's words describe a real relationship, a two-way interchange of ideas and responsibilities. God demonstrated His lavishly great love by sending His Son Jesus to destroy the devil's work (see 1 John 3:8), thus releasing us from our bondage to sin (see Paul's discussion of this idea in Rom. 6:15-23).

Continue in Him

John stressed his "theology of relationship" in this passage by using a Greek word, *meno*, three different times. The *New International Version* translates it as "continue" (1 John 2:28), "lives" (3:6), and "remains" (3:9). Translated in other versions as "abide," *meno* was the term John used in reporting Jesus' allegory of the vine and the branches: "Remain in me, and I will remain in you. No branch can bear fruit by itself; it must remain in the vine. Neither can you bear fruit unless you remain in me." (John 15:4). This verse tells us that "remaining in Him" helps us bear fruit, or grow spiritually.

Lest we consider this remaining in Him an optional step, Jesus warned: "If anyone does not remain in me, he is like a branch that is thrown away and withers; such branches are picked up, thrown into the fire and burned. If you remain in me and my words in you, ask whatever you wish, and it will be given you . . . . If you obey my commands, you will remain in my love, just as I have obeyed my Father's commands and remain in his love" (John 15:6,7,10). From these verses we learn that remaining (*meno*) results in answered prayer, but it also involves obeying commands. John further defined *meno* by stating that one who claims to live in Him must walk as Jesus walked (see 1 John 2:6). God designed a balance between privilege and responsibility.

With this background, we can greet John's imperative statement in 1 John 2:28, "continue in him," (*meno*) with a better understanding of what he meant.

Because we have this continuing relationship with God, which enables us to avoid sinning, we will be able to greet Him unashamed at His next coming.

He Demands, Yet Enables

The key word, *meno*, appears next as "lives" (see 1 John 3:6). John said that no one who lives in Christ keeps on sinning. This statement may appear to contradict John's other words: "But if anybody does sin, we have one who speaks to the Father in our defense . . . Jesus Christ, the Righteous One" (1 John 2:1,2,). How can one who does not keep on sinning still sin? John used the Greek past tense in chapter two, implying an individual act. He used the Greek present tense in chapter three, referring to a continual state. So we may conclude that the one who remains (*meno*) in God may sin, but not continually or habitually. Knowing Him, being His child, having His life in us precludes continuous sin (see 3:6). In this way God enables His children to begin the process of becoming like Him. As our Father He cheers us on, wanting us to grow and to become all that we can be. He demands obedience, but then He draws alongside to help us obey (see John 14:16,17). As Paul wrote, "continue to work out your salvation with fear and trembling, for it is God who *works in you* to will and to act according to his good purpose" (Phil. 2:12,13, emphasis added).

John added that no one who is born of God will continue to sin because God's seed remains (*meno*) in Him (see 1 John 3:9). John's fellow apostle, Peter, was led by the Holy Spirit to write to Christians: "For you have been born again, not of perishable seed, but of imperishable, through the living and enduring word of God" (1 Peter 1:23). He identified the imperishable seed as the living and enduring Word of God. So we see that God's Word plays an important part in building a relationship between God and a believer.

He Considers Us Worthy

God chose to have a close relationship with us—not a distant one. He promises that we will one day be like Him and see Him as He is. "Now we see but a poor reflection; then we shall see face to face" (1 Cor. 13:12). And in the meantime, as we look forward to seeing Him, we purify ourselves. Even while we are in this life we can become more and more like our Father—though the process will not be completed until we come into His presence.

It is a joyful experience to know that God actually wants to have fellowship with us. Within that fellowship relationship, God chooses to respect us, to honor us with the privilege of seeing Him and becoming like Him (see 1 John 3:2). As Christians we hold no righteousness of our

own, but stand before God as sinners saved by grace. Our justification is a gift from God, nothing that we can earn (see Rom. 3:23-25). Yet God chooses to enable us to stand confident and unashamed at the second coming, eager to see our Father. We will be able to present ourselves as children He knows well through the relationship nurtured during our lifetime. This will be possible, not because God is an indulgent "softy" but because He enables us to live up to His demand that we obey Him out of the love He poured into our hearts through the Holy Spirit.

John's Model

John's very language in this passage points to the relationship issue. His terminology reveals his fatherly affection for his readers. He called them "dear children" (see 1 John 2:28; 3:7) and "dear friends" (see 3:2). He issued forth his theological precepts and warnings in words of encouragement, even endearment. Perhaps this "son of thunder" learned this skill from his Master.

Then, as if talking to small children whose relationships with God might be stunted by not seeing Him in the flesh, John reminded them twice that they would see Him ("when he appears," see 2:28; 3:2) and that just a few years ago some *did* see Him ("he appeared," see 3:5). These appearances of God portray a Father who earnestly desires to help His children.

A Relationship Helps Teenagers

At a time in their lives when senior high students have majored in relationships with others and minored in obeying rules, this lesson may prove a great source of comfort. A relationship with God as an ideal Father can fill the *loneliness* many of them feel, for in God they discover Someone whose "telephone line" is never busy and whose love fulfills all the generous promises of 1 Corinthians 13. This Father lavishes His love to the point of sacrificing His Son, a test of love that surpasses any teenager's demands.

This relationship with a Father God also answers the need for *purpose* many young people feel. The need to make choices about career, friends, dating partners, or time priorities overwhelms them. They need to know that their Christianity is not a lot of rules or merely a social unit, but a relationship with Someone who is guiding their lives.

To the surprise of some adults, many high school students are looking for responsibilities and challenges in their Christian walk. In God they find a Father who not only presents the challenges but also supplies the tools (Scripture, the Holy Spirit, fellow Christians) to conquer such tasks. His practice of facilitating our obedience allows us the privilege of having

God work through us to accomplish His work on earth.

Teenagers need to view God as a Person, as an ideal Father. Yes, He makes demands, but then He also enables us by coming to live inside us in the form of the Holy Spirit. All of us, not just students, welcome His presence as He fills us with *faith* in His ability to equip us.

Students also need to know that God is just—even when it may not seem like it. Even though He rules the universe, God treats us with dignity—allowing us to see Him as He is and to become like Him, wanting us to be able to stand confident and unashamed at His coming. While young people see the world's version of authority figures lording it over each other, they appreciate Christ's example of telling the greatest to be the servant of all (see Luke 22:24-27). Teenagers like a leader who lets them function at their highest capacity, who equips them to be all they can be. Being equipped instead of trodden down gives them *hope*.

Students need to see God as an ideal Father who proves His love with actions. Although God gives us countless examples of His love, the young person who first hears about Christ understands His love best when expressed by "someone with skin on"—you or a youth sponsor or a friend. The sacrifices and emulation of Christ, the lavishing of love by such people help the teenager understand God's love and, in turn, begin to *love* Him.

THIS WEEK'S TEACHING PLAN

APPROACH TO THE WORD

APPROACH: (3-5 minutes)

Materials needed: Copies of Student Guide sheet "Whose God?" and extra pens or pencils.

Distribute Student Guide sheet "Whose God?" and

R Is for Relationship
Winter #7

Walking in God's Light

Whose God?

So you think you're a history whiz, huh? Let's see! Listed below are the legendary gods of various cultures. Match the name of the deity with the description in the right hand column.

Janus __c__

Bacchus __e__

Osiris __b__

Molech __f__

Pele __g__

Thor __a__

Buck __d__

a. A Scandinavian god who possessed great strength. He was supposed to have gotten his jollies by beating up all the demon-type gods.

b. The Egyptian god of the underworld; a funerary god.

c. The Roman god of the door from whom we get the name of one of the months. He was thought to be one of the many gods who resided in homes.

d. A small paper deity worshiped in the western hemisphere in the twentieth century.

e. The Greek god of wine.

f. A god worshiped by the Ammonites. He was appeased by the sacrifice of children on his fiery arms.

g. The Hawaiian goddess of the volcano. She literally blew her top when she was displeased.

---

introduce the activity: **"People through the ages have had different kinds of gods. Take a look at the Student Guide and try to match up the people with their gods and what the gods were known for."**

After allowing a few minutes for students to complete the activity, regain their attention. Ask for their responses, and give any correct answers that may be needed. (See answers on this page.)

Make a transition to the Bible Exploration by saying something like this: **"The Apostle John lived in a time when people worshiped many gods, and when there were conflicting views about the God of the Jews and the Christians. He wrote parts of 1 John to tell his readers about the truth of God's nature and His relationship with His people. We're going to look at this topic today."**

ALTERNATE APPROACH: (8-10 minutes)

Materials Needed: Large piece of butcher paper with marking pens or chalkboard and chalk.

Before students arrive, hang a piece of butcher paper on the

wall and write this phrase on it with a marking pen: "Some people think that God . . . "

As students arrive, give them marking pens and tell them: **"Write on the butcher paper your ideas about how people view God. Feel free to use some of the opinions you have heard from your teachers or friends or relatives. This activity has no right or wrong answers—just opinions both positive and negative. If seeing someone else's answer jogs your thinking, you may add a second answer."**

When you are ready to begin class, have students sit down. Read some of their "graffiti" comments and thank them for their participation. Lead into the Exploration by stating: **"The Apostle John wrote during a time when the popular religions included Gnosticism, which taught that matter was totally evil, so that God could not have taken on a human body, and Romanism, which said that the gods toyed with people for their own pleasure. John wrote to set the record straight about how the true God related to people."**

BIBLE EXPLORATION

EXPLORATION (30-40 minutes)

Materials needed: Bibles, pens or pencils, paper, copies of Student Guide sheet "Fact Finder," chalkboard and chalk or overhead projector with transparencies and pens.

Step 1 (15-20 minutes): Guide students in forming groups of four to six. Give each learner a copy of the "Fact Finder"

Fact Finder

Read the passage printed below. Then underline words and phrases that portray the way God relates to His people. Circle words and phrases that show how God wants His people to relate to Him.

"And now, dear children, continue in him, so that when he appears we may be confident and unashamed before him at his coming.

If you know that he is righteous, you know that everyone who does what is right has been born of him.

How great is the love the Father has lavished on us, that we should be called children of God! And that is what we are! The reason the world does not know us is that it did not know him. Dear friends, now we are children of God, and what we will be has not yet been made known. But we know that when he appears, we shall be like him, for we shall see him as he is. Everyone who has this hope in him purifies himself, just as he is pure.

Everyone who sins breaks the law; in fact, sin is lawlessness. But you know that he appeared so that he might take away our sins. And in him is no sin. No one who lives in him keeps on sinning. No one who continues to sin has either seen him or known him.

Dear children, do not let anyone lead you astray. He who does what is right is righteous, just as he is righteous. He who does what is sinful is of the devil, because the devil has been sinning from the beginning. The reason the Son of God appeared was to destroy the devil's work. No one who is born of God will continue to sin, because God's seed remains in him; he cannot go on sinning, because he has been born of God. This is how we know who the children of God are and who the children of the devil are: Anyone who does not do what is right is not a child of God; neither is anyone who does not love his brother."

---

sheet. Ask them to study the Scripture passage and mark words and phrases that portray the relationship God wants to have with people.

Allow students to work for five to eight minutes, warning them when two minutes remain. Then regain their attention and ask them to report what they have found about the way God wants to relate to people and the way He wants us to relate to Him.

Emphasize God's love, His purity and righteousness, His unselfishness (demonstrated by sending His Son to die for our sins), His willingness to help us do what He wants us to do (by having His seed in us). Point out that God actually desires to have fellowship with us, as evidenced by the promise that we will see Him.

God asks us, in turn, to be righteous and pure, to make the effort to refrain from habitual sinning, and to love one another.

Step 2 (5-7 minutes): Explain, **"It's not enough to know and discuss the facts about the relationship God wants to have with us. We need to take active steps to cultivate that relationship. Let's think about that for a bit."** Have students suggest some of the obvious, basic elements of a relationship with God while you list their ideas on the chalkboard or overhead transparency. These ideas will probably include Bible study, prayer, fellowship with other believers and so on.

Then say something like this: **"These are all good ideas. They're the basics of developing a relationship with God. But sometimes it's easier to list them than it is to do them. Let's see if we can get a little deeper."**

Step 3 (8-10 minutes): Have students return to their groups. Assign to each group (or let groups choose) one of the topics listed on the chalkboard or overhead. Then explain, **"Take your topic and ask yourselves some questions about it, then come up with answers to your questions. For example, you could ask, What are some ways Christians can do this more effectively? What are some problems Christians have with this activity? How can we make it work better? How can we make it more interesting? One person in each group should record the group's answers. After you've had some time to come up with ideas we'll get back together and share."** (You might want to write the suggested questions on the chalkboard or overhead transparency.)

Allow time for students to work. Then regain their attention and ask them to report their ideas as you list them on the chalkboard or overhead transparency. Affirm their efforts, then make a transition to the Conclusion by saying something like this: **"It has been interesting to talk about the relationship God wants to have with us and how we can cultivate that relationship. Let's take a few moments to decide on a specific action we will take this week."**

ALTERNATE EXPLORATION: (40-60 minutes)

Materials needed: Bibles, pens or pencils, copies of Student Guide sheet "Fact Finder," butcher paper, felt pens, chalkboard and chalk or overhead projector with transparencies and pens.

Steps 1 and 2 (20-27 minutes): Follow Steps 1 and 2 in the original Exploration.

Step 3 (10-15 minutes): Explain, **"We're going to write jumbo brochures describing the 'care and feeding' of a relationship with the heavenly Father."**

Have students return to their groups. Provide butcher paper and felt pens. Assign to each group (or let groups choose) one of the topics listed on the chalkboard or overhead during Step 2. Then explain, **"Take your topic and ask yourselves some questions about it. Then come up with answers to your questions as the content for your brochure. For example, you could ask, What are some ways Christians can do this more effectively? What are some problems**

Christians have with this activity? How can we make it work better? How can we make it more interesting? After you've had some time to come up with ideas we'll get back together and share." (You might want to write the suggested questions on the chalkboard or overhead transparency.)

Explain that each group should determine a title for its brochure. Then group members should write an introductory paragraph describing the importance of the topic assigned to the group. Finally, they should write several sections giving their responses to the questions you have suggested. Encourage students to think of the brochures as being directed to newer Christians who are having some difficulties with the basic practices of Bible study, prayer, and so on.

Step 4 (10-15 minutes): Reassemble the class and let the groups share their brochures. Make positive comments about their ideas, and add any of your own that have not been mentioned. Display the brochures in your classroom as a reminder of today's session. You may want to make arrangements later to display the brochures on a central church bulletin board in order to share with the rest of the congregation what your students are learning.

Make a transition to the Conclusion by saying something like this: **"We've had an interesting time discussing the kind of relationship our loving heavenly Father wants to maintain with us, and how we can maintain that relationship. Let's think about our own personal response for a few moments."**

CONCLUSION AND DECISION

CONCLUSION (5-7 minutes)

Materials needed: Ideas listed on chalkboard or overhead transparency from original Exploration, or brochures from Alternate Exploration, paper, pens or pencils.

Direct students' attention to the chalkboard or overhead, or the brochures. Ask them to take a few minutes to prayerfully consider the various ideas listed for cultivating a relationship with God. They are to choose at least one activity to do this week. It should be something that they are not already doing regularly—something in which they would like to improve. They should write the action they choose on a sheet of paper, initial it, and give it to you as the class ends.

After allowing a few moments for students to pray and to mark their papers, close in prayer.

During the week read students' papers and pray for them as they attempt to improve in their development of their relationship with God. At the next session take a few minutes to ask how it went and to listen to students' responses.

ALTERNATE CONCLUSION (5-10 minutes)

Materials needed: Construction paper or card stock in various colors, felt pens in various colors.

Explain that one way people sometimes maintain their relationships with one another is by sending friendship cards. These can be serious or lighthearted. The messages can be short or long. Today your class will create friendship cards conveying messages to God. Students may wish to thank Him for His love and His provision of Jesus Christ. They may wish to express their feelings about the fact that He wants to have a close, loving, Father-child relationship with His people. Or they may have other ideas of their own. Provide paper and pens and let them get to work.

Near the time to end the session, ask if any students would care to show and read their cards. Do not pressure anyone to do this, as the messages may be private.

Close in prayer.

Put God's Love to Work in You

KEY VERSE
"If anyone has material possessions and sees his brother in need but has no pity on him, how can the love of God be in him?" 1 John 3:17

BIBLICAL BASIS
1 John 3:11-18

FOCUS OF THE SESSION
Godly love involves giving practical help to those in need.

AIMS OF THIS SESSION
You and your students will have accomplished the purpose of this Bible study session if you can:
  • DETERMINE what the Bible says about showing love through giving practical help to others;
  • CONSIDER ways Christian students can show God's love to people in your community;
  • CHOOSE a specific way to show God's love to someone in need.

TEACHER'S BIBLE STUDY

Most high school students are interested in love! And many young people are idealistic enough to want to show love in practical ways to people around them. As described in 1 John 3:11-18, God's kind of love majors in action.

The Universal Command
As he answered the false teachers who were trying to lead the believers astray John emphatically stated, "This is the message *you heard from the beginning*: We should love one another" (1 John 3:11, emphasis added). He earlier used a similar expression: "This is the message *we have heard from him* and declare to you . . . " (1 John 1:5, emphasis added). Though the false teachers declared mystical doctrines of secret origins, Christ's teaching through the apostles was on public record. The gospel had not changed! The believers could correctly identify false teaching if they remembered what they had heard from the beginning—the apostle's teaching.

Likewise this verse speaks to those who maintain that the Old Testament re-

veals an angry God while the New Testament presents a loving Jesus. They read the accounts of the judgment of the evil nations surrounding Israel and overlook the complete picture of God's loving actions in preserving Israel. He patiently cared for the disobedient children of Israel on their journey from Egypt, through their conquest and settlement of the Promised Land, and with their wayward kings. He sent prophets to warn Israel, only to see His messengers scorned.

Through his own life, Hosea painted a picture of God, the faithful husband, waiting to forgive and love his unfaithful wife, Israel, if she would just return to Him (see Hosea 1-3). Even after their captivity, He waited only seventy years to restore His people.

Jesus drew the greatest commandments—loving God and loving our neighbor—from the Old Testament Scriptures (see Matt. 22:36-40; Deut. 6:5; Lev. 19:17,18). In the midst of Jesus' miracle working and acts of mercy, He publicly scolded both King Herod and the Pharisees (see Mark 8:14-21; Matt. 23:1-39)

and issued tough demands to people like Nocodemus, to the rich young ruler, to His disciples, to the crowds and even to a fig tree! (See John 3:1-21; Luke 18:18-30; 9:1-6; 14:25-35; Matt. 21:18-22.) Jesus introduced the concept of hell in the New Testament; the Old Testament referred only vaguely to an afterlife in Sheol. Both Testaments reflect God's love and justice.

Love's Opposites
The following paragraphs summarize the contrast this passage draws between the world's hate and God's love:

Hatred is typical of the world (1 John 3:13); was modeled by Cain (v. 12); originated in the devil (v. 12); is motivated by evil deeds (v. 12); produces murder (vv. 12, 15); is directed toward those who do good deeds (v.12); is evidence of spiritual death (vv. 14,15).

By contrast, **love** is typical of the church ("brothers," v. 17); was modeled by Christ (v. 16); originated in God (v. 16); is motivated by Christ's sacrifice (v. 16); produces self-sacrifice (v. 16); is directed to-

45

ward those in need (v. 17); is evidence of eternal life (v. 14).

John uses the account of Cain's jealousy of his brother Abel's sacrifice to illustrate hatred and to further declare that hatred is a form of murder. Instead of accepting God's encouragement when his sacrifice was not accepted ("If you do what is right, will you not be accepted?"—Gen. 4:7), Cain turned his hatred of Abel into murder. Contrary to suspecting Abel of being evil, Cain hated Abel because Abel's actions were righteous and his own were evil! A person's own evil deeds cause him or her to hate another whose deeds are righteous. Sensing the mystery of this fact, John exhorted, "Do not be surprised, my brothers, if the world hates you" (v.13). A Christian's righteous deeds will earn him the hatred of those who pursue evil. John probably remembered when Jesus made a similar statement: "If the world hates you, keep in mind that it hated me first. If you belonged to the world, it would love you as its own" (John 15:18,19).

John contrasted the world's hatred with the Christians' knowledge that their love for their brothers proves that they have "passed from death to life" (1 John 3:14). The one who does not love has not become a new person, but "remains in death" (v. 14). Interestingly, John used the word "remain" (the Greek word, meno; see Session 7, Teacher's Bible Study). But in this instance the person remains, abides or continues in death instead of in God. In the next verse, John stated that no murderer has eternal life abiding (meno) in him (see 1 John 3:15, KJV). The one who hates or murders has not chosen to live in God, nor to let God live in him. The result is death. The opposite of hatred and murder is love. And so love for fellow Christians is the test of faith, even an advertisement of it (see John 13:35).

John tied together the sins of those who remain in death by saying that anyone who hates his brother is a murderer! (see 1 John 3:15). Like Jesus, who extended the condemnation of murder to anger and bitter name calling (see Matt. 5:21,22), John discerned the heart condition of the murderer and the hater to be the same.

The Indifferent

This passage condemns not only those who hate, but also those who do not love—those who are indifferent. "Anyone who does not love remains in death" (1 John 3:14, emphasis added). The imperative of this first paragraph about Cain is to love, not just to refrain from hating. Certainly the priest and the Levite in the parable of the Good Samaritan did not show hatred for the beaten man; they did not add to his injuries or comment joyfully on his misfortune. They just passed by (see Luke 10:25-37).

In some circles of the "civilized" world where hatred is no longer fashionable, indifference remains most acceptable. Our complacency needs to be shaken by John's call for a love so intense that we are willing to lay down our lives for fellow Christians.

Surrendering One's Life

Having commanded love, illustrated what love is not, and linked love with a regeneration of life, John explained what it would look like if someone took a picture of it. This agape love—doing what's best for the other person—involves giving what has value to us to enrich the life of someone in need. Jesus' love caused Him to offer the most precious possession He had, His life (see John 15:13; Rom. 5:6-10). Cain's hatred caused him to steal the most precious possession Abel had, his life. John commanded us to follow in Jesus' steps, to lay down our lives for our brothers.

Anticipating the quandary of those who have no occasion or opportunity actually to die for another person, John interpreted the laying down of life in alternative terms: "If anyone has material possessions and sees his brother in need but has no pity on him, how can the love of God be in him?" (1 John 3:17).

Just as Jesus, in His earthly ministry, cared for the poor, the sick, the hungry, and the tormented, His followers must fulfill this role today.

John established two prerequisites for showing this kind of love: having possessions and seeing a fellow Christian in need. In societies in which it is relatively easy to get a job and earn money, some may feel that John was endorsing a sort of "Christian welfare state" in which some people work and support others who do not work. This would contradict Paul's axiom, "If a man will not work, he shall not eat" (2 Thess. 3:10). But Paul was speaking of those who chose not to work, whereas John was speaking of a Christian who was in need. In refusing to support the former, Christians must not refuse to help the latter.

Considering the complex differences in circumstances, God wisely chose a caring body of believers, the church, to discern who is in need and then supply those needs. John's second prerequisite, seeing a fellow Christian in need, requires us to become skilled in seeing others' needs. We must acquire and practice Jesus' art of noting the needs of others (see Mark 5:25-34, for example).

Most people become quite good at noticing and meeting their own needs. When we have a relationship with God we must allow Him to radically change our values and teach us to detect the needs of others.

Once we have fulfilled the prerequisites—we have material possessions and

we have discerned another believer's need—we must "have pity on" the person in need. We are not to "shut our eyes—and our heart" (Phillips). If we fail to meet this demand, we may not have the love of God in us! (see 1 John 3:17). John made no allowance for the possibility of indifferent, apathetic Christians.

Love with Legs on It

Leaving no doubt that the pity he called for was more than emotion, John concluded with a gentle reminder, "Dear children, let us not love with words or tongue but with actions and in truth" (v. 18). John emphasized the person's actions: Cain's evil deeds made him hate Abel; love must show itself by its deeds. People who do not demonstrate love in action are condemned by their own indifference. Verse 18 pinpoints the sign of a hypocrite: talking about love, but not doing anything about it. John's statement allows for no split in functions among Christians—those who philosophize or theologize versus those who meet practical needs.

This concept is supported by the well-known passage by James: "What good is it, my brothers, if a man claims to have faith but has no deeds? Can such faith save him? Suppose a brother or sister is without clothes and daily food. If one of you says to him, 'Go, I wish you well; keep warm and well fed,' but does nothing about his physical needs, what good is it? In the same way, faith by itself, if it is not accompanied by action, is dead. But someone will say, 'You have faith; I have deeds.' Show me your faith without deeds, and I will show you my faith by what I do" (Jas. 2:14-18).

The one who has no deeds actually has no faith. Similarly, the one who has no deeds also has no love.

If anyone is tempted to perform good deeds without love, he or she should take note that John added the phrase "in truth" (v. 18). We must perform helpful deeds with the proper motivation—to serve Christ, not to glorify self. Jesus said, "When you give to the needy, do not let your left hand know what your right hand is doing" (Matt. 6:3). He warned against announcing good deeds with trumpets in order to be honored by men. Those people already have their reward. Our giving must be in secret with a sincere heart (see Matt. 6:1-4).

Teenagers and Deeds of Love

What a timely truth to share with teenagers! Aiding the needy is one of those practices of Christianity that comes easier the earlier one learns it. If any of your students have not encountered this concept of love, pray that the Holy Spirit will use this class session to reveal to them one of God's central concerns.

Though the spheres in which teenagers can help the needy may seem limited, they possess time, energy, skills, and money. Many young people already give their **time** to volunteer activities at school or in the community. Perhaps this session will motivate some of your students to give up an activity that is solely for their own benefit and instead volunteer to help someone in need during that time slot.

Energy and **skills** go hand-in-hand with time. Encourage your students to put their strength and abilities to work in creative ways to help people who have needs.

Money is "coined life"—hours of work that have been exchanged for currency. Whether Christians have a lot or a little, they need to be surrendering something of themselves to enhance the life of someone who is in need.

People in Need

Jesus mentioned the hungry, the thirsty, the strangers, the poorly clothed, the sick and those in prison as the "least of these my brethren" (see Matt. 25:34-46). He considered those who helped these groups of people as having done it for Himself.

James identified those who practice a pure and faultless religion as those who care for the widows and orphans in their distress and keep themselves from being polluted by the world (see James 1:27).

More than thirty Old Testament passages refer to the necessity of helping the fatherless and the widows.

One way students can demonstrate their Christian love is by attending service activities of their youth group with the same loyalty and enthusiasm they give to the social activities. Other ways they can reach out include the following:

The hungry, the thirsty: Buy groceries; cook a meal for a family whose chief cook is out of town, in the hospital or inundated with responsibilities; give money to denominational or parachurch agencies devoted to relieving hunger.

The stranger: Invite newcomers at church, in the neighborhood or at school to join them in activities; help them get acquainted with opportunities and facilities in the neighborhood; introduce newcomers to their friends; make an effort to be friendly to the friendless person at school.

Those needing clothes: Buy or make clothes for someone whose budget barely covers food and shelter; hand down good but outgrown clothes to a family who needs them.

The imprisoned: Be friendly to teenagers from a local juvenile home; contact a prison chaplain to see what needs teenagers could meet there.

The sick or shut in: Visit someone who is recovering from a long illness or accident: play table games with them, wash their hair, bring books, offer to run errands. The older people in your church would be a good place for students to start.

The fatherless, orphaned: Play "big brother" or "big sister" regularly to a child with one parent or none; baby-sit free of charge, do yardwork, run errands for a single parent; contact an orphanage about special needs at Christmas or throughout the year.

The widows (or any older people living alone): do yard work or chores; take them to their doctor appointments; listen to a story even if they've heard it many times before!

To help students expand their awareness of community needs, you may wish to plan a trip to a local orphanage or retirement home soon after the class session. (You may wish to coordinate such a trip with the youth pastor or volunteer youth group sponsors.)

To follow up on the needs of the world, suggest to people in your church who are in charge of need-meeting boards and committees that they include young people on their committees. Ask visiting missionaries how teenagers could help meet needs of the people they work with.

Young people need models. We cannot expect them to do as we say unless we, too, are doing it. Are you providing a good example of love in action?

THIS WEEK'S TEACHING PLAN

APPROACH TO THE WORD

APPROACH: (5-8 minutes)

Materials needed: Student Guide sheets "One Fine Day in a Traffic Jam" and "The Last Frame," pens or pencils.

Give students copies of the Student Guide sheet "One Fine Day in a Traffic Jam." Explain, **"This cartoon is based on a true incident. Read the cartoon and notice that the last panel is blank. Draw what you think the ending would be."**

After allowing a few minutes for students to work, ask them to share their drawings. Then display the Student Guide sheet "The Last Frame" and say, **"This is what really happened. It shows us that our actions are very important—they speak about our Christianity to those around us. Let's see what John's letter has to say about the way Christians should act toward other people."**

ALTERNATE APPROACH: (8-10 minutes)

Materials needed: A piece of paper for each student.

Distribute paper as the students arrive. Guide students in forming groups of three or four. Explain, "Tear your pieces of paper into shapes that represent love in action." Show an example that you have made—perhaps a bag representing a sack of groceries given to someone in need.

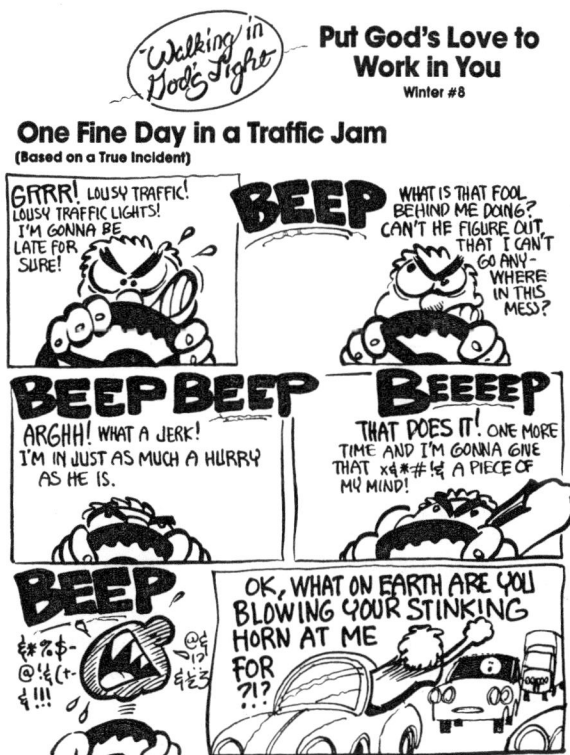

Walking in God's Light
Put God's Love to Work in You
Winter #8

One Fine Day in a Traffic Jam
(Based on a True Incident)

After five minutes, ask volunteers to display and explain their symbols. Move into the Exploration with thoughts such as these: "We're going to take a look at what 1 John has to say about love in action."

BIBLE EXPLORATION

EXPLORATION: (35-45 minutes)

Materials needed: Bibles, paper, pens or pencils, a cardboard box (about the size of a shoebox), copies of Student Guide sheet "What Can a Poor Kid Do?"

Step 1 (5-10 minutes): Distribute paper and pencils. Provide Bibles to students who need them. Ask students to read 1 John 3:11-18 silently. After allowing a few moments for them to do this, explain, **"I'm going to assign part of this passage of Scripture to each of you. I want you to make up a question based on your assigned section. Later we'll try to answer each other's questions. Put the verse number or numbers on your paper, and include your name or initials."**

Assign one or more verses to each student. If you have more than eight students, assign each person only one verse, and duplicate verse assignments as needed. If you have fewer than eight students, combine two or more verses for each assignment.

Allow time for students to think and write.

Step 2 (8-10 minutes): Regain students' attention. Pass around a cardboard box and ask them to place their papers in it. When all the papers are in the box, redistribute them, making sure you don't give anyone his or her own question. Allow time for students to read the questions they have received and to write down their answers. If a student has difficulty understanding the question, he or she may ask the author to explain it.

Step 3 (8-10 minutes): Regain students' attention. Taking the questions in the order of the verse numbers (moving from verse 11 to verse 18), ask learners to read the question they received, the verse or verses on which it is based, and the answer they wrote down. If a student is unclear about the correct answer, ask the author of the question to explain what he or she had in mind.

Continue by asking any of the following questions not covered in the question box discussion.

- What are the sources of love and hate? God (v.17); the devil (v.12).
- What does 1 John say motivated Cain to kill Abel? Cain's own evil actions (v.12).
- What motivates Christians to lay down their lives for their brothers? Christ's example of laying down his life (v.16). Students may consider having material possessions and seeing a brother in need (see v. 17) as their motivation. These are not bad reasons for giving, but love for Christ is the ultimate motivation.
- Who is the target of the hateful person? The righteous person (v.12,13).
- Who is the "target" of the loving person? The one in need (v.17).
- What does 1 John say about the one who does not love? He or she remains in death (v.14). Point out that such a person does not necessarily hate, but simply is indifferent—a failure to love.

Step 4 (13-15 minutes): Summarize in this manner: **"This Scripture is straightforward about the importance of giving practical help to those in need. Sometimes we would be happy to help, but we simply don't know what is needed or how we can help. Let's see if we can work together to get some ideas."**

Guide students in forming pairs. Distribute copies of Student Guide sheet "What Can a Poor Kid Do?" Assign two or three categories from the sheet to each pair and tell students,

What Can a Poor Kid Do?

Read Matthew 25:34-46; Luke 14:12-14 and James 1:17. Make a list of the examples of people in need that are given or implied in the Scripture. Next, try to describe the situation in your community which most closely parallels the biblical example.

Finally try to give a good example of what a person your age could do to help correct the situation or show caring in the situation.

Biblical Examples	A Parallel in My Community	What Could Be Done to Help

"Read the Scripture, then write down some ideas about the closest thing in our community to the kind of need described. Then list some things that could be done by Christians to meet that need."

After allowing students time to work, regain their attention and ask them to report their ideas and to take notes on the others' ideas. Provide any additional ideas that may be needed, using material from the Teacher's Bible Study.

Make a transition to the Conclusion by saying something like this: **"God's love clearly calls us to make an effort to meet the practical needs of other people. Let's think further about how we personally could do this."**

ALTERNATE EXPLORATION: (30-45 minutes)

Materials needed: Bibles, paper, pencils, large sheets of butcher paper (one sheet for every 14 students), felt pens, copies of Student Guide sheet "What Can a Poor Kid Do?"

Step 1 (10-12 minutes): Provide paper and pencils. Explain, **"Here's your big chance to do what people have been doing to you for years—giving you tests. Work on your own to read 1 John 3:11-18 and make up a five-question test about the passage. Then we'll trade test papers and try to answer them. Make your questions tough, but be sure they can be answered from the Scripture passage."**

Step 2 (10-12 minutes): After allowing time for students to work, collect their papers and redistribute them, making sure no learner receives his or her own paper. Give students time to answer the questions. Then regain their attention and ask them to read the questions and answers. Suggest any additional ideas that should come out of a study of the passage, using material given in the original Exploration.

Step 3 (10-20 minutes): Guide students in forming pairs. Distribute copies of the "What Can a Poor Kid Do?" sheet.

Assign one category from that sheet to each pair. Tell students, **"Look up the Scripture indicated for your category. Fill in the sheet as indicated by the headings. When you have finished doing that, you will contribute to a mural by drawing a picture of love in action. Your picture should show a Christian student doing one of the loving actions you have suggested on your student sheet."**

Since there are seven categories on the student sheet, provide one sheet of butcher paper for every seven pairs. (If you have a smaller class, assign more than one category to each pair.) Stress the importance of getting their ideas across—artistic skill is not the point here.

After students have had time to do their study and their drawing, reassemble the class and let each pair explain what they have drawn.

Move to the Conclusion by saying something like this: **"God helped us when we were in need by giving His Son to provide our salvation. This great gift should motivate us to give practical help to people who are in need. We have explored different ways of giving such help. Let's take some time to think about what we can do personally."**

CONCLUSION AND DECISION

CONCLUSION: (3-5 minutes)

Materials needed: Copies of Student Guide section "Personalize . . . ," pencils.

Distribute the "Personalize . . . " sheet and explain, **"Copy the verse printed in the student guide, but substitute your name for the word 'anyone'; substitute a person in need that you know for the words 'his brother in need'; and substitute something you could do to help them for the words 'has no pity on him.' Then read it again several times."**

Personalize . . .

If anyone has material possessions
(your name)

and sees his brother in need but
(someone in need)

has no pity on him, how can the
(something you can do to meet his or her need)

love of God be in him?

1 John 3:17

Rewrite this verse and personalize it.

After students have finished, close in prayer thanking God for giving them ideas for showing love and asking Him to help them follow through.

ALTERNATE CONCLUSION: (5-8 minutes)

Materials needed: Flip chart and felt pens.

Preparation: Come to class prepared with two or three suggestions for acts of service. For example, you might suggest something like a "Send the Janitor to Lunch Day," in which students provide funds for the janitor to take his or her family to lunch while students do the clean-up work for the day. Or suggest that groups of two or three can visit older people from the church family, taking flowers and spending time letting their hosts enjoy their company. Then they can meet and cook hamburgers and share what they have experienced. Another suggestion is to host a "Senior Citizens' Salad Bar Lunch" at the church. Or students could plan a night when they will get together at church to provide free baby-sitting to enable young parents in the church family to have an evening out.

Explain to students that one way to put love into action is to get involved in a service project such as those you are prepared to suggest. Give students your examples, and let them suggest other ideas. Write all the ideas on the flip chart, and work with your class to select at least one to follow through on. Remember that any such project must be carefully planned in advance. And remember to keep it interesting. Serving others can be fun—and will encourage students to be open to doing it again.

Cultivate Godly Characteristics

Unit Focus

With this unit your students will learn more about how God cultivates maturity through teaching Christians faith, love, and obedience. Faith assures Christians of their salvation and allows them to experience God's love in such a great way that they begin to love others with God's love. Faith and love facilitate an obedience that is not burdensome.

Session 9

Get God's Assurance
Biblical Basis: 1 John 3:19-24; 4:1-6
Focus: God helps Christians who are struggling with doubts and questions.

Session 10

Buy into God's Kind of Love
Biblical Basis: 1 John 4:7-12,19-21
Focus: Love permeates everything God does. His love motivates us to love others.

Session 11

Let God In
Biblical Basis: 1 John 4:13-18
Focus: As we live in God and He lives in us, we can nourish our relationship with Him through Christian disciplines such as Bible study and prayer.

Session 12

Resolve the Obedience Riddle
Biblical Basis: 1 John 5:1-12
Focus: Faith that Jesus is the Christ and love for God and others produces a natural sort of obedience to God's commands that is not burdensome. Students will identify the correct motivations for obedience and determine ways they can improve both love and obedience in their lives.

Session 13

Step up to Maturity
Biblical Basis: 1 John
God gives Christians guidelines that help us mature. In this session students will review these tips for growth from the entire study of 1 John.

Unit Aims

After completing this unit, your students should be able to:
- DISCOVER the meaning of godly (agape) love and how it precipitates obedience;
- CONSIDER ways to nourish faith, love, and obedience in their lives;
- CONTINUE abiding with God through Bible study and prayer.

Get God's Assurance

KEY VERSE
"The one who is in you is greater than the one who is in the world." 1 John 4:4

BIBLICAL BASIS
1 John 3:19-24; 4:1-6

FOCUS OF THE SESSION
God helps the Christian who is struggling with doubts and questions.

AIMS OF THIS SESSION
You and your students will have accomplished the purpose of this Bible study session if you can:
- IDENTIFY some of the ways God helped Bible people who were struggling with doubts;
- DESCRIBE ways people today can deal with doubts and questions about spiritual things;
- EVALUATE your need to seek God's help in dealing with doubts

TEACHER'S BIBLE STUDY

The people to whom John originally wrote his letter must have been experiencing turmoil. The confusion caused by the false teaching of the antichrists was apparently causing some of them to question their salvation. Some may have come from a pagan background in which people were involved in elaborate outward displays to please their gods. The simplicity of the Christian faith may have been unfamiliar to them. Others may have tasted the sting of persecution; if they had failed their Lord under that pressure, they may have wondered if their relationship with Him was now lost. Others may have been basing their spirituality on feelings rather than on the reliability of God and His Word.

John provided his readers with a means of finding assurance of their standing with God. At the same time he reinforced the warning against the false teachers and added another way to test religious teachings.

In 1 John 2:22 the criterion of truth in doctrine is the acknowledgement that Jesus is the Christ. We saw in an earlier lesson that this refers to His deity. In 4:2,3 the test is the acknowledgement that Jesus Christ has come in the flesh. These two statements combatted the false teachings

in the early church, and they combat much false teaching today. Many unbiblical doctrines have at their core some error about Jesus. These errors boil down to the same thing: a denial of His God-in-a-human-body nature. Yet Jesus Himself accepted the title of "Christ" and "Son of God" and did not contradict those who said He was claiming to be God (see Matt. 16:13-17; John 10:22-28).

No wonder the people were confused! Was Christ who He and the apostles said He was? Or were those who taught differently correct? It must have been difficult to know what God was really like.

And so John brought much-needed words of assurance. He provided objective tests for evaluating a doctrine, as we have seen. He emphasized and re-emphasized the love of God and the tangible way it was demonstrated in Christ. He urged his readers to obey one of God's most fundamental commands by loving one another with active, tangible deeds. And he tied his statements of assurance to the doing of those deeds.

Assurance through Checking Life
John said, "This then is how we know that we *belong to the truth,* and how we set our hearts at rest in his presence when-

ever our hearts condemn us. For God is greater than our hearts, and he knows everything" (1 John 3:19,20, emphasis added). "Belonging to the truth" probably refers to having eternal life since "the truth" in the New Testament usually alludes to the gospel. John was addressing people who wanted to know if they were truly Christians. "This" refers to the previous paragraph (vv. 16-18) which teaches that Christians should display the kind of love that Jesus did—laying down their lives for one another. John first mentioned this concept earlier when he said that loving their brothers proved that they had passed from death to life and had eternal life in them (see 1 John 3:14,15).

When people doubt their salvation, they need to look at their lives for evidence that they belong to Christ. One such evidence is that they are learning to treat others with Christlike *agape* love.

Do not confuse *agape* love with *philia* love (friendship). The Bible does not suggest that Christians must establish affectionate friendships with everyone, but that Christians should try to do what is best for others.

Certainly on one would pass this test of love all the time; but Christians should check for improvement. Our relationship

51

with God should be teaching us more about love all the time; it should be spilling over into our actions. Growing in love signifies that we belong to the truth.

God Is Greater Than Our Hearts

But what if checking up on our love makes us feel defeated? Maybe we have not been living out God's love in our actions as we ought. John's letter has another word for us. John said that God is greater than our hearts and that He knows everything. He created us and knows our secret thoughts and motives; He sees the changes in our hearts while others look only on outward actions. God "knows how we are formed" and "remembers that we are dust" (Ps. 103:14).

The "Assured" Life

John described the benefits of knowing that we have eternal life ("if our hearts do not condemn us," 1 John 3:21) in terms of a dynamic relationship with God. First, we have confidence before God. Rather than cowering before God in fear, we trust Him. This confidence produces the boldness to make requests to Him in prayer (see v. 22), for if we trust Him with eternal salvation, we can trust Him with other matters also. We receive answers because we obey God's commands and do the kind of things that please Him. God answers prayer not as a reward for righteous obedience, but on the condition that the requests are truly in tune with His desires (see 1 John 5:14,15).

Mutual Abiding

What sort of obedience does God want? "And this is his command: to believe in the name of his Son, Jesus Christ, and to love one another as he commanded us" (3:23). Once again the law, the prophets, and the gospel have been capsulized into the two greatest commandments (see Matt. 22:34-40).

What is the result of this obedience? "Those who obey his commands live in him, and he in them. And this is how we know that he lives in us: We know it by the Spirit he gave us" (1 John 3:24). Once again John used the Greek word, *meno*, meaning abide, continue or remain, to speak of the mutual abiding of God and His child as that child obeys Him (see John 15:1-17). Obedience is the condition of mutual abiding; the working of the Spirit is the evidence of mutual abiding.

The Spirit works by teaching believers the truth (see 1 John 2:20,27; John 16:13-15) and by producing love, joy, peace, patience, kindness, goodness, faithfulness, gentleness, and self-control (see Gal. 5:22,23). As we see in ourselves these evidences of our relationship with God we are assured of our salvation and we are encouraged to obey God more and more.

Assurance Through Testing the Spirits

Moving from the thought of God's Holy Spirit to the thought of the ungodly spirits that were opposing the truth, John wrote, "Dear friends, do not believe every spirit, but test the spirits to see whether thy are from God, because many false prophets have gone out into the world" (1 John 4:1). Perhaps his readers were accepting without discrimination teachings that seemed to be inspired by the Spirit.

John urged them to test each spirit for its source. There are spirits from the antichrist (see v. 3). As Christians we are responsible to judge the origin of the teaching we hear.

John then gave his readers two vehicles for testing the spirits: the content of the message (see vv. 2,3) and the nature of the audience (see vv. 4-6).

The message must agree with the litmus test for true doctrine: "Every spirit that acknowledges that Jesus Christ has come in the flesh is from God, but every spirit that does not acknowledge Jesus is not from God" (vv. 2,3). This statement that he "has come in the flesh" clearly countered the Gnostic belief that Jesus never had become an actual man, but had remained a god even in His earthly existence. Even today many believe that God never came in the flesh, but that God's spirit descended on the man Jesus at baptism and left Him at the cross.

John must have stilled his readers' fears with his clear-cut, commonsense test after issuing such a strong command to test the spirits. He required no mystical enchantments as proof from the false prophets, only that confession which is the first step in Christianity—that Jesus is the Christ.

God Is Greater than the Antichrists

To further encourage them, John guaranteed their victory over the false teachers by comparing the strength of their sources of power. "You, dear children, are from God and have overcome them, because the one who is in you is greater than the one who is in the world" (v. 4). God's power and His Spirit provide security against the evil forces.

Because they were equipped with God's power and His Spirit, believers who had walked and talked with God recognized and listened to the apostolic teaching ("whoever knows God listens to us," v. 6). But God's truths meant nothing to those of the world. The antichrists were from the world and spoke from the viewpoint of the world and the world listened to them (see v. 5). John assured the believers that those who refused to listen to biblical teaching were not from God. As Christians we should not be offended if our message is rejected by the world. We should, in fact, expect that it might be. We

should not let this rejection affect our zeal. The people from the world have a spiritual problem—they look at life from the viewpoint of the world and do not see the heavenly realities that believers see. If the audience will not listen to biblical (apostolic) teaching, we know that they are not from God but from the world.

When John said, "This is how we recognize the Spirit of truth and the spirit of falsehood" (v. 6), he referred to the preceding verses. Christians recognize the false message because it does not credit Jesus as Messiah; we recognize an audience as "of the world" when they refuse to listen to the teaching of the apostles—the gospel of the Bible.

Your Students and Their Doubts

Adolescence is a time of life often characterized by self-doubt. So it is not surprising that teenagers may suffer uncertainty about their salvation and about other aspects of spiritual life. Some days they may wake up just not feeling like Christians. At other times they may become acutely conscious of their own sinfulness (possibly because they have sinned a lot) and doubt that such sinful beings can belong to God. Some may not doubt their salvation, but may have unspoken questions or doubts about the reliability of Scripture or the nature of God.

All too often adult Christians act as if it were impossible for a real believer ever to entertain a doubt about God and His love. It may be surprising to note that people we consider great men of God had severe moments of doubt. God has a habit of doing things that mystify our human logic. This gap between God's ideas and our ideas (see Isa. 55:8) can plunge us into deep canyons of doubt.

Moses, for example, doubted his ability to be the kind of leader that God asked him to be. He doubted that anyone would pay attention to him. God had to prod him time and time again until he reluctantly agreed to give God's plan a try (see Exod. 3:11—4:13,20).

Gideon complained to a stranger (who was actually a heavenly messenger) that God had brought His people out of Egypt only to abandon them. "Where are all of his wonders?" was Gideon's question (Judges 6:13). He was afraid and lonely. He couldn't even see that this messenger was going to do something mighty for God's people. The strength of the enemy forces was all that occupied Gideon's mind. God's response was to prove His love and His presence to this now-famous leader (see Judges 6:1-18).

Peter, in a great exercise of faith, walked on water of the stormy sea. But in the middle of this experience, he looked at the situation around him—the weather, the rolling waves, the astonished disciples in the boat—and as his faith sank into doubt his body sank into the sea. Jesus chided him for his doubt but did not leave him struggling in the water (see Matt. 14:22-33).

Thomas doubted that which he had not seen. (his is a position that many take today about spiritual things.) Thomas was not willing to be persuaded by the testimony of others that Christ had risen from the dead, so Jesus provided him with tangible proof that met his need. Our Lord also pronounced a blessing on those who would believe in His resurrection by faith rather than by sight (see John 20:24-29).

Share with your students that it is not uncommon to experience doubts in many or all of the areas in which other people of God have experienced them. What is important is that we do not let that doubt devour our faith, and that we actively seek resolution to it, no matter how long that may take. The suggestions provided in this session should help students find ways to settle their doubts.

THIS WEEK'S TEACHING PLAN

APPROACH TO THE WORD

APPROACH (5-7 minutes

Ask students to form pairs. Have partners share with each other their answers to the question "When did you first begin to doubt Santa Claus?" After allowing a couple of minutes for sharing, regain their attention and ask for a few volunteers to report to the whole class what they have said.

Make a transition to the Bible Exploration by saying something like this: **"Santa is a made-up being that our society has as part of our overall culture. Sometimes it can be a shock to a kid to find out that this person he or she has believed in is not real. It can shake a person up and make him or her wonder about other things such as God and Jesus Christ. There are many other situations that can also cause us to wonder about God or about our relationship with Him. There's nothing wrong with wondering, as long as we are willing to look for and listen to the answers. Let's take a look at what 1 John says about doubts and how to deal with them."**

ALTERNATE APPROACH (5-7 minutes)

Ask, **"Is there anyone here that resembles another member of your family so much that people, without being told, know that you are related?"** Allow a few moments for responses. If no one responds, expand the explanation by pointing out that there are some people who look just like a parent or brother or sister. (Identical twins are another matter. If anyone brings up twins known to them, thank them for the idea, but push on for non-twins who look a lot alike.) If no one in the class seems to have such a resemblance to a relative, ask if there is any family in the church that has two or more members who resemble each other strongly. Keep the discussion lighthearted.

Move to the Bible Exploration by saying something like this: **"We've been talking about how people in a family may resemble or 'take after' one another. Similarly, in God's family we should 'take after' our heavenly Father. When we see that our lives are becoming more like His, we gain assurance that we really do belong to Him. Today we're going to look at a section of 1 John and some other Scriptures that can help us consider what we should do when we're not quite sure if we are God's children, or if we have other doubts or questions in spiritual areas."**

BIBLE EXPLORATION

EXPLORATION (30-45 minutes)

Materials needed: Copies of Student Guide sheet "I'm Not Sure," Bibles, paper, pens and pencils, chalkboard and chalk; optional—copies of Student Guide sheet "Tips on What to Do."

Step 1 (10-12 minutes): Guide students in forming groups of four to six. Direct attention to a chalkboard on which you have written the following Scriptures: 1 John 3:19—4:6; Exodus 3:11—4:13; Judges 6:1-8; Matthew 14:22—33; John 20:24-29. Explain, **"John was writing to a group of people in a church who must have been having some doubts about their relationship with God. These other Scripture passages describe other people who had doubts and questions about God or about their own ability to do what God wanted them to. Read the passage in 1 John and at least one other passage. Then work together in your groups to come up with some way to act out the story found in the second passage. You might do a straight drama, a television talk show interview, or a phone call in which the central character describes his experience to a friend. In your skit be sure to indicate who the central character is, what the doubt was about, and what the solution as. Limit your skits to three minutes."**

If students need additional guidance, you might suggest that they follow this order of action: read the passage; determine the central character, the basic doubt, and the solution; determine in what form they will present the material; write a script; assign actors; rehearse.

Warn students when five minutes and then two minutes are left.

Step 2 (6-12 minutes): Reassemble the class and have groups present their skits. (If you have a large class, you may wish to have half the groups present their skits to one another under the supervision of an adult helper while the other half presents them to each other under your supervision.)

Point out that there are all kinds of doubts—doubts about whether we are actually God's children, doubts about God's nature—"How can He be a loving God and let this bad thing happen?"—doubts about our own ability to do what He has asked us to do. Sometimes we get confused when people express philosophies or religious beliefs that do not fit in with what the Bible teaches. God doesn't expect us never to have doubts, but we should certainly be willing to take the steps necessary to get those doubts resolved. John pointed out some important things in his Epistle.

For example, he pointed out that God is greater than our hearts—He knows if we are truly His children even when our hearts condemn us. And He is greater than the spirit of antichrist, the power behind the false teachings in the world. So student who are uncertain about their relationship with God because of the accusations of their own hearts or because they have been confused by false teachings can have confidence in God's power to keep them in His family.

John pointed out that there are ways to check out whether we belong to God. We can look for evidence of His presence in our lives. If we believe in Jesus Christ, if we are seeking to love one another as He commanded us, if we have experienced the Spirit our lives (for example, if we can see the fruit of the Spirit as described in Galatians 5:22,23), than we know that God is in our lives. We don't have to be perfect, but we should be growing.

John also pointed out that there is no need to become confused by false teachings; all we have to do is determine what they say about Jesus Christ. If they do not portray Him as the Bible does—as God in human flesh—than there's no need to let them upset us.

John's Epistle does not deal directly with the other types of doubts suggested in the Scripture studied. You may wish to go over these tips for dealing with doubt (they are also found on the Student Guide sheet "Tips on What to Do," which you may wish to distribute):

Tips on What to Do

1. Investigate, study, explore. Truth can stand investigation. Research until the doubt dies.

2. Make sure of your commitment. Some people use doubts as excuses for not having to live the way God wants them to.

3. Trust God's promises, not your own emotions.

4. Reinforce yourself with the assurance that "Everything is possible for him who believes" (Mark 9:23; see also Phil. 4:13). Depend on God to help develop your skills and your character.

5. Look for signs of His love. It's even OK to be emotional in your search. The writers of some of the Psalms cried and pleaded for God to reveal Himself to them. Just be careful that you aren't so caught up in your own problems and emotions that you miss the indications of God's love when they come!

6. Put your faith and trust in God. Don't look back at what happened in the past. Fix your focus on God and keep walking with Him.

---

1. Investigate, study, explore. Truth can stand investigation. Research until the doubt dies.

2. Make sure of your commitment. Some people use doubts as excuses for not having to live the way God wants them to.

3. Trust God's promises, not your own emotions.

4. Reinforce yourself with the assurance that "Everything is possible for him who believes" (Mark 9:23; see also Phil. 4:13). Depend on God to help develop your skills and your character.

5. Look for signs of His love. It's even OK to be emotional in your search. The writers of some of the Psalms cried and pleaded for God to reveal Himself to them. Just be careful that you aren't so caught up in your own problems and emotions that you miss the indications of God's love when they come!

6. Put your faith and trust in God. Don't look back at what happened in the past. Fix your focus on God and keep walking with Him.

Step 3 (8-10 minutes): Have students return to their groups. Provide copies of the Student Guide sheet "I'm Not Sure." Assign to each group one of the case studies on the

---

I'm Not Sure

Read the case study assigned to you. Then determine what the person should do, based on the Scripture you have studied in 1 John, to develop assurance of his or her salvation.

Steve

Steve accepted Christ several years ago, but recently he has begun to question whether he really has eternal life. His grandfather died not long ago, and Steve was very upset. He missed his grandfather so much that he questioned God's goodness and love. Now he wonders if that time of doubt means that he is not saved.

Lisa

Lisa works at a hamburger place after school. Some of the other people who work there believe that Jesus was a man who was temporarily filled with God's Son, but was not actually God in the flesh. Lisa isn't sure what to make of this teaching or how it stacks up against the Bible. It is confusing her so much that she is no longer sure of her own relationship with God.

Don

Don is a person almost everybody likes. He's willing to go out of his way to help others, especially those in some sort of need. He received Christ several years ago, and his kindness has been increasing ever since. But Don is very sensitive to sin. He has become terribly aware of his own sinful nature, and has begun to wonder how he can possibly be God's child.

Theresa

Theresa has been going to church all her life. Some of her earliest memories involve her parents telling her how much Jesus loves her. When she was a small child she decided that she loved Jesus and wanted Him to be part of her life. Now that she is older, though, that childhood decision seems rather dim and remote. She just isn't sure any more if she really belongs to God or not.

---

sheet. Ask learners to follow the directions on the sheet as they work together.

Step 4 (8-9 minutes): Regain students' attention and ask the groups to report. Summarize their ideas and how these relate to the Scripture in 1 John and to the tips given in Step 2.

You may want to stress once again God's power. He is greater than our doubts, greater than the pressures that come to us, greater than the forces of antichristian teaching in the world.

Make a transition to the Conclusion by saying something like this: **"We've seen that God will help us through our times of doubt, and we've looked at some suggestions for what we can do when we have those times. Let's take a few minutes to think and pray about our own needs in this area."**

ALTERNATE EXPLORATION (30-40 minutes)

Materials needed: Bibles, copies of Student Guide sheets "Frankly . . . I Doubt It!", "What Would You Do About It?", and "Tips on What to Do," paper, pens or pencils.

Step 1 (10-15 minutes): Guide students in forming groups of three or four. Distribute copies of the Student Guide sheet "Frankly . . . I Doubt It!" Explain, **"John wrote to church**

Frankly . . . I Doubt It!

John wrote his Epistle to Christians who were having some doubts about their relationship with God and some struggles about doctrine because they had been influenced by false teachers. Other people of God down through the years have also struggled with doubts. In our age, unfortunately, some Christians have made people with honest doubts feel very unwelcome. (An honest doubt is one which we will actively try to resolve; it's not something we are using as an excuse to avoid God.)

Fortunately, God is able to use people in spite of their apprehensions about themselves and even their questions about Him.

Read 1 John 3:19—4:6. Then read at least one of the additional passages listed below. For each passage, fill in the chart.

Additional passages: Exodus 3:11—4:13,20; Judges 6:1-18; Matthew 14:22-23; John 20:24-29.

Who Was Having a Problem with Doubt?	What Was the Doubt About?	What Was the Solution to the Doubt?

Write a paragraph giving an example of how the kind of doubt in the passage(s) you have read might show up in a group like yours.

---

people who were experiencing some doubts about their relationship with God and who were troubled by some false teachings about Jesus Christ. Other people through the ages have had struggles with other kinds of doubts and questions—about God's nature, about their own ability to do what God wanted them to, and so on. Today we're going to take a look at what John said and then at the experiences of some other biblical people who struggled with doubts. Begin by reading 1 John 3:19—4:6. Then read at least one of the other Scripture passages indicated on your Student Guide sheet. Follow the instructions on your sheet for responding to the Scripture. We'll come back to the part that asks for a paragraph, so you don't need to work on it right now." (Let groups choose which Scripture to study, or assign them in order to assure complete coverage.)

Allow time for students to work. Then regain their attention and ask them to share what they have discovered.

Summarize what students have said, beginning with the basic concepts in the 1 John passage—that God is greater than our own self-condemnation and greater than the powers behind false teaching; that He assures us that we belong to Him; that we can reassure ourselves by noticing that we believe in Christ and that we love fellow believer; that we live in God and He lives in us; that we respond to the true biblical teachings about Christ.

Move on to the lessons learned from the other Scriptures—that no matter what kind of doubt we are struggling with, our Lord will help us and meet our need for assurance.

Step 2 (10-12 minutes): Have students return to their groups. Provide paper and pens or pencils. Direct attention to the section at the bottom of the "Frankly . . . I Doubt It!" sheet which asks students to write an example of how the sort of doubt they dealt with in Step 1 might show up in a church or youth group today.

Allow time for students to write; then regain their attention and ask them to read what they have written.

Step 3 (10-12 minutes): Have students remain in their groups. Distribute copies of the Student Guide sheet "What Would You Do About It?" Ask students to work in their groups to complete this sheet. After allowing time for them to work, regain their attention and ask for their ideas.

What Would You Do About It?

For each category described below, write some ideas about what you could do to resolve doubts in that area.

1. Doubt about the historical reality of some events in Scripture (such as the resurrection of Christ, the Flood, or the origin of the Bible).

2. Doubt about personal salvation.

3. Doubt about your ability to do what God has asked of you.

4. Doubt about God's love, care, presence and protection.

Share suggestions from the Student Guide sheet "Tips on What to Do" that were not covered by students. You may wish to distribute copies of the sheet for learners to take home. (These tips are also listed in Step 2 of the original Exploration.)

Make a transition to the Conclusion by saying something like this: **"We have talked about some of the kinds of doubts that Christians may struggle with, and we have discussed what we can do about them. We need to take some time now to think and pray about our own needs in this area."**

CONCLUSION AND DECISION

CONCLUSION: (5-7 minutes)

Materials needed: Copies of Student Guide sheet "Review Your Assurance Policy," pens or pencils.

Distribute the "Review Your Assurance Policy" sheet and tell students, **"Complete the paper thoughtfully and prayerfully."**

Review Your Assurance Policy

Do you need God's assurance? If yes, complete this section.

~ Assurance of Salvation ~

Evaluate your life for the last three months by marking the chart with a 1, 2, or 3 for each area.

1 = never   2 = sometimes   3 = usually

	three months ago	two months ago	last month
I treated my family with consideration.			
I went out of my way to help other people.			
I treated my friends well even when they didn't do so to me.			
I believed that Jesus is God in the flesh.			

If you don't see any improvement in your capacity to show selfless love or in your convictions about Christ, note any struggles and improvements in attitude that only God knows about.

_____

Do you have God's assurance? If yes, complete this section.

Thank you Father, because . . .

_____

Do you need to commit yourself to God? Talk to Him about it in prayer. (You can do this inside your head, or write a prayer on a piece of paper.)

Are you unsure about God or about what you want to do? Maybe talking it over with your teacher or pastor will help. Don't be afraid to say, "I don't understand."

Close in prayer, thanking God for the help He gives in dealing with various kinds of doubts.

ALTERNATE CONCLUSION (5-10 minutes)

Materials needed: Copies of Student Guide sheet "I Tend to Have Doubts."

Distribute the Student Guide sheet "I Tend to Have Doubts."

I Tend to Have Doubts . . .

. . . in the area of:

Next time I have these doubts, I will take the following steps to resolve them:

Even if I've never had a doubt in my life, I can make some plans for handling doubts if they ever come. I plan to:

Ask students to complete it prayerful and thoughtfully. After allowing time for them to work, close in prayer, thanking God for the help He gives in dealing with various kinds of doubts.

Buy into God's Kind of Love

KEY VERSE
"Dear friends, since God so loved us, we also ought to love one another." 1 John 4:11

BIBLICAL BASIS
1 John 4:7-12, 19-21

FOCUS OF THE SESSION
God's love motivates us to love others.

AIMS OF THIS SESSION
You and your class will have accomplished the purpose of this session if you can:
- EXPLAIN how God demonstrates His love to us;
- CONSIDER ways you can show God's love to others;
- CHOOSE one way you can show God's love to at least one person.

TEACHER'S BIBLE STUDY

"The human race needs a good lecture on loving each other," one angel said.

"God should give them rewards—like a new car every six months—if they'll just show more love!" urged another angel.

"No, I think threats of punishment would whip them into shape," suggested another.

But another angel insisted, "I think God will convince them by living in them, loving them and showing them how to love others."

This imaginary dialogue introduces the topic of the session: How does God persuade Christians to obey His command to love? He modeled it by giving His Son; He plants it in our hearts as He lives within us; He teaches us about it through His Word, the Bible. The Supreme Motivator helps Christians want to love by generously dispensing love from its source—Himself.

The Source of Love

John addressed the issue of Christians loving one another several times in his letter. He had already mentioned that loving others offered evidence of being in God's light (see 1 John 2:7-11) and of having eternal life (see 3:14,15). In the passage examined in this session he showed how Christians are to reflect God's nature: He is the source of love, so we are to love one another (see 4:7-12). (Note that the Scrip-

ture studied in this session is 1 John 4:7-12, 19-21. Verses 13-18 deal with another concept and are discussed in Session 11.)

Within this paragraph John offered three reasons for loving one another. His first reason was that **love comes from God** (see vv. 7,8). Loving one another proves that we have experienced a new birth and are getting to know God better. Loving others and knowing God are so intricately woven together that one who does not love does not even know God (see v. 8). Not loving others (or being indifferent to their needs) but claiming to know God is like "claiming to be intimate with a foreigner whose language we cannot speak or to have been born of parents we do not in any way resemble. It is to fail to manifest the nature of Him whom we claim as our Father (born of God) and our Friend (knoweth God)."[1]

God Is Love

By saying in verse 8 that God is love, John was saying that God loves to the extent that one might say He **is** love! Love is not just something God does; it is an attribute that permeates everything He does. It is part of His nature.

Love entails a choice, an act of the will. We choose to love Him. Robots do not choose to love, they act as they are programmed.

Love explains God's mercy. If He were

not love, but only law and justice, He could have let humans die in their sin and let the earth sustain itself as best it could. His love, however, caused Him to offer a plan of redemption through the death of Christ.

John also stated that God is spirit and light (see John 4:24; 1 John 1:5). This teaching countered the Gnostics' belief that God was spirit and light but not love.

Agape Love

The early Christians used *agape*, one of the Greek words translated by our single (and sometimes inadequate) word love, to describe a love that causes one to want and to actively seek what is best for the other person. *Agape* means being concerned for the other person. It may lead us to give what we have to strengthen and benefit the lives of others. That giving may take the form of material things, money, spending time with the person, sharing our skill in a certain area, or other forms of help. Christian writers used *agape* to describe the mark of a disciple, the reason that Christ died for undeserving sinners, the unbreakable bond between God and Christians, the central characteristic of a Christian, and the source of Christian maturity (see John 13:35; Rom. 8:35,39; 1 Cor. 13:1-3, 8-12).

Another term used in some parts of the Bible is *philia,* meaning friendly affection, warm devotion or mutuality. John used this type of expression to describe God's love for man in terms of warm, fatherly feelings (see John 16:27). The word is also used in the Bible to express love for one's own life, for family members, and for things of the world (see John 12:25; Matt. 10:37; 23:6).

There is some overlap between the meanings of *agape* and *philia*. But *agape* is used of love by choice, love that can be commanded as in "love your neighbor." This kind of love entails an active effort to do what will benefit the loved person. *Philia* is used more for the love that comes from the emotions—good feelings toward another person.

The English word love also translates the Greek word *eros*—romantic and erotic love. God gives *eros* and *philia* to human beings as part of our nature; He gives *agape* love as a special gift to those who are born of Him (see 1 John 4:7). For "God has poured out *his love* into our hearts by the Holy Spirit, whom he has given us" (Rom. 5:5, emphasis added).

As Christians we channel *agape* love with our minds and wills; this enables us to put aside our feelings and thus love our enemies (see Matt. 5:43-48). We do not just "feel" this kind of love; in fact, we may not feel it at all. But we can put it into action regardless of feelings (see 1 John 3:18). (And sometimes the feelings—the *philia* love—will follow the actions—the *agape* love.)

Agape love enables us to see people as God sees them and to value them as God values them. God's love is so great that Christ died for all of us while we were yet sinners (see Rom. 5:8).

The Atoning Sacrifice

John's second reason for Christians to love one another was that by so doing **we follow God's example of love in sending His Son as the atoning sacrifice for sin** (see 1 John 4:9,10, *NIV*; other Bible versions use "propitiation" or "expiation"). The *New International Version* uses the phrase "his one and only Son" in v. 9 (and in John 3:16) to describe Jesus as a Son who is the only one of His kind. We become God's children when we are born again, but the Son of God has been the Son of God from the beginning (see John 1:1,2,14). God described Him as "my chosen one in whom I delight" (Isa. 42:1). However, God also loved the world to the extent that He was willing to give the one He loved so much to save weak, ungodly sinners (see John 3:16; Rom. 5:6-8; 1 Tim. 2:4). God's bountiful love held nothing back, even though the world had done nothing to deserve such a gift.

John stated the purpose for God's action: "that we might live through him" (1 John 4:9). We live through Him not only in the sense that our eternal destination is assured, but also in the sense that every-day life here on earth is transformed because He lives in us and gives us purpose, strength and peace. Jesus' life demonstrated the abundant life available by abiding in Him (see John 10:10).

Before John painted the picture of Christ's loving sacrifice, he dismissed any notions that a Christian's love for God had initiated the relationship or defined love: "This is love: not that we loved God, but that he loved us and sent his son as an atoning sacrifice for our sins" (1 John 3:10). The Christian's love, then, is but a reflection of the spontaneous, freely-given love of God. Our Father does not love in response to something we do; He does not love us "because of" any reason we can offer Him for doing so. God's love is self-starting. Love is the way He is.

Pass It On

John's third reason for showing love to others was that **Christians become the advertisements for God's love** as "God lives in us and his love is made complete in us" (v. 12). God's love was not just a single historical event; it continues as He lives in the Christian. His love is made complete by the tangible, concrete ways Christians practice it on each other. Since no one has seen God (see v.12), Christians help other people see Him through His effect on them.

John explained that God's love and a believer's love for others are so tightly bound together that a person who loves God but not his brother is a liar (see v. 20). John used the simple reasoning that a person who fails at an easier task will not be graduated to a more difficult task. It is easier to love a visible, in-the-flesh human being. If we cannot do that, we cannot show love to an invisible spirit—God. An inability to love other humans does not make a person unable to love God, but rather proves that he or she does not.

John fused the two already inseparable greatest commands of loving God and loving others: "Whoever loves God must also love his brother" (v. 21). This is not a "must" of coercion, but of motivation. God's character and example move us to imitate His love. As we receive His love we are able to show love to others.

What Is Love?

Your students need to know what love is and what it is not. They often feel that the easy, agreeable people love them while the tough, demanding people do not. Fortunately, the Greek language had precise words for love so that the early Christians communicated God's kind of self-giving love by the word *agape,* which was described earlier in this session. Contemporary usage of the English language has clouded the meaning of the word love by overusing it in sentences such as "I love pizza" or "I love rock music." Students need to define God's love in terms of taking practical action to benefit another person.

God's love must not be demoted to merely a warm emotional bond. He offered His love along with His challenges, as if to say: "I am loving you; now show my love to other people." That balance must be maintained to give young people an accurate picture of the God who wants to be their Father. Some people think they can live as they please and then expect a loving God to deliver them from the consequences of their actions. But He doesn't work that way. Because He loves us He wants us to live up to His standards, and He will permit us to experience the consequences of straying from them. He is love and He is also just. It would not be loving or just to let people get away with sin. At the same time, His love and His justice worked together to provide our salvation through Christ—His costly gift to His sinful people.

Since God's love is the proper motivation to love others, Christians must be keenly aware of the greatness of that love. We must not let our familiarity with the fact of Christ's sacrificial death numb our spirits to His love. Nor should we take His deity for granted by thinking that since He was capable of such great virtues and miracles, His sacrifice was minimal. We must not forget that Christ was with God in the beginning and that God treasured Him and fellowshipped with Him in a heavenly relationship far beyond our understanding. Yet He gave up that fellowship for a time in order to live among us, die for us, and then rise again in order to give us new life and hope.

A question that often comes up when discussing God's love is, "If God is love, why do people suffer?" There are no simple answers, but we can look at several aspects of the issue. One is that **suffering and evil are related to human sin.** They were not part of God's original plan for the human race; they entered our experience when Adam and Eve chose to disobey God. Another thing we need to consider is that "permitting human suffering was no easy thing for God. In Christ God entered our world to suffer with us and for us. He suffered in an ultimate way we may not even be able to understand in eternity. For now, we can only trust that God, whose wisdom is beyond our own, understands the necessity that we cannot."[2]

Scripture makes it clear that we will suffer (see John 15:18-27; Rom. 8:17). It also makes it clear that God can use our suffering for His glory and for our good (see Rom. 5:3-5; 8:28,29; Jas. 1:2-4; 1 Pet. 3:13-16; 4:12-16). **Suffering can make us more like Christ,** refining our character as a metal worker refines silver and gold (see Zech. 13:9). As people see our Christian response to suffering, we gain opportunities to share Christ with them.

Looking at Christ's sufferings can help reassure us about our own trials. Christ was sinless and good—He did not suffer for any fault of His own. Thus we can realize that our sufferings need not be identified as punishment for sin. (Of course, if we have sinned, we may suffer the consequences; but many people unnecessarily torture themselves by trying to dredge up nonexistent sins when they find themselves having trials.) In addition, we know that Christ was raised from the dead and now enjoys the Father's presence and glory. One day we, too, will be released from suffering and will enjoy being with God.

Learning to Love Others

Your students can use this session to examine the love they show to their families, their friends, and even their enemies. In the **family,** taking time to consider oth-

ers' needs might even result in a young person taking out the garbage without being asked! Stepping into a brother's or sister's shoes might help explain that person's attitudes and behavior. A family serves as the laboratory of life; if teenagers can begin to show love by noticing and trying to meet their family's needs, it will affect all parts of their lives.

Christian love should extend to **friendships** as well. Your students need to ask themselves if they like their friends just because their friends please them, or if they are willing to do what is best for their friends. For example, they may need to ask, "Am I willing for my friend to make a decision that will benefit him or her, even if it excludes me?" Of course, the best thing any believer can do for a friend who is not a Christian is to introduce that friend to Christ.

Taking stock of their **enemies'** needs might provide some surprising informa-

tion. Perhaps the "enemy" is a shy person whose reticence has been mistaken for snootiness. Perhaps the feelings of antipathy have arisen through some misunderstanding. An act of genuine love might break the ice with the shy person or clear up the misunderstanding with the other. If students did what was best for their enemies, would they still dislike each other?

Christian teenagers need to notice the people around them, to discern others' needs and ask God what He wants them to do to improve others' lives.

Footnotes

1. John R.W. Stott, *The Epistles of John* (Grand Rapids: Eerdmans Publishing Co., 1976), p. 161.

2. Lawrence O. Richards, *The Believer's Guidebook* (Grand Rapids: Zondervan Publishing House, 1983), p. 476.

THIS WEEK'S TEACHING PLAN

APPROACH TO THE WORD

APPROACH: (5-8 minutes)

Materials needed: Self-adhesive name tags, pen.

Preparation: On each name tag, write a word describing various conditions of life, such as born blind, a paraplegic, born into a wealthy family, has a learning disability, an orphan, a refugee, a skilled musician, a very poor person, and so on. Make a name tag for each student in class. Be sure they are balanced between positive and negative conditions.

As your students arrive, hand each one a name tag to wear. When class begins, explain, **"Move around the class and find people who have name tags describing conditions that are similar to yours. For example, if your name tag describes someone who has been blessed by life, look for others who have also been blessed by life. Your name tags will not be identical. After you have found others with whom you can get together, talk among yourselves and come up with a one-sentence description of God. Keep in mind what you have been blessed or handicapped with as you consider your description."**

After allowing time for students to follow the instructions, regain their attention and ask the groups to report the concepts of God that they came up with. Some groups may present ideas that do not portray God as being loving—especially those whose name tags suggested disabling or disadvantaged conditions. Those with name tags representing more fortunate conditions may come up with statements that tend to show God's love. Be prepared for surprises.

Ask students some questions like these: **How did you come to that conclusion about God from the position you hold in life? How do you think people who really have these handicaps would feel? How might some extremely disadvantaged people respond to the idea that God is love? How would you tell a disadvantaged person that God is love?**

Make a transition to the Bible Exploration by saying

something like this: **"Today we are going to look at a statement about God that we have heard for years—that God is love. As you can see, there are some complications that we need to consider as we think about this truth."**

ALTERNATE APPROACH (8-10 minutes)

Materials needed: One or more chenille-covered wires for each student.

Have students form groups of five or less and give each student one or more chenille-covered wires. Explain, **"Use this wire to symbolize God's love in some way."** Show them an example such as a cross, a heart or a triangle.

After allowing students to work, regain their attention and ask them to share and discuss their symbols in their small groups. Use a transition like this: **"God's love is different from traditional ideas of love. We're going to examine His love today and talk about how He wants us to reflect it to other people."**

BIBLE EXPLORATION

EXPLORATION: (30-45 minutes)

Materials needed: Shelf paper, pencils, paper, felt pens, copies of Student Guide sheets "Take Apart Love," "For Instance," and "Brain Busters."

Step 1 (12-15 minutes): Guide students in forming small groups of two or three. Explain, **"Sometimes Scripture is so packed with important ideas that it's a little hard for our minds to take in. Today's passage is like that. So we're going to try taking it in small chunks and seeing what we can do with one chunk."**

Give each student one section of the Scripture passage, cut from the "Take Apart Love" Student Guide sheet. (If there are more sections of Scripture than students, give some who read well an extra section.) Give each group a strip of shelf paper and a felt pen. Explain, **"Each person will take the passage of Scripture that you have been given and think about**

Buy into God's Kind of Love
Winter #10

Walking in God's Light

Take Apart Love

Dear friends, let us love one another, for love comes from God. **1.**	We love because he first loved us. **8.**
Everyone who loves has been born of God and knows God. **2.**	If anyone says, "I love God," yet hates his brother, he is a liar. **9.**
Whoever does not love does not know God, because God is love. **3.**	For anyone who does not love his brother, whom he has seen, cannot love God, whom he has not seen. **10.**
This is how God showed his love among us: He sent his one and only Son into the world that we might live through him. **4.**	And he has given us this command: Whoever loves God must also love his brother. **11.**
This is love: not that we loved God, but that he loved us and sent his Son as an atoning sacrifice for our sins. **5.**	
Dear friends, since God so loved us, we also ought to love one another. **6.**	
No one has ever seen God, but if we love each other, God lives in us and his love is made complete in us. **7.**	

1 John 4:7-12, 19-21, *NIV*

what it means. Then come up with a rebus to express that meaning. Each member of a group should write his or her rebus on the shelf paper. A rebus is a way of expressing a statement with words and pictures." Show students this example:

"GOD IS LOVE" (GOAT-AT + DOG-OG IS GLOVE-G.)

After allowing time for students to work, regain their attention. Call the numbers of the Scripture sections in order and have students tape their shelf paper to the walls of the classroom, making a continuing rebus that may wrap around the room once or twice.

Provide paper and pencils and ask students to follow the rebus and decipher the entire passage.

When students have completed the task, regain their attention and spend a few minutes discussing the passage. Ask students what they think the main points are. Then summarize what they have said and stress these points: God is the source of love; He demonstrated His love by giving His Son so that we might have life; because God loves us, we should love others. Use material from the Teacher's Bible Study as needed in your discussion. (If students bring up any difficult questions about God's love versus the suffering in the world, ask them to hold those questions. They will have an opportunity to examine them a little later in the session.)

Step 2 (10-12 minutes): Have students remain in their groups. Have each group send one student to the rebus to select a passage (not one their group worked on). Provide copies of the "For Instance" Student Guide sheet, or give

For Instance

Sometimes we can read a whole passage of very deep thoughts without very much of it sinking in. Some parts of 1 John are like that.

Try taking a verse from 1 John 4:7-12 or 19-21 and giving it roots by describing a "for instance" from everyday life.

Here's an example taken from 1 John 4:6, which says, "We are from God, and whoever knows God listens to us":

For instance, if a group of us are in a discussion at lunch time and some spiritual idea comes up, those who are Christians or who are open to God will not shut out what is being said. Those not interested in God may not listen, and might even get up and leave.

students the information verbally. They are to write a paragraph describing an example from everyday life illustrating the selected passage.

After allowing time for students to work, regain their attention and ask them to share their "for instances." Compliment them on their ideas before moving on to Step 3.

Step 3 (10-15 minutes): Have students remain in their groups. Distribute copies of the "Brain Busters" Student Guide

Brain Busters

The problem with love is that some people feel that they have not received their fair share. Look at the ideas below and come up with a good answer for at least one of them.

1. If God is love, He can't send people to hell!

2. God cannot be a God of love and allow people (especially believers) to suffer.

3. A loving God will not be strict with His children.

4. Why would a loving God make a lot of rules to spoil our enjoyment of live?

59

sheet. Assign to each student (or let them select) one of the problems from the sheet. Ask students to answer based on what they have studied in 1 John and on what they know from other Scripture.

After allowing time for students to work, regain their attention and ask for their responses to the "Brain Busters." Try to arrive at satisfactory answers for all the problems on the sheet. If more help is needed, ask for volunteers to study during the week and report back next time.

Make a transition to the Conclusion by saying something like this: **"We've spent some time talking about God's love and some ways it can be demonstrated in daily life. Let's take a few moments to consider our personal response."**

ALTERNATE EXPLORATION (30-35 minutes)

Materials needed: Copies of Student Guide sheet "Determine God's L. Q.," Bibles, pens or pencils, chalkboard and chalk or overhead projector with transparency and pens.

Step 1 (10-12 minutes): Guide students in forming pairs. Distribute "Determine God's L. Q." sheets and assign to each

---

Determine God's L.Q.*

Read 1 John 4:7-12, 19-21 and answer at least one set of questions.

*Love Quotient

God and love (verses 7-10)

1. What is the source of love, according to verse 7?

2. What do you think John meant when he said that God is love (verse 8)?

3. How do you define God's kind of love? (For further help, see 1 Corinthians 13:4-8.)

Christ's sacrifice (verses 9,10)

1. What do you think John meant by "his one and only Son" in verse 9?

2. Describe God's probable feelings about sending His Son. (See Isaiah 42:1.)

3. Why did John include "not that we loved God" in verse 10?

Loving others with God's love (verses 11,12,19-21)

1. Compare the reason why most people love others with John's reason for loving other people (verses 11, 19). What difference does it make?

2. "If we love each other, God lives in us and his love is made complete in us" (v. 12, NIV). What does that mean? What does that have to do with no one having seen God?

3. John said that people who claim to love God, yet hate their brothers, are liars (see verse 20). Why is this so?

---

pair one of the three sets of questions from the sheet. Explain, **"In his letter John repeated certain themes several times. One such theme is love. He considered that it was so important it was worth discussing several ways. We're going to take a look at what he had to say about it in 1 John 4:7-12,19-21. Work together in your groups to read the Scripture and then answer the questions assigned to your group. If you finish before the others, work on another set of questions."**

Step 2 (8-10 minutes): After allowing students time to work, regain their attention and ask them to share their answers. Use information from the Teacher's Bible Study and the following suggested answers as you guide your students in discussion:

God and love

1. God is the source of love.
2. This answer has room for individual ideas. God's very nature is love, and love derives its nature from God.
3. God's kind of love was illustrated in His gift of Jesus Christ to help us have new life. Attributes of love are given in 1 Corinthians 13:4-8.

Christ's sacrifice

1. This answer has room for personal interpretation. John probably meant that Jesus is God's Son by His very nature, in contrast to people, who must be born again to become God's children. Jesus is a "one of a kind" Son.
2. Jesus was God's special Son. God must have grieved at losing Jesus' fellowship, even for a time, and at watching His suffering at the hands of human beings.
3. John was illustrating love. God's giving of Himself pictures love better than human attempts at love.

Loving others with God's love

1. People often love others because the others have helped them or pleased them. Scripture says Christians should love others because God loved us first. If people base their love on the actions of other people, they will probably stop loving if the actions cease to please them. If they love because God loved them first, they will continue to love no matter what happens.
2. God sends the Holy Spirit to live inside Christians. Other people cannot see God or His Spirit, but they can see acts of love performed by the Christian. These loving acts serve as a way for them to learn about God.
3. It is easier to love a visible, in-the-flesh person than an invisible Spirit such as God. If a person cannot do the easier task—loving someone who can be seen—he or she will not be able to do the more difficult one—loving a God who cannot be seen. Thus a person who claims to love God but does not love people is not telling the truth.

Thank students for their work and summarize by saying something like this: **"God is the source of *agape* love, the kind of love that makes a practical effort to do something good for other people. God gave what was most precious to Him, His Son, in order to provide a way for us to know the exciting life He has available for us. Realizing the great love God has for us motivates us to be like Him and to show His love to others."**

Step 3 (10-12 minutes): Draw this chart on the chalkboard or transparency:

	Parents	Friends and Siblings	Enemies
Needs			
Ways to Show Love			

Give students these directions: **"In order to show the kind of love that tries to meet needs, let's consider the typical needs of these groups of people and how teenagers could try to show love by meeting those needs. This might mean giving something of value, such as time, energy, or money, to help someone else. For example, many parents have undesirable jobs or heavy time pressures. A teenager can show love by being patient when they come home from work or by running errands to save them time. What are the needs you can think of?"**

Write students' suggestions on the chart (or appoint a recorder to do so). If the students need ideas for ways to show love ask them to consult the attributes of love described in

1 Corinthians 13:4-8, then translate these characteristics into positive actions. For example, if love is not rude (see v. 5), a way to show love might be, "Responding politely, not just grunting when Mom asks about my day."

Provide ideas of your own if students have any difficulty in coming up with several suggestions for each section of the chart.

They may particularly need help perceiving needs of "enemies" and ways to show love to "enemies." Spend some time talking about what an enemy is. Students are not likely to have enemies who are out to kill them. But they probably know some people that they don't like and perhaps would be glad to see get a bad grade in school or earn the disfavor of a teacher. On the other hand, your students may not have any negative feelings toward people, but may be on the receiving end of dislike—perhaps through no fault of their own. Jesus said we should love our enemies (see Matt. 5:44). He would not command us to feel an emotion that we are not able to control easily. So He was not talking about the emotional feeling of being warm towards and liking the person. Rather He meant that we were to love by choice—to *decide* to do something that will benefit the other person. This is the way we love our enemies—by praying for them, to start with, and then, as God directs, to meet even such simple needs as the need for a friendly greeting. Amazing things can happen in the lives of both parties when a Christian reaches out in this way.

Make a transition to the Conclusion by saying something like this: **"Considering a person's needs is the first step in showing love. God saw our need for salvation and had a plan to meet that need. Think about the needs of your parents, brothers and sisters, friends, and even enemies. God wants you to show His love to them by what you do to enhance their lives."**

CONCLUSION AND DECISION

CONCLUSION: (7-10 minutes)

Materials needed: Copies of Student Guide sheet "Because He Loves Me . . . ," pens or pencils.

Because He Loves Me . . .

In the space below write some ideas about ways you could respond to God's love for you.

Distribute pencils and Student Guide sheet "Because He Loves Me . . . ." Give directions such as these: **"Write some ideas about ways you could respond to God's love for you. Maybe you want to write a note thanking Him for loving you. Maybe you want to show His love in practical ways to the people around you. Jot down a number of ideas, then select one to start with this week."**

After allowing time for students to write, close in prayer thanking God for His love and asking Him to show all of you ways to share that love with others.

ALTERNATE CONCLUSION (5-8 minutes)

Materials needed: An index card for each student, pens or pencils.

Instruct students in this manner: **"Pick a person or persons in your life to whom you need to show God's love. Determine some specific ways you can show God's love to them. Draw at least two cartoons on this card, showing yourself meeting the needs of the person or persons. You may use simple stick figures to insure that you finish on time. Keep your card with you this week and try to look at it at least once a day. Ask God to help you actually do the things you have depicted."**

Close in prayer, thanking God for His special love and for the ways He has shown it. Ask Him to help the students show His love to those around them.

Let God In

KEY VERSE

"And so we know and rely on the love God has for us. God is love. Whoever lives in love lives in God, and God in him."
1 John 4:16

BIBLICAL BASIS

1 John 4:13-18

FOCUS OF THE SESSION

As we live in God and He lives in us, we can nourish our relationship with Him through Christian disciplines such as Bible study and prayer.

AIMS OF THIS SESSION

You and your students will have accomplished the purpose of this Bible study session if you can:

- IDENTIFY from Scripture evidences and results of the Christian's relationship with God;
- EXPLORE ways Christians can nurture their relationship with God;
- PRACTICE a devotional time in class.

TEACHER'S BIBLE STUDY

Can simple, finite humans have a close relationship with an infinite, powerful Creator? We can—but only through God living in us and we in Him. The strength of this mutual relationship sets aside any fear we might have of Him and replaces it with confidence.

John mentioned the benefits of God living in Christians throughout his Epistle, but in 4:13-18 he concentrated on the evidences and results of mutual abiding. (Abiding, dwelling, and living are different words used to translate the same idea.) Because this reciprocal relationship contributes to maturity in the Christian, we will also explore ways to help students nurture their relationship with the Lord.

In 1 John 4:13-18, John elaborated on two phrases he had used in 1 John 4:12: "God lives in us" and "his love is made complete in us." John listed evidences of God living in Christians in verses 13-16:

the Spirit (see v.13);

our conviction that Jesus is the Son of God and Saviour of the world (see vv. 14,15);

a life of love (see v. 16).

God's love is made complete in Christians as they come to know and rely on God's love (see v. 16). The mutual abiding of God and the Christian in each other

results in confidence at the day of judgment since the relationship has banished the fear of God.

The Holy Spirit Within

As Christians we can confidently acknowledge that we and God dwell together because **God has given us His Spirit** (see v. 13). The Holy Spirit is God Himself present in the Christian. The Spirit plays an integral part in the abiding process, for by His presence we can call God "Abba, Father" (see Rom. 8:15). "Abba" is an Aramaic term of affection similar to "Daddy." It shows the close, tender relationship God wants to have with us. He loves us with an intimate love that invites us to draw close to Him.

The Spirit also helps us with our prayer life: "We do not know how we ought to pray, but the Spirit himself intercedes for us with groans that words cannot express . . . in accordance with God's will" (Rom. 8:26,27). When we don't know what to pray or how to put into words the desires of our hearts, the Spirit assists us.

Acknowledging Christ

The second evidence of mutual abiding is our **conviction that Jesus is the Saviour and the Son of God** (see vv.

14,15). This faith is further evidence of the Spirit's work (see 1 John 4:2).

Love

The third evidence of our relationship with God is **love** (see v. 16). We do not know the nature of love nor how to truly love others until we open ourselves to the Spirit whose first fruit is love (see Gal. 5:22). Mature love develops as we live in God and He lives in us, for God is love and to partake of God is to learn love.

Results in Confidence

When we experience God's love, we have confidence in our relationship with Him. We don't have to worry about the day of judgment (see 1 John 4:17) because we know that our loving Father has forgiven our sins and freed us from their penalty through the work of our Saviour (see vv. 17,18,14). John had previously stated that continuing in God (or abiding) equipped us to be confident and unashamed at His coming (see 2:28); in 4:17 he added that mature love produces this confidence at judgment "because in this world we are like him." We can be like God in this world because Christ lives His life through us (see Gal. 2:20).

The confidence we gain through living

in God and having Him live in us spreads through our life. It encourages us to make requests in prayer and receive what we ask for because we are obeying God and doing what pleases Him—including asking for the things He wants us to ask for (see 1 John 3:21,22; 5:14,15).

As the mutual abiding grows we learn more and more about Jesus. We find that He is our high priest, who was tempted just as we are (see Heb. 4:15). This allows us the freedom to "approach the throne of grace with confidence, so that we may receive mercy and find grace to help us in our time of need" (Heb. 4:16).

No Fear in Love

Mature love drives out fear because fear has to do with punishment (see 1 John 4:18). We cannot have a true love relationship with a person we fear, for our fear shows our lack of confidence in the person's love for us. Fear involves a dread of what the person might do to us—the very opposite of the joyful anticipation involved in a love relationship. If we fear God we cannot develop a mature love for Him. Fear and love are incompatible: fear inhibits, but love frees; fear separates, but love unites; fear encourages violence, but love produces acceptance. God wants Christians to be so confident in His love that we are fearless even when we think about the future judgment.

Does eliminating fear contradict other teachings in the Bible? Although the phrase "the fear of the Lord" is mentioned more than twenty times in the Old Testament, the expression has to do with worshiping and having faith. The nations surrounding Israel did not fear (worship, have faith in) the true God; instead they trusted in idols. The "fear" of the Lord included: having wisdom, hating evil, prolonging life, producing a fountain of life, not envying sinners (see Prov. 1:7; 8:13; 10:27; 14:27; 23:17). Even though service and worship involved fear ("My flesh trembles in fear of you; I stand in awe of your laws," Ps. 119:120), those who worshiped experienced reverence or awe, not terror.

There are some New Testament commands to fear, but these actually entail awe of the greatness of the issue involved—usually salvation. After speaking about those who chose not to believe, Paul told the Christians: "Do not be arrogant, but be afraid. For if God did not spare the natural branches, he will not spare you either" (Rom. 11:20). Even the command, "work out your salvation with fear and trembling" does not refer to terror of God but reverence for the gravity of eternal salvation, for the rest of the sentence continues, "for it is God who works in you to will and to act according to his good purpose" (Phil. 2:13). Terror does not mix with intimacy. Throughout the Bible, fear in the sense of terror existed for

the habitual sinner who did not accept Christ (see Heb. 10:27; Prov. 18:1).

God encourages confidence, not terror in His children. "For you did not receive a spirit that makes you a slave again to fear, but you received the Spirit of sonship" (Rom. 8:15). "For God did not give us a spirit of timidity, but a spirit of power, of love and of self-discipline" (2 Tim.1:7). When we abide in God and He abides in us we develop faith in Him, not fear of Him.

Learning to Abide

Abiding in God affords distinct advantages. Those who abide do not continually sin (see 1 John 3:6); they acknowledge that Jesus is the Son of God (see 4:15); they have confidence (see 2:28); they obey his commands (see 3:24); they overcome the evil one (see 2:14); they develop mature love for others (see 4:12,16); and they see evidence of the Spirit (see 3:24; 4:13). This session gives students three tests of mutual abiding: the presence of the Spirit, their faith that Jesus is the Son of God, and their life of love.

But no matter how many evidences the students perceive in their lives, they will never "arrive" at mutual abiding. They must continue to grow. A relationship, like any living thing, must be nurtured.

Help your students grow in the Lord by strengthening their communication lines with Him. Students need to share their lives with God on a regular basis. Even Jesus, who knew God so well, needed "quiet times" with Him. After a tiring day of teaching in the synagogue, casting out a demon, healing Peter's mother-in-law, and concluding with a healing session in front of the whole city, Jesus still got up early in the morning while it was still dark and went off to a solitary place to pray (see Mark 1:21-37). How much more Christians need to spend time with the Lord.

Young people need to open up to God by sharing their needs and requests with Him no matter how large or small they may be (see Phil. 4:6). As they talk over their desires with God, they can look at those requests in the light of what they are learning from Him. Sometimes they will discover for themselves that a particular request does not fit in with His scheme of things. Sometimes they will still need for Him to answer yes, no, or wait. In addition, these sharing times will give God the opportunity to speak to them through His Word or through the quiet inner voice of conviction.

As students thank God (see 1 Thess. 5:18) for blessings of all types, they will see His hand on their lives. They will realize that He is not off somewhere riding shooting stars, but is working diligently in their lives to help them come to maturity. Confessing their sins to Him (see 1 John 1:9) closes the gap between God

and themselves, relieves them from their guilt and assures them that God does love them to forgive them of so much. Confessing to God also prepares them for learning to confess to their brothers and sisters in Christ when that is appropriate.

Perhaps most challenging of all, prayer teaches teenagers to worship as they learn to praise God (see James 5:13; Heb. 13:15). Finite minds and worldly cares cloud our ability to understand God's great qualities. Praise can push aside the clouds and help us see more clearly. If we are beginners at this, we can learn to praise God by using the words of those who know Him better: Psalms, hymns and Christian songs can help us verbalize the qualities of God. Eventually we can learn to put into words our own thoughts of praise to Him.

Letting God Talk

A relationship cannot survive on one-way communication. Believers must learn to let God speak to them regularly. Their "quiet times" or "devotions" must include input from God's Word. Getting it second hand from a teacher, youth director, or minister will probably not foster an abiding relationship, for the Word of God should live in a Christian (see 1 John 2:14). Maturity necessitates growth in God's Word. The writer of Hebrews began his warning against falling away from God (see Heb. 5:11—6:12) by encouraging his readers to quit living on the milk of God's Word but to move on to solid food. Reading only certain favorite passages in the Bible is the first step to atrophy of spiritual muscles.

The precepts in God's Word must also be applied continuously. Young people usually find straightforward books of the Bible such as Proverbs, James, or Mark the easiest books to understand and appropriate. They must develop the habit of reading the Bible regularly, even just a few verses. They should use it as a mirror to examine themselves, being careful not to walk away without applying it (see James 1:22-25).

One way to encourage your students' growth in God is to urge them to use easy-to-read Bibles. Many young people do not read well, and their lack of comprehension leads to lack of response. You may be disappointed in students' lack of excitement about the wonderful truths of God's Word, not realizing that they are simply not understanding those truths. A Bible version more appropriate to their level of reading comprehension may become the door to new appreciation for God and what He has done for His children.

A regular, even if brief, communication with God will help students have confidence in their salvation. Students can know that they have eternal life because of God's great love for them and the provision He made through the death of Christ, not from any merit of their own. A "quiet time" better acquaints them with His love so as to make His mercy believable and trustworthy. You can help students by sharing how you schedule time to be with God. Be honest about the struggles this entails as you have to set priorities and perhaps forego other activities. Be honest, too, about the benefits and blessings you experience as you make this effort to nurture your growth.

THIS WEEK'S TEACHING PLAN

APPROACH TO THE WORD

APPROACH TO THE WORD (5-8 minutes)

Select one to four students who can stand up to a bit of embarrassment. Explain that you're going to have these students present a charade and the rest of the class is to guess its meaning. Tell the selected students that they must present a charade on the word "abide." Keep the whole experience lighthearted. Probably no one in the class will guess the charade, since it is a difficult concept to convey without words. On the other hand, your students may surprise you with their insights! Either way, thank everyone for their efforts. If they have guessed correctly, congratulate them on their intelligence. If they did not guess, commiserate with them on the "dirty trick" you have pulled on them by giving them such a difficult assignment.

Make a transition to the Exploration by saying something like this: **"Although we don't use the word 'abide' very much in conversation, the concept of abiding permeates 1 John. We will be studying that concept today."**

ALTERNATE APPROACH (8-10 minutes)

Materials needed: Index cards, envelopes, pen.

Preparation: Write the words of 1 John 4:16 ("Whoever lives in love lives in God, and God in him") on index cards (one word per card). Make one set of these cards for each four to six students. Place each set in an envelope. (Or you may write the verse in a scrambled order and make copies for students to unscramble individually.)

Have the students form teams of four to six and give these instructions: **"Arrange the words of this unfamiliar verse so that it makes sense. When I say 'Go,' you may begin. Go!"** Ask the team that finishes first to read the verse aloud.

Make a transition to the Bible Exploration by saying something like this: **"All those repetitions of the little word 'in' complicated the game, didn't they? We can simplify the theme of that verse by using the term 'mutual abiding.' God abides or lives in us and we in Him. We're going to study that concept today."**

BIBLE EXPLORATION

EXPLORATION (25-30 minutes)

Materials needed: Extra Bibles, paper, pencils or pens, chalkboard and chalk or overhead projector and transparency and pens.

Step 1 (10-12 minutes): Explain, **"The section of 1 John we're going to look at today talks about living in God and God living in us—a process that we're going to call mutual abiding. We're going to see some of the benefits we receive from this relationship. To get started, we need to see what John says about mutual abiding. We're going to read the passage. Then, to make sure we really focus on the meaning and understand what it says, I'm going to ask you to rewrite it so that a third grader could understand it. For example, suppose that your assignment included 1 John 4:12, which says: 'No one has ever seen God; but if we love each other, God lives in us and his love is made complete in us.' Rewritten so that younger kids could understand it, it might sound like this: 'We can't see God. But when we do loving things for other people, they find out that He loves them.'"**

Guide students in forming groups of three or four. Distribute paper and pencils. To half the groups assign 1 John 4:13-15; to the other half assign 1 John 4:16-18. Circulate among the groups, making yourself available to answer questions about the assignment or to give some assistance in coming up with ideas for the rewriting.

Step 2 (8-10 minutes): After allowing students time to work, regain their attention and ask students to share their versions of the Scripture. Then ask this question: **"John mentioned the mutual abiding of God and the Christian three times: in verses 13, 15, and 16. He listed at least four results or evidences of that abiding. What are they?"** Students should note: the Spirit (v. 13); acknowledging Jesus as Lord (vv. 14,15); knowing and relying on God's love—living in love (v. 16); confidence at judgment (v. 17); not fearing God (v. 18). Use information in the Teacher's Bible Study to build on students' comments or to answer questions.

Step 3 (8-10 minutes): Lead a brief brainstorm, asking students to think of at least ten ways Christians can grow or stay close to God. Write their suggestions on the chalkboard or transparency. Remember, in brainstorming there is no evaluation of the quality or appropriateness of the ideas suggested.

Ask students to call out the items listed that deal with prayer and mark these with a *P.* Make certain the prayer category includes any item listed that deals with praise, worship, confession, thanks or requests. Then ask them to call out any items that deal with reading or studying the Bible. Mark those with a *B.* Do the same for meditation (*M*) and obedience (*O*). You may add other categories if you wish.

Summarize by saying: **"The items we've marked deal with the ways God communicates with us and we communicate with Him. It's a two-way conversation. We generally think of prayer as our communication with God, and it is that; but sometimes He speaks to us as we are praying about a matter. He may give us an idea of a way we can solve our problem, or He may suggest to us something we can do to help the person we are praying for. Then obedience enters the picture, for we need to do what He asks us to do. Similarly, in Bible study we are examining God's message to us. He may draw a certain passage to our attention in a particular way. We may want to spend some time meditating on that passage, really soaking in the various details of what it says. Another time God may show us something we need to do—and that's obedience again. Or we may pray a verse back to Him. For example, we might repeat some of the praise Psalms as our own praise to Him. Or we might pray using ideas such as those we have studied today in 1 John 4, by asking Him to help us understand them and** to live them out in practical ways. Prayer, Bible study, meditation and obedience work together to nurture our relationship with God."

Make a transition to the Conclusion by saying something like this: **"We've talked today about our mutual abiding relationship with God. Let's take some time now to think about our personal response."**

ALTERNATE EXPLORATION (30-35 minutes)

Materials needed: Bibles, copies of Student Guide sheet "Live-in Help," pens or pencils, chalkboard and chalk or overhead projector with transparencies and pens.

Step 1 (10-12 minutes): Explain, **"The section of 1 John we're going to look at today talks about living in God and God living in us—a process that we're going to call mutual abiding. We're going to see some of the benefits we receive from this relationship and what we can do to nurture it. To get started, we need to see what John says about mutual abiding."**

Guide students in forming groups of four to six. Distribute copies of Student Guide sheet "Live-in Help." Explain, **"Read

---

Walking in God's Light

Let God In

Live-in Help

The letter of 1 John talks about believers living in God and God living in us. Read 1 John 4:13-18. Then create a job description that shows what a Christian needs to do as "live-in help," living for Christ. Also list the benefits of this job.

The person who lives in God needs to do the following:

The benefits of this position include the following:

---

the Scripture listed on the sheet. Then work together to create a job description that shows what a Christian needs to do as 'live-in help'—living for Christ. Also list the rewards or benefits of this job."**

Allow time for students to work. Be available to groups if they have questions about the assignment or need help understanding the Scripture. Then reassemble the class and ask for groups to read their work.

Summarize the points students have made. Point out that we need to acknowledge that Jesus is the Son of God and the Saviour of the world; that we are to rely on God's love; that we are to have confidence in Him. Benefits include having the Saviour, having the Spirit in our lives, having God's love, not having to be afraid about our relationship with Him. Use ideas from the Teacher's Bible Study and your own study of God's Word as needed in your discussion of the passage.

Step 2 (10-12 minutes): Explain, **"Now that we've had a look at the basic concepts in the passage, let's see how they should work out in everyday life. Let's work together to brainstorm a list of the some of the basic actions we need to take as we live in God and He lives in us."**

Write students' ideas on chalkboard or overhead as they suggest them. If they need help getting started, you might point out that prayer and Bible study are two obvious basic necessities.

After several minutes of brainstorming, go back through the ideas suggested and work with students to identify several large categories for them, such as everything having to do with prayer, everything relating to Bible study, to meditation, to obedience, and so on.

Step 3 (10-12 minutes): Explain, **"We have listed some excellent activities that all Christians need to be involved in. Sometimes, though, we have trouble figuring out how to get started, or exactly what to do, or how to work it into our schedule. I want to spend a little time thinking about the really practical aspects of these important activities."** Have students return to their groups. Assign to each group (or let them select) one of the broad categories determined in Step 2, such as prayer, Bible study and so on. Each group should work together to come up with at least five practical steps that will (1) help the average Christian to build this activity into his or her life or (2) guide the average Christian in actually doing the activity. These steps can be quite simple, such as "Go to bed half an hour earlier so you can get up early and read the Bible," or "Keep a list of the people you want to pray for."

After allowing time for groups to work, reassemble the class and ask for reports. Thank students for their efforts.

Make a transition to the Conclusion by saying something like this: **"We've spent some time today talking about our mutual abiding relationship with God and about practical ways we can nurture that relationship. Let's take some time now getting a little practice in one of the activities that contributes to our relationship with Him."**

CONCLUSION AND DECISION

CONCLUSION (10-12 minutes)

Materials needed: Sample devotional books or booklets, copies of Student Guide section "Devotional," pencils, Bibles.

Explain, **"A tool that many people use to help them in their times with God is the devotional book. It suggests a portion of Scripture to read each day and then gives some thoughts on the passage, or suggests questions to consider."** Show sample devotional books. Pass them around the class if time and the size of your class permit.

Tell students, **"I want you to try writing one page in a devotional book about 1 John. Choose one or more of the verses we have studied today. Use the sheet I'm about to give you. Sign your name as the author, then list the verse or verses and your thoughts on the passage and/or a question to consider. Then we'll put these together as a class devotional booklet."**

Distribute the "Devotional" sheet and allow time for

Devotional

By:

Read:

Some thoughts on this passage:

---

students to work. Then ask for a few volunteers to read what they have written. Collect the sheets and close in prayer.

During the week duplicate enough copies of the completed sheets for everyone in your class. Use some of the clip art from this book to add graphics to your book. Design a cover using clip art, rub-on letters or hand-lettered information, such as "A Devotional in 1 John 4:13-18 by the members of the high school class at the Neighborhood Church." Distribute the booklets at your next session.

ALTERNATE CONCLUSION (15-20 minutes)

Materials needed: Bibles, pencils, Student Guide sheet "Something to Ponder."

Explain to students, **"Spending time with God regularly is essential to maintaining our relationship with Him. We need to do this regularly—daily if possible, or at least several times a week. Today we're going to get a little practice at doing this."**

Distribute the "Something to Ponder" sheet. Explain to students that using questions like those on the sheet can help us focus on Scripture and get more out of our reading. Students might wish to use these questions in their own study at home. For now, ask them to re-read 1 John 4:13-8 and to answer one or more of the questions.

Allow students time to work on this part of their devotional period. Then quietly suggest that they now spend a few minutes in silent prayer. They may wish to make brief written notes of their prayer requests or of the names or initials of the people for whom they are praying. Again, using pencil and paper can help focus attention and produce a more effective time with the Lord.

Dismiss class when time is up for this session.

Something to Ponder

Sometimes we can get more out of our Bible study if we focus our attention on a series of questions and use paper and pencil to note our ideas. The questions listed here will help you do this. You may wish to use them in your personal Bible study at home. For now, read 1 John 4:13-18 and answer one or more of the questions.

What does this tell me about God?

What does this tell me about myself?

What promise does this give me?

What instruction do I find here?

What part of this Scripture do I want to try to remember throughout the day?

Resolve the Obedience Riddle

KEY VERSE
"This is love for God: to obey his commands. And his commands are not burdensome, for everyone born of God overcomes the world." 1 John 5:3,4

BIBLICAL BASIS
1 John 5:1-12

FOCUS OF THE SESSION
Our obedience to God should be motivated by love.

AIMS OF THIS SESSION
You and your learners will have accomplished the purpose of this Bible study session if you can:
- IDENTIFY from 1 John 5:1-12 correct motivations for obedience;
- DISCUSS how the motivation of love makes obedience more enjoyable than is possible with other motivations;
- DETERMINE ways to improve in both love and obedience.

TEACHER'S BIBLE STUDY

"There is a story about a schoolboy who was asked what he thought God was like. He replied that, as far as he could make out, God was 'The sort of person who is always snooping round to see if anyone is enjoying himself and then trying to stop it.'"[1] The issue of Christian obedience often produces the same image in people's minds—that it interferes with having a good time. But in 1 John 5:1-12 John argued that obedience flowed from love and faith without burdening the Christian.

This session culminates a study of the tightly woven pattern of faith, love and obedience. A faith that God will save those who commit themselves to Christ puts a Christian on the road to love and obedience. Through this generous gift of salvation, he or she begins to learn God's ways of *agape* love, doing what is best for others. The mutual abiding of God in Christians and they in Him produces love, faith, and an obedient spirit.

John had previously devoted sections of his letter to love (2:7-11; 3:11-18; 4:7-12), faith (2:18-27; 4:1-6), and obedience (2:3-6; 2:28-3:10). Now in chapter 5 he established their interdependence upon one another, intertwining them together in one passage.

The Path to Obedience
John began his treatise on learning obedience through faith and love by reviewing the basics of both in verse 1 of 1 John 5. Faith that Jesus is the Christ brings a person into the family of God through the new birth; experiencing God's love enables us to love His children.

In verse 2, John said, "This is how we know that we love the children of God: by loving God and carrying out his commands." So John tied obedience and love together. Love, as explained in Session 10, is not just an emotional bond, but a concern for the other person and a willingness to make a practical effort to benefit that person. Our love for God takes the form of desiring to "do what pleases Him" (1 John 3:22). It pleases Him when we love our brothers and sisters by giving them practical help (see 1 John 3:17,18).

The distasteful reputation of obedi-ence must be universal, for John quickly added an explanation after his statement about obeying commands: "And his commands are not burdensome, for everyone born of God overcomes the world" (1 John 5:3,4). John did not say that the commands were not difficult, but that they were not heavy or irksome as the Pharisees' commands had been. Their Sabbath rules tied up "heavy loads and put them on men's shoulders" (Matt. 23:4), but Jesus' yoke was easy and His burden was light (see Matt. 11:30).

God, the Great Enabler, in whom all things are possible (see Mark 10:27), gives power to obey just as He gives the desire to obey; He gives strength to obey along with the need to obey as illustrated in this passage: "I pray that out of his glorious riches he may *strengthen* you with *power* through his Spirit in your inner being, so that Christ may dwell in your hearts through *faith*. And I pray that you, being rooted and established in *love,* may have power, together with all the saints, to grasp how wide and long and high and deep is the love of Christ, and to know this love that surpasses knowledge—that you may be filled to the measure of all the fullness of God" (Eph. 3:16-19, emphasis added). God enables Christians to obey by equipping them with power and love and faith.

When we respond in love, no duty is too difficult, no task too great to attempt for the One who loves and enables us. When we abide in God, we find that obedience is a privilege rather than a burden. But when we focus on our own desires in opposition to His, we may consider His commands to be burdensome. No one can serve two masters (see Matt. 6:24).

Right Thing, Wrong Reasons

There is another side to the obedience coin, and that is the problem of doing the right thing for the wrong reason. We have established that God wants His children to obey Him. We must remember, however, that His first priority is the condition of our hearts. We can be going through the motions of obedience without having the right attitude behind those motions. Here are some poor reasons for obeying God:

Super-spirituality: Characterized by feelings of being an extra-special, better-than-average Christian; taking credit for goodness rather than giving God the credit.

Guilt: Characterized by an attitude that makes it difficult to accept God's forgiveness.

Fear: Being more conscious of the scary consequences of wrong actions than of the reasons for behaving as God would have us behave.

Negotiation: Trying to bargain with God—"I'll be good, if you will . . . ." Or an attempt to keep "one little sin" in exchange for keeping the rest of our life holy.

Doing Right for the Right Reasons

It isn't necessary to struggle along, feeling burdened with the need for obedience. It isn't necessary to obey out of fear or other wrong motivations. God has a way of enabling us to obey because we *want* to.

Through the new birth God equips Christians with faith that facilitates our obedience (see 1 John 5:4). Believing that Jesus is the Son of God reassures us that God cared for us enough to come to earth in Jesus. It assures us that He now shares life with us through His Spirit. "God's heredity" (the Phillip's version's terminology for the new birth) takes Christians out of the world and puts them into the family of God; it "rescued us from the dominion of darkness and brought us into the kingdom of the Son he loves" (Col. 1:13).

Lest his readers underestimate the power of faith, John repeated three times in three sentences that faith "overcomes the world." The victory that "has overcome" the world refers possibly to the readers' conversions or their rejection of false teachers. John probably saw this overcoming of the world in terms of spiritual warfare where Jesus reigns over the powers and principalities of the air (see Rom. 8:37-39). Jesus conquered the world in the true sense in a way the powerful Roman armies in John's day could never do.

Proofs of Faith

Since only the one who believes that Jesus is the Christ overcomes the world, John provided the evidence to support this important belief. Inasmuch as a personal faith depends on reasonable, valid testimony, John described the nature of the witnesses as well as their testimony. He presented two objective, historical witnesses, the "water" and the "blood" (1 John 5:6), referring to Christ's baptism and His death. In saying, "He did not come by water only" (v. 6), John denounced the Gnostics' belief that Jesus was an ordinary man who became divine following His baptism yet reverted to His human state before His death on the cross. On the contrary, Christ's death on the cross provided the only acceptable sacrifice for sin while enabling Jesus to taste human suffering. As a result, He has become a high priest able to understand human struggles (see Heb. 4:15), thus increasing a Christian's faith in Him.

The Spirit, the subjective personal witness, testifies because He is truth (1 John 5:6). John spotlighted the Spirit's role in aiding believers to discern spiritual truths in chapter 4. The Spirit also helps non-Christians unravel the truth concerning Jesus' Lordship (see 1 Cor. 12:3), freeing them to accept Christ and grow in Him. John carefully noted that the three witnesses agree since Jewish legal procedures required two or three witnesses to establish the truthfulness of an issue. Together these witnesses constitute God's testimony (1 John 5:9).

The one who accepts God's testimony "has this testimony in his heart," reassuring him or her that it is true. This results in an ever-increasing faith. But the one who rejects God's testimony is calling God a liar. Belief in Jesus is like a gate into a courtyard; it gives people access to God. Unless we believe that Jesus is Lord, we cannot get in.

John then explained the essence of God's testimony: "God has given us eternal life, and this life is in his Son. He who has the Son has life; he who does not have the son of God does not have life" (vv. 11,12). Jesus is the Life-Giver, the Saviour of the world. The offer of this great gift, once accepted, inspires obedience to the One who cancels the debt of sin and promises us a heavenly home (see Rom. 3:24-26; John 14:2-4).

A sharp student might question you regarding parts of verses 7 and 8 being omitted in some Bible versions. The omitted parts read: " . . . bear record in heaven, the Father, the Word and the Holy Ghost: and these three are one. And there are three that bear witness in earth, . . . " Some newer versions delete this segment, while others, such as the King James Version, retain it. The oldest available New Testament manuscripts are thought by some scholars to be the most accurate texts. These manuscripts exclude this phrase, so many scholars conclude that an overzealous scribe probably inserted his three-fold witness of verses 7 and 8 as a plug for the Trinity when he copied the manuscripts. Or perhaps someone had written the words as a marginal note and a later copyist mistook them for part of the Scripture itself.

Relating to Obedience

This session should enable students to elevate obedience from the "dirty word" category and view it as a natural result of love and faith. Although obedience is a duty, it surpasses duty. Obedience overflows from the two-way relationship between the Christian and the Lord. Through their reciprocal communication, God convicts us that certain actions are important for us to do. Obedience causes us to offer ourselves as "living sacrifices, holy and pleasing to God—which is your spiritual worship" (Rom. 12:1). Some translations use the words "reasonable service." Service and worship are actually so similar that the Greeks used the same word for both concepts. A Christian's service (or obedience), when offered out of love and faith instead of duty, worships God in praise and thanks.

Students especially need to learn this truth because they have not lived long enough or experienced enough to see the logic of many of God's commands. They have not witnessed the eventual consequences of promiscuity, bitterness or rebellion, so the commands about purity, forgiveness and obedience to authority do not always make sense to them. They must trust God enough to accept His Word, obey Him and look for the fruit of their obedience. Establishing a quiet time, as mentioned in a previous session, will nurture their relationship with the Lord and help them develop assurance that obedience is the right path.

Since this issue is largely an attitudinal one, review comments that students have made in the past to determine if any of them feel that Christianity is a matter of "have to" rather than "want to." If so, encourage them to work at getting better acquainted with God. As they get to know Him better, their love and their faith will increase and their perception of obedience will develop into a more accurate view.

Some students may believe that Jesus

is the Christ, but they may not have accepted Him as Lord and put their faith in Him. Others may have assimilated someone else's unbalanced view of obedience which stressed duty and minimized love. Still others may have accepted Christ out of guilt feelings over sin or desire to escape hell, shortchanging both faith and love. All need your prayers for the help of the Holy Spirit in correctly understanding what God has for them and what He wants them to do.

Your goal in this session is to help your students see the proper motivations for obedience—to urge them to grow in faith and love by continuing to build their relationship with God.

Footnote
1. C. S. Lewis, *Mere Christianity* (New York: The Macmillan Co., 1970), p. 69.

THIS WEEK'S TEACHING PLAN

APPROACH TO THE WORD

APPROACH (5-8 minutes)
Materials needed: Chalkboard and chalk or overhead projector with transparency and pen.

Print the word "obedience" vertically on the chalkboard or transparency and add a crosswise word as an example for the students; for example, cross the N in learning with the N in obedience.

Give directions such as these: **"Think of definitions or feelings that you associate with obedience and write those words crosswise on the chalkboard as I have done. I chose learning because I'm still learning to be obedient."**

Provide chalk or pens; allow students time to think and then to add their words to the acrostic. As they write note any words that express ideas of duty and drudgery related to obedience. Summarize in this manner: **"The idea of obedience comes up a lot in the Bible. Many people feel that obedience involves being a spoilsport or trying desperately to be good. Today we're going to study God's message to us to get a more realistic view of what obedience is all about— and we're especially going to look at the question of why we obey."**

ALTERNATE APPROACH (8-10 minutes)
Materials needed: Copies of Student Guide sheet "Pick from the Pile . . . ," pens or pencils.

Distribute copies of the "Pick from the Pile . . ." Student Guide sheet. Ask students to work individually to select a word from the "pile" that best describes *all* the illustrations on the page. (The word is obedience.)

Make a transition to the Bible Exploration by saying something like this: **"People have all different kinds of reasons for obedience. We obey because someone barks orders at us or has some way of threatening us into obedience. How often do we think of obeying because a person loves us and we love that person? Today we're going to take a look at the motivation for obedience."**

BIBLE EXPLORATION

EXPLORATION (20-30 minutes)
Materials needed: Chalkboard and chalk or overhead projector with transparencies and pens, Bibles, pens or pencils, copies of Student Guide sheets "Hidden Highlights" and "Good Ol' First Church."

Step 1 (5-7 minutes): Tell students, **"Before we discuss what motivates us to obey, let's think a little more about obedience itself."** Using chalkboard or overhead, ask students to help you list:
1. People or rules that we have to obey if you want to live in freedom;
2. People or rules that we should obey;
3. People or rules that we want to obey.

Ask, **"Which of these is the most enjoyable form of obedience? Why?"** Obviously it's most enjoyable to obey because we want to . . . and that is what God wants for us.

Step 2 (8-12 minutes): Guide students in forming pairs. Distribute copies of the "Hidden Highlights" Student Guide.

Resolve the _____ Riddle
WINTER #12

Walking in God's Light

Pick from the Pile . . .
The best word to describe the idea conveyed by all the pictures

Kindness   Spirituality
Faithfulness
Self-discipline
Love
Stewardship
Obedience   Service
Forgiveness
Trustworthiness
Responsibility

Yeah, I guess I could spare a little more...

Hidden Highlights

Read 1 John 5:1-12. Some key words from this Scripture passage are hidden in the word puzzle below. Circle the words (look across, up and down and diagonally).

List the reasons highlighted in these verses for obeying Christ:

Have pairs read 1 John 5:1-12 and then search the puzzle for important concepts from the Scripture.

After allowing time for students to work, regain their attention and ask for the words they have found. (See illustration on this page for answers.) Spend a few minutes talking about the main points of the Scripture passage, using ideas from the Teacher's Bible Study and from your own study of God's Word. Be sure you include the following ideas:

1. John defined loving the children of God as loving God and carrying out His commands (v. 2).
2. John defined loving God as obeying His commands (v. 3). Many of His commands help us learn to know Him and love Him. For example, He asks us to read the Word, pray, and fellowship with other Christians.
3. John said God's commands are not burdensome because those who are born of God overcome the world. Our relationship with God gives us the power to obey as well as the motivation to obey.

Step 3 (8-10 minutes): Distribute copies of the Student Guide sheet "Good Ol' First Church." Have students work in

Good Ol' First Church

The high school crew at First Church (Podunk, U.S.A.) is an obedient lot. But they could be a dud of a youth group if they obeyed for the wrong reasons. (In fact, they could be downright dangerous if they obeyed God for the wrong reasons.) Fill in the thought balloons in the first set of pictures as if these people were being obedient because of fear, peer pressure, guilt, or other not-so-good motivations. Then fill in the thought balloons of the second set of pictures showing the same group being obedient because they love God.

their pairs to read the instructions and fill in the cartoons. After allowing a few minutes for them to work, regain their attention and ask for their responses. Express appreciation for their efforts and their insights.

Make a transition to the Conclusion by saying something like this: **"Today we've been talking about what motivates our obedience. Let's take a few minutes to think about how we want to respond to what we have examined in this session."**

ALTERNATE EXPLORATION: (35-50 minutes)

Materials needed: Bibles, pens or pencils, paper, chalkboard and chalk or other writing surface.

Step 1 (5-7 minutes): Follow Step 1 in the original Exploration.

Step 2 (10-15 minutes): Have students form groups of four or five. One person from each group is given a piece of paper and asked to act as recorder. Ask students to read 1 John 5:1-12 and list all the reasons for obeying God or things that would make a person want to obey God that they find in the passage.

After allowing time for students to work, regain their attention and ask for their ideas. Summarize what they have contributed. Point out that our main motivation for obeying should be that God loves us and we love Him. His love is demonstrated in the fact that He sent Christ to die for us and that He gives us His Spirit to live in us. Our love can be demonstrated in our obedience.

Step 3 (3-5 minutes): Ask students to help you brainstorm a list of wrong reasons for obeying God. For example, one might obey God out of fear. Write their ideas on the chalkboard or other surface as they share.

After students have suggested a number of wrong reasons, point out that obeying God may have positive results no matter what the motivation is; but with the wrong reasons for obedience, a person's relationship with God is stripped of its joy. Obedience becomes a burden rather than a pleasure.

Step 4 (15-20 minutes): Have students return to their groups. Provide paper. Explain, **"Work together to create a short jingle that 'advertises' the value of obedience through love. Use a familiar tune from a song or an existing commercial. Then create another jingle—using the same tune if you wish—that shows what is missing when we obey God for any reason other than love."**

Allow about 7-10 minutes for students to write their jingles. Then regain their attention and ask them to read their work. (They don't need to *sing* their jingles unless they really want to.)

Summarize the insights students have shared through their jingles. Make a transition to the Conclusion by saying something like this: **"We've talked about obedience and why we obey. It's important to obey—and to do it for the right reason. Let's take a few minutes to think about our own motivations and actions."**

CONCLUSION AND DECISION

CONCLUSION (5-7 minutes)

Materials Needed: Copies of Student Guide sheet "Bite the Bullet," pens or pencils.

Distribute the "Bite the Bullet" sheet and ask students to complete it prayerfully and thoughtfully. After allowing a few minutes for them to do so, close in prayer.

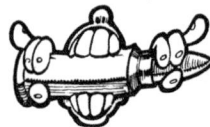

Bite the Bullet

1. Name an area of your life in which you need to initiate more obedience.

2. How could love and/or faith make it more enjoyable to obey?

ALTERNATE CONCLUSION (5-8 minutes)

Ask students to memorize 1 John 5:3-5 as a symbol of their desire to live a life of obedience based on love for God.

After allowing a few minutes for students to work, close in prayer.

Step up to Maturity

KEY VERSE
"We know also that the Son of God has come and has
given us understanding, so that we may know him who is true.
And we are in him who is true—even in his Son Jesus Christ."
1 John 5:20

BIBLICAL BASIS
1 John

FOCUS OF THE SESSION
God gives Christians guidelines that help us mature.

AIMS OF THIS SESSION
You and your students will have accomplished the purpose of
this Bible study session if you can:
- REVIEW or PREVIEW the Scriptures and applications
  from the other sessions in this course;
- DISCUSS ideas for maturing as Christians;
- EVALUATE past improvement and choose three steps to
  effect maturity in your lives.

TEACHER'S BIBLE STUDY

John wrote his Epistle to encourage Christians to grow spiritually in spite of the pagan, perverse world they lived in. They had been unsettled by the false teachers and they needed criteria to guide them in testing their beliefs and their actions. John reiterated for them the truth about God and His Son, Jesus Christ; he shared with them attitudes and actions that would help them mature as Christians.

Since we too live in a world that ignores and opposes God, we need John's directions to obtain maturity in Christ today.

John gave his readers specific instructions that would help them attain fellowship and joy as they matured. He directed them to *deal with sinful tendencies* by listening to God's truth, by confessing their sin, by rooting out continual sin and by ridding themselves of worldly desires. They needed to *major in the central issues* of proclaiming Jesus' messiahship against the cults, establishing a relationship with God as their Father and demonstrating love with selfless actions. Finally, John encouraged them to *cultivate godly characteristics* such as faith and love which, in turn, produce obedience.

John took several strands of thought such as those just mentioned and wove

them together, discussing a theme, moving to another one, then repeating an earlier thought with a new emphasis. He returned to several of these themes one last time in 1 John 5:13-21. This session, while completing the study in 1 John by examining those last verses, may also serve as a review or preview of the concepts in the course. It can also serve as a mid-course change of pace. Before teaching the session you may wish to review or preview the key verses, focuses, and aims of the other sessions in the course.

Root Out Sin
Early in his letter, as examined in Session 1, John introduced the need to listen to God's teaching in order to acquire the fellowship and joy that his readers may have lacked. He set the tone immediately by stating, "our fellowship is with the Father and his Son, Jesus Christ" (1 John 1:3). He was calling for a loving relationship between Father and child, which would result in joy (see v.4).

Then John explained that the relationship between God and believers is enhanced when we deal with our sins by getting them out in the open with Him. He gave the reassurance that if we confess our sins, God is faithful and just to forgive

and purify us (see 1 John 1:9). You and your students saw in Session 2 that confession frees us to relate to God without the interference of barriers caused by unconfessed sin.

Session 3 pointed out the need for believers to adopt the life-style of Jesus. While humans will not attain His sinless perfection, we can strive to eliminate habitual sin and to adopt His kind of love toward others.

Part of following Jesus' life-style will involve avoiding a love for the world. In Session 4 your students examined three statements that further describe love of the world: "the cravings of sinful man, the lust of his eyes and the boasting of what he has and does" (1 John 2:16). The world and its desires will pass away, but the person who does God's will will live forever (see v.17).

John felt the pull of evil so strongly that he closed his letter with a short warning: "Dear children, keep yourself from idols" (1 John 5:21). Idol worship was part of the "world" that believers are not to love.

Solidify Key Issues
John moved on to emphasize the central issues of Christianity. He demon-

71

strated his own *agape* love for his readers by warning them about antichrists in a tactful, straightforward way.

Session 5 described the chief characteristic of the antichrists: they deny that Jesus is the Christ, or God in a human body (see 2:22; see also 4:2,15; 5:1,10,11).

Session 6 examined ways Christians can respond in love to people who believe false doctrines about Christ, while at the same time standing firm for the truth.

In 1 John 5 John further emphasized the true identity of Christ as the Son of God (see v. 20).

John covered another central issue regarding the relationship Christians have with God as their Father. God lavished His tender love on mankind to the point of sending His Son as a sacrifice for their sins. In Session 7 your students examined this relationship and how they can cultivate it.

No action characterizes Christianity more than love, and John dealt with this topic more than once in his letter. In Session 8 your students examined the idea that *agape* love involves giving practical help to those in need.

Grow in Godliness

A Christian cultivates godly characteristics as a result of abiding in God. Session 9 examined ways believers can resolve their doubts and questions and thus build their faith. One of John's reasons for writing the letter was to assure his readers that they had eternal life: "I write these things to you who believe in the name of the Son of God so that you may know that you have eternal life" (1 John 5:13).

Session 10 presented students with the fact that God's great love for them should motivate them to show that love to others. John illustrated this love in the last part of his letter by asking his readers to pray for those who had committed sins that "do not lead to death" (5:16,17). We do not know exactly what John meant by this expression. Some Bible students feel that he was referring to people for whom hope still existed because they had not yet (a) become so degraded that they gloried or reveled in sin or apostasy or (b) committed the unpardonable sin of attributing the Holy Spirit's work to the devil (see Matthew 12:31,32). Rather than gossip about or browbeat those who have sinned, a believer should demonstrate love by praying for them. Instead of doing good deeds grudgingly, out of a sense of duty, a Christian gladly demonstrates love because of God's love.

Next John concentrated on the concept of mutual abiding—God living in Christians and we in Him. This relationship with God is nurtured as we practice basic Christian disciplines such as Bible study, prayer, meditation, and obedience.

In Session 12 your students examined the importance of obeying for the right reasons—out of love rather than because of fear, guilt, or other motivations. Obeying God because He loves us and we love Him takes the burden out of obedience.

You may wish to sum up the course for students in terms of these basic themes: Knowing the true identity of God and Christ; sharing a mutual love relationship with God; obeying God by rooting out sin and by caring for the needs of others.

THIS WEEK'S TEACHING PLAN

APPROACH TO THE WORD

APPROACH (5-7 minutes)

Materials Needed: Chalkboard and chalk or overhead projector and transparencies.

Write this statement on the chalkboard or transparency: "A person who has been a Christian a long time is spiritually mature." When you are ready to begin, ask students who agree

> A PERSON WHO HAS BEEN A CHRISTIAN A LONG TIME IS SPIRITUALLY MATURE.

with this statement to raise their hands. Then ask those who disagree to raise their hands.

Explain, **"A person who has known the Lord for a long time may or may not be spiritually mature. Years are no guarantee. Today we're going to look at some elements of Christian maturity."**

ALTERNATE APPROACH (10-12 minutes)

Ask students to describe a child having a temper tantrum. What does the child do? (Screams, kicks, etc.) Then ask about a junior high age person having a temper tantrum. What elements are the same and what are different? Finally, ask, **"Have you seen an adult having a temper tantrum? What did he or she do? How does it make you feel to see an adult acting like a kid?"**

Make a transition to the Bible Exploration by saying something like this: **"You can get older but not grow up.**

Calendar years do not necessarily make a person wise and mature. The ideas we have been studying in this course are designed to help us grow up spiritually. Today we're going to review some of them."

BIBLE EXPLORATION

EXPLORATION (25-35 minutes)

Materials needed: Copies of Student Guide sheet "The Abbreviated 1 John," Bibles, pens or pencils.

Step 1 (15-20 minutes): Guide students in forming pairs. Give each student a copy of "The Abbreviated 1 John" sheet.

Walking in God's Sight

Step Up to Maturity

Undigested Reader Department

The Abbreviated 1 John

Together with a friend, read over 1 John in your own words abbreviate the book to fit on this page by pulling out the main thoughts and ideas from the book and stating them simply

Tell them to read through the entire book of 1 John and then to abbreviate it by writing down the main thoughts and ideas. You might want to suggest that they break this task down into smaller pieces by reviewing each chapter, then writing down one or two main ideas for that chapter before moving on to the next one.

Step 2 (10-15 minutes): Regain students' attention and ask them to read their work. Comment on the main ideas of each chapter, using material from your own study of 1 John and from the Teacher's Bible Studies of the thirteen sessions. You may want to put special stress on these points: knowing the true identity of Jesus Christ; maintaining and building a two-way love relationship with God; obeying God and loving others because of the love He has for us.

Post students' "The Abbreviated 1 John" sheets around the room.

Make a transition to the Conclusion by saying something like this: **"Today we have reviewed some of the key themes from the book of 1 John. Let's take a few moments to think about our personal response to what we have learned."**

ALTERNATE EXPLORATION (30-40 minutes)

Materials needed: Index cards, pens or pencils, copies of Student Guide sheet "Key Verses," hat or box.

Step 1 (10-15 minutes): Guide students in forming groups of three or four. Give each group 40 index cards and copies of the "Key Verses" Student Guide sheet. Explain, **"Work**

KEY VERSES

Deal with Sinful Tendencies

1. "We proclaim to you what we have seen and heard so that you may have fellowship with us. And our fellowship is with the Father and his Son, Jesus Christ. We write this to make our joy complete." (1 John 1:3,4)

2. "If we confess our sins, he is faithful and just and will forgive us our sins and purify us from all unrighteousness." (1 John 1:9)

3. "My dear children, I write this to you so that you will not sin (continually). . . . But if anyone obeys his word, God's love is truly made complete in him." (1 John 2:1a, 5a)

4. "Do not love the world or anything in the world. If anyone loves the world, the love of the Father is not in him." (1 John 2:15)

Major in Central Issues

5. "Who is the liar? It is the man who denies that Jesus is the Christ. Such a man is the antichrist—he denies the Father and the Son." (1 John 2:22)

6. "Now the Bereans were of more noble character than the Thessalonians, for they received the message with great eagerness and examined the Scriptures every day to see if what Paul said was true." (Acts 17:11)

7. "How great is the love the Father has lavished on us, that we should be called children of God! And that is what we are!" (1 John 3:1)

8. "If anyone has material possessions and sees his brother in need but has no pity on him, how can the love of God be in him?" (1 John 3:17)

Cultivate Godly Characteristics

9. "The one who is in you is greater than the one who is in the world." (1 John 4:4)

10. "Dear friends, since God so loved us, we also ought to love one another." (1 John 4:11)

11. "And so we know and rely on the love God has for us. God is love. Whoever lives in love lives in God, and God in him." (1 John 4:16)

12. "This is love for God: to obey his commands. And his commands are not burdensome, for everyone born of God overcomes the world." (1 John 5:3,4)

Maturity

13. "We know also that the Son of God has come and has given us understanding, so that we may know him who is true. And we are in him who is true—even in his Son Jesus Christ." (1 John 5:20)

All Scriptures quoted in this page are from NIV.

---

together in your groups to copy each key verse on an index card."

Circulate among the groups. When most are nearly finished with the copying, give the next instruction: **"Distribute the verse cards fairly equally among the members of your group. Each person should have two or three cards. Take the first verse card that you have and think about a practical example of the verse in action. Write that example on a blank index card. Then, on another blank card, write an example of what might happen if the verse**

is not heeded. Do the same for your remaining verses."

Step 2 (20-25 minutes): Collect all the cards and place them in a box or hat. Select a person from one group to come to the front and draw a card at random. Explain, **"Return to your group and work together to prepare a short pantomime or a 30-second skit or a 30-second chalkboard drawing to represent the verse or the example that you drew. You have only about 45 seconds to prepare."**

After giving the group time to prepare, ask them to present their work. Members of other groups are to raise their hands if they think they know what verse is being portrayed or can guess the nature of the example. The first group to get it right then selects an index card and tries their skill.

If the game bogs down, have a student from each group select a card. Then all the groups will be working on their presentations at the same time.

If you have a large class, you may want to form two or more large groups, each with an adult to supervise. Each larger group can then play the game described in this step.

When time is up, regain students' attention and make a transition to the Conclusion by saying something like this: **"We've had some fun today as we have reviewed some of the basic concepts in the book of 1 John. Now let's take a few moments to think about our personal response to what we have learned."**

CONCLUSION AND DECISION

CONCLUSION (5-8 minutes)

Materials needed: Shelf paper, poster paints, brushes, masking tape, paper towels, pre-moistened towelettes or other clean-up materials, aprons or old men's shirts or other protective garments. (Or, if you prefer to avoid clean-up problems, use felt pens instead of poster paints.)

Guide students in forming groups of four to six. Provide art materials and explain, **"Carefully consider the ideas you have reviewed today from 1 John. Then work together to create a banner that expresses a thought from 1 John that particularly struck you. State that idea in your own words on your banner."**

After students have had time to prepare their banners, regain their attention. Have them share and explain their work. Then post the banners in the room. (You may also wish to post them in other parts of the church facility in order to share with others what your class is dong.)

Close in prayer.

ALTERNATE CONCLUSION (5-7 minutes)

Materials needed: Paper, pens or pencils.

Provide paper and pens or pencils. Ask students to work individually. Tell them, **"Write a hymn of praise or thanksgiving to God for something that He has shown you or reminded you of in 1 John. If you wish you can take a song that you know and write new words that could be sung to the tune. Or you can even take a familiar song and just write a few new words to make it apply."**

(If some students find this too difficult, ask them simply to write a prayer of thanksgiving to God for what He has done.)

After allowing time for students to write, regain their attention and ask for volunteers to read what they have written. (Don't make them sing!)

Close with a prayer of thanksgiving.

Student Guide Section

The following pages are the

Student Worksheets

for this course.

For complete instructions, please turn to pages 3-5 at the beginning of this book.

Walking in God's Light

Get with It, Gang
Winter #1

Scrambled Definitions

This word means		
sharing between two or	more people	
who have something	in common.	It invol
joint participation.	Christians have in com	
with each other	their relationship to Chris	
the Holy Spirit,	and God	the Father,
with all the spiritual resources		that God

This word means	delight and exultatio	
In the Christian context	it is	
not merely an emotion	but a charac	
produced by the Holy Spirit.	It is no	
affected by circumstances;	in fact,	
in spite of	or even as a result of suf	

Walking Along

Think of some steps you need to take to follow Jesus more closely. Write your ideas on the signposts below.

75

Get with It, Gang
Winter #1

Scrambled Definitions

This word means

sharing between two or more people

who have something | in common. | It involves

joint participation. | Christians have in common

with each other | their relationship to Christ,

the Holy Spirit, | and God | the Father,

with all the spiritual resources | that God provides.

This word means | delight and exultation.

In the Christian context | it is

not merely an emotion | but a character quality

produced by the Holy Spirit. | It is not

affected by circumstances; | in fact, it may exist

in spite of | or even as a result of suffering.

How It Works

If we have fellowship . . .
(see 1 John 1:3)

. . . Then we will experience joy
(see 1 John 1:4)

Read the Scriptures listed below and summarize what they tell you about fellowship and joy.

1 John 1:7

John 17:20-23

Philippians 1:3-6
(If your Bible says "partnership" it means the same thing as "fellowship" in this context.)

John 15:9-11

Romans 15:13

Galatians 5:22,23

James 1:2-4

Assignment one

Kim's family just moved to a new area. Kim is a Christian but her parents do not attend church regularly, and they have not yet tried to find a church in their new town. Kim is getting lonely for other Christians. One day she takes a Christian book to school with her. She is sitting alone in the cafeteria, eating lunch and reading her book, when . . .

Complete the story, using ideas about Christian fellowship and joy which you have studied today.

Assignment two

David is walking home from school, discouraged because he is not doing well in algebra. He seems to be slower than the other students in grasping what he is supposed to do. Once he learns something, however, he really knows it and does well. But the teacher can't spare any time to give David individual help. As David walks along, his friend Mark catches up with him. Mark is the top student in the algebra class.

Complete the story, using ideas about Christian fellowship and joy which you have studied today.

Assignment three

The tenth-grade class at First Church of the Neighborhood is just getting started on Sunday morning. The students have been together for several months and really enjoy getting together each Sunday morning to study God's Word with their teacher. Just as everyone is milling around finding chairs and getting ready to start, the door opens and another high school age person walks in. No one knows this girl—she has never been to this class or this church before.

Complete the story, using ideas about Christian fellowship and joy which you have studied today.

Time Will Tell

If joy in our lives is dependent upon the quality of our fellowship with Christ and others, then it is worth our time and effort. What things can you do this week to get to know Christ better? How can you be a better Christian friend?

Use this space to identify ways you can help strengthen and improve fellowship with God and what you can do to make yourself a better friend.

I want to be joyful so . . .

. . . I will work at getting to know Christ

. . . and my Christian friends.

Own Up to What You Are

Winter #2

Figure out the clues listed on the left, then fill in the words that answer those clues, placing one letter on each blank. When you have answered all the clues correctly, the specially-marked letters will spell an additional word from top to bottom.

Puzzler

Bravery □ _ _ _ _ _ _

Not remember _ □ _ _ _ _

Truthfulness _ _ □ _ _ _ _

A good relationship □ _ _ _ _ _ _ _ _ _ _ _

Be sorry for, turn from _ □ _ _ _ _

Without deceit □ _ _ _ _ _ _

Transgression, wrongdoing □ _ _ _

Stranger Than Fiction

The paragraphs below describe how people of other cultures and religions seek forgiveness and approval. Read the paragraphs and answer the questions.

The sacrifice of a black llama and subsequent drinking of its blood mixed with cornmeal is a ritual performed even today by Peruvian Indians. This is a part of a week-long tribute to the sun god in which the Indians seek forgiveness and blessing.

The English word "thug" comes from the name for a group of devotees of Shakti, a Hindu sect, called Thugi. Thugi ravaged the countryside of India in the 1800s, strangling human victims to satisfy Shakti's desire for blood. The Thugi believed that by satisfying Shakti, they would be granted her favor.

In the Buddhist system a person is looked upon as being holy or unholy based upon the pluses or minuses accumulated in life through good or bad deeds. People are "destined" to either paradise or purgatory.

Shiite Muslims believe the death of Mohammed's grandson Husein in battle several hundred years ago atoned for their sins.

During the Middle Ages some Christians believed forgiveness could be purchased by giving money to profiteering monks and priests.

Which of the above statements seems the strangest to you? Why?

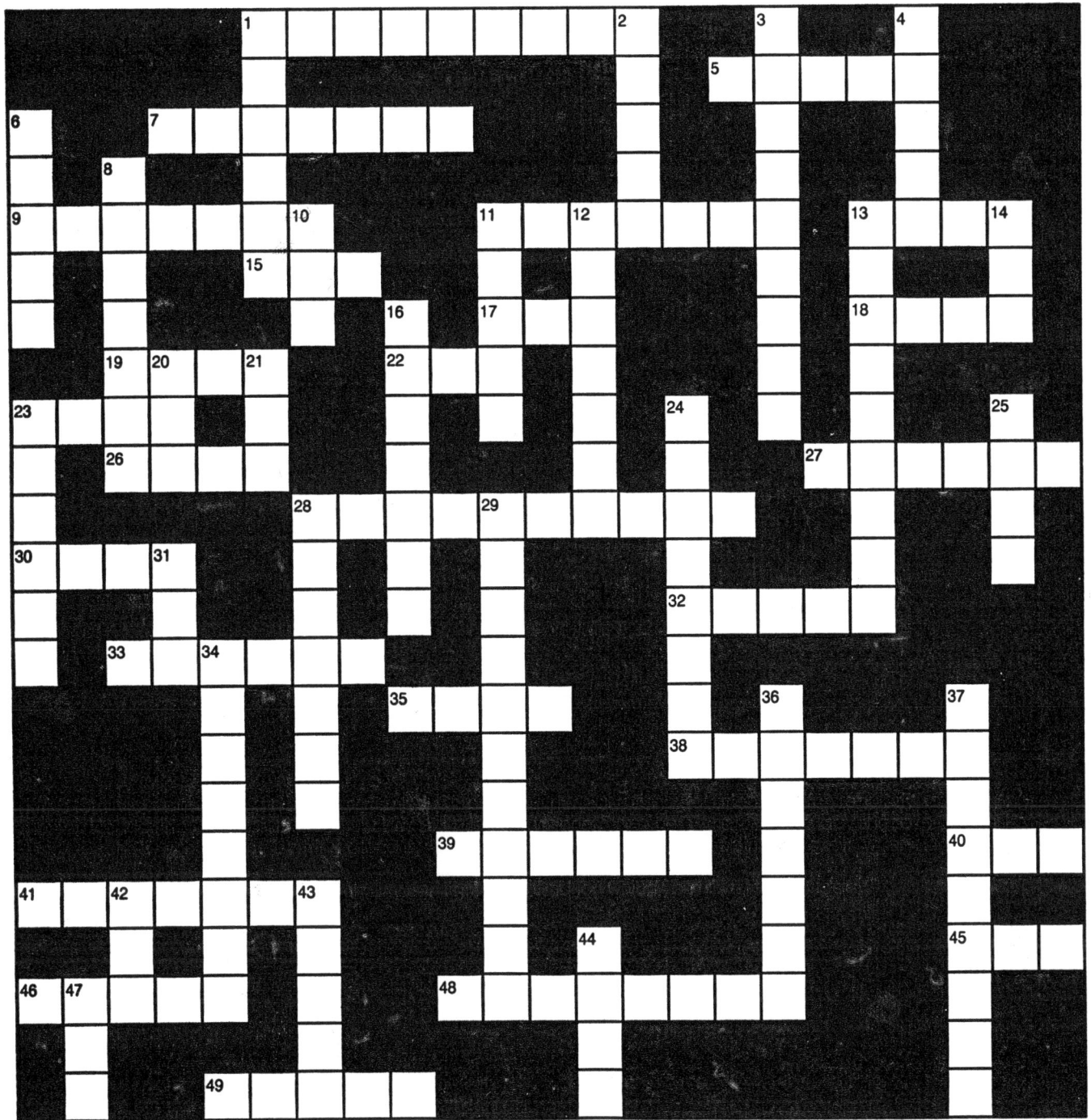

Confession and Forgiveness

Read these Scriptures: **1 John 1:5-10; Ezra 9:6,10,11; Psalms 38:18; 51:1,2; 103:12; Proverbs 28:13; Isaiah 55:7; 59:12; Jeremiah 31:34; Luke 15:7.**

Then work on this crossword puzzle. The biblical words are based on the *New International Version (NIV)*. If your Bible is a different version, it will have similar words and ideas. In some cases we have paraphrased the Scripture. Note: Just to make it more of a challenge, we have included clues and words that have nothing whatever to do with the Bible.

Across

1. The middle of the week.
5. God is _____: There is no darkness in Him. (1 John 1:5)
7. Our sins _____ against us. (Isa. 59:12)
9. See 8 Down.
11. God will always _____ our (18 Across). (1 John 1:9)
13. Uses chemicals to change the color of something.
15. This is a good _____ for repenting and being forgiven.
17. Baseball official.
18. Wrongdoings; trespasses. (Ezra 9:6)
19. Where the sun rises.
22. Singular of 18 Across.
23. To tell a secret.
26. You might want to _____ with joy when your sins are forgiven.
27. God will freely _____ those who forsake evil and turn to Him. (Isa. 55:7)
28. God shows great _____ towards us. (Ps. 51:1)
30. We should not _____ that we are sinful people. (1 John 1:7)
32. Jesus' _____ will (33 Across) us. (1 John 1:7)
33. See 32 Across.
35. Don't let anyone pull the _____ over your eyes: You don't have fellowship with God if you don't (29 Down) your (22 Across). (1 John 1:8)
38. We _____ ourselves if we say we are without (22 Across). (1 John 1:8)
39. God will _____ our transgressions as far as the (19 Across) is from the (44 Down). (Ps. 103:12)
40. (2 Down) and _____ alike need to (28 Down).
41. He will _____ me from my sin. (Similar to 1 Down). (Ps. 51:2)
45. Some people get so sad about their (18 Across) that they _____.
46. Say the same as.
48. God will not _____ our sins any more. (Jer. 31:34)
49. Those who sin can ask for God's _____. (Isa. 55:7)

Down

1. Being forgiven of our sins is like being _____. (Ps. 51:2)
2. See 40 Across.
3. We should not _____ God's commands. (Ezra 9:10)
4. We all tend to _____ from the straight and narrow.
6. How you can feel after you (28 Down) your (18 Across).
8. If you _____ your (22 Across) you will not (9 Across). (Prov. 28:13)
10. A cheer.
11. The lost is _____.
12. There is (37 Down) in heaven when a sinner _____. (Luke 15:7)
13. Ezra felt _____. (Ezra 9:6)
14. Emergency code.
16. How we might feel when we (22 Across). (Ezra 9:6)
20. Short name for a U.S. president and a Hebrew patriarch.
21. Child's toy.
23. A heavy weight; the way some people experience their (18 Across) before being forgiven.
24. We should be _____ by sin. (Ps. 38:18)
25. God's _____ has no place in our lives if we claim we have not sinned.
28. Tell God about our (18 Across).
29. We should _____ our iniquities. (Isa. 59:12)
31. Second person singular.
34. If we _____ our (22 Across) we find (49 Across). (Prov. 28:13)
36. More frightening.
37. See 12 Down. (Luke 15:7)
42. Make a mistake.
43. When we know how great it feels to have God (11 Across) and (41 Across) us, we are _____ to (28 Down) our (19 Across).
44. Where the sun sets.
47. Sticky stuff.

Forgiveness in Action

Create a short contemporary situation about a high school student who sins and needs forgiveness.

For example: Debbie Smith was barely passing math, so
when a friend offered her the answers for an upcoming
quiz she was thankful. Now she doesn't feel right about it . . . .

Share what the student in your story could ask of God. Use Psalms 32 and 51 as examples and guides.

Sticky Questions

The subject of forgiveness can raise some sticky questions. There are principles in Scripture that answer these questions, but it takes some work to dig them out and apply them correctly. Challenge your brain by taking at least one of the questions on this sheet and seeing if you can find the biblical answer in the Scriptures listed.

Matthew 6:12,14,15; 12:31,32; 18:2-5; 18:21,22;   Mark 3:29; 4:12; 11:25;   Luke 7:47; 17:4;   Acts 2:38;   Romans 2:1-4; 2:12-16;   Ephesians 1:7-10;   Colossians 3:13;   Hebrews 8:12;   1 John 1:9

Can you sin with the intent of asking for forgiveness later?

What about the person who has never heard of Christ?

What is the unforgivable sin?

If Hitler repented on his deathbed would he be forgiven?

What happens to small children who die?

Will God hold it against me if I do something that I do not know is a sin?

Will God forgive you if you carry a grudge?

Will God forgive you if you do the same thing over and over again?

Answer sheet

Get Your Priorities Together

Walking in God's Light

List Your Likes

Number the items listed below in order of your preference, with number one being the item you like best. (This is not to say that you necessarily like everything on the list. The higher numbers may represent things you don't like at all.)

Eating this food: _____

Sleeping in

Math class

Writing letters

A sunny day

Spearmint chewing gum

Reading a mystery novel

Watching reruns

Playing _____
(sport)

Bubonic plague

The flu

Pizza

Sand in your hot dog

Sand in your shorts

Going to the dentist

Getting a flu shot

A runny nose and no Kleenex

Cats

Dogs

The World According to John

Read 1 John 2:15-17.

Now summarize the main truth of that Scripture in 20 words or less:

Definition:

   When John said that we are not to love the world, he did not mean that we are not to enjoy and care for the world of nature, nor did he mean that we are not to love human beings. Rather he was saying that we should not put anything in the world before God in our lives. The world around us opposes God or ignores Him. We are to love Him totally and give Him top priority.

Everything in the World

Think of some typical situations at school, in your neighborhood or at home that might fit into one of these categories from 1 John 2:15-17. Use extra paper, if necessary, to write a story or draw a cartoon strip showing one of these situations.

"The cravings of sinful man." —————————————————

Definition: This description involves the desires of that part of our nature which is ours because we belong to the human race. These cravings may involve sexual sin, selfish ambition, and our tendency to measure everything by material standards. This category includes our demand to satisfy our own desires at another's expense.

"The lust of his eyes." —————————————————

Definition: This category involves the temptation to exploit those things that can be seen. The world offers all sorts of pageantry, glory and outward show. It tempts us to think we can find happiness in the things we can buy and display. It places ultimate value on material possessions.

"The boasting of what he has and does." —————————————————

Definition: This phrase has to do with the attempt to feel superior to someone else. It is a self-centered desire to be somebody special by putting others down. It is pride in wealth, talent, education or any other area of achievement. This pride is not simply a realistic recognition that God has given us gifts and abilities, it is thinking that these gifts and abilities make us better and more important than other people.

Reminder Card

Balance the Books

List some of the attractions the world offers and some of the benefits that God offers. (Remember that "world" here means the world system that leaves God out and is opposed to Him.)

If you need some reminders about what God offers, check out some of these verses: **John 3:16-18; 4:13,14; 10:10; 11:25,26; 14:2,3,16,17; 15:11**

The World	God

The bottom line: Which has more to offer you—God or the world?

When you've overspent in one area . . . what are the consequences?

Which Way to the Game?

Hurry! You're almost late for the biggest basketball game of the year. You need to get to the Sports Arena as quickly as possible.

Instructions: Cut out the traffic signs below. By trial and error, place all signs in the appropriate spots on the maze. Only one combination of signs will correctly complete the maze.

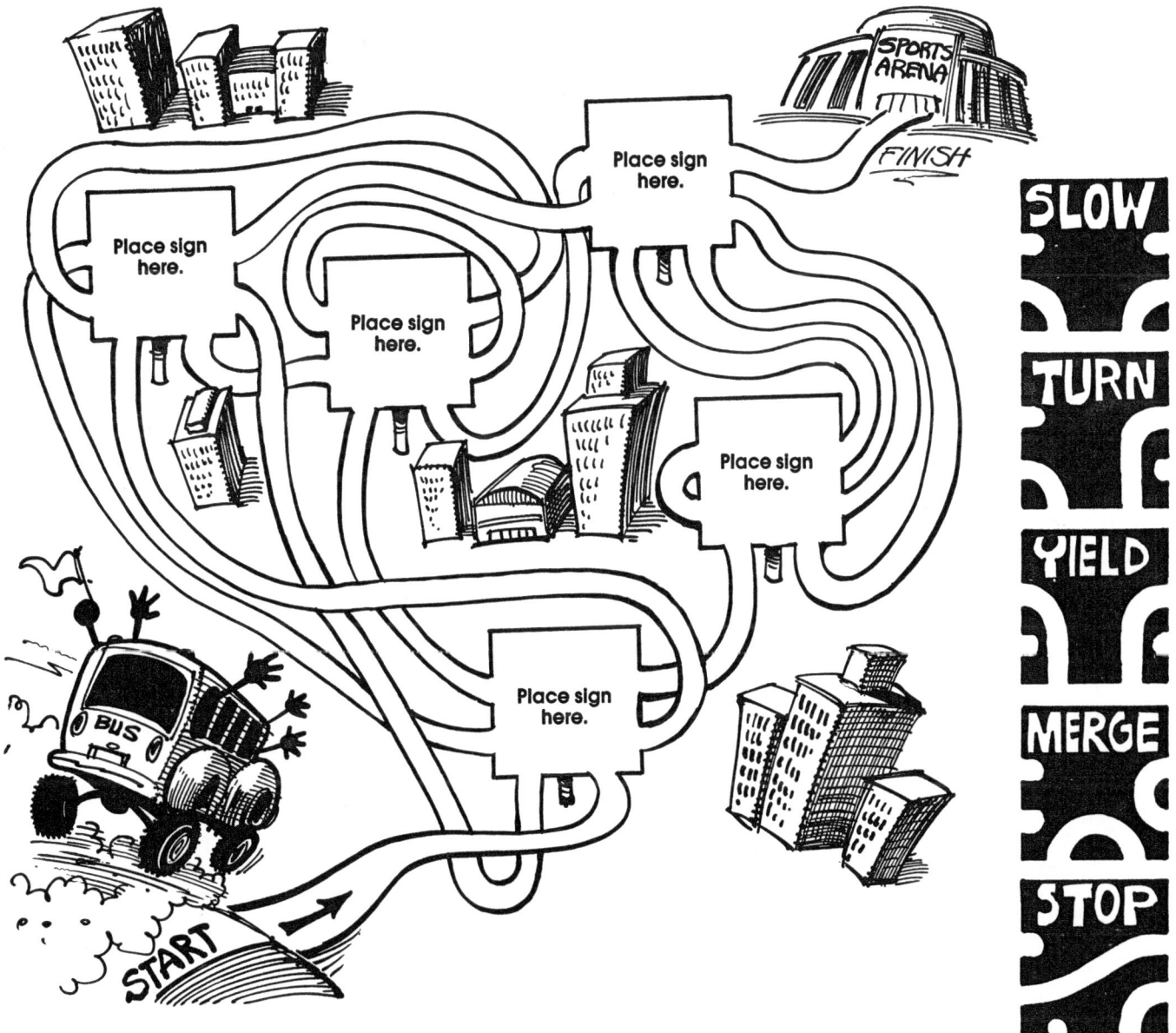

Place sign here.

Place sign here.

Place sign here.

Place sign here.

Place sign here.

Place sign here.

SPORTS ARENA

FINISH

BUS

START

SLOW

TURN

YIELD

MERGE

STOP

Put Them to the Test _____

According to the Scriptures listed below, what standard should we use to measure the truth of statements about Christ?

1 John 2:22,23:

1 John 4:2,3

We must also acknowledge the facts about Christ that are stated in the following passages. Look up each one and summarize it.

Matthew 12:30

Luke 24:1-7,36-39

John 1:14

John 10:22-33

1 Corinthians 15:3,4

Can You Spot Flak from the Antichrists?

Ask just about anyone in your church what the mark of the antichrist is and they will probably tell you that it is the number 666, which might be glued, stapled, pinned, or tattooed to obvious parts of a person's anatomy. Wrong.

While the Bible does talk about 666 in other passages and in a slightly different context, John (you know, the author of the Gospel of John, of 1, 2, 3 John, and of the Revelation; the disciple, the apostle—**that** John) says that the mark of the antichrist is to deny that Jesus is the Christ.

Multiple Choice

The word **Christ** is:

☐ the last name of Jesus

☐ another way to say Rabbi or great teacher

☐ the same as Bwana, Kimo Sabe, Guru, Swami

☐ not the kind of question that I can compute before lunch

☐ the Greek word for Messiah or the Promised One of God.

Obviously the people who think that Jesus was just a great guy fall into the category of having the mark of the antichrist.

A careful reading of 1 John 2:18-23 will show us that the term "antichrist" can mean anyone who denies the reality of who Jesus is—God come to earth in the flesh. In the light of this knowledge the category of antichrists suddenly fills up with a lot of quasi-Christian religious groups.

For further reading on the fact that Jesus is actually God see: John 10:23-33; John 1:1 with Revelation 19:11-16; John 14:11, Matthew 11:27; 16:16; Acts 2:36; Hebrews 1:1-3.

Truth or Consequences

Read one or more of the following situations. Then answer the questions that follow the description of the situation. If a Scripture from the "Put Them to the Test" sheet seems appropriate in responding to the situation, jot it down.

Number 1: Molly invited Susie to her church for some special classes they were offering. After attending one class, Susie was excited about everyone's friendliness and love toward her; she was eager to come to more classes. When Susie's mom asked her what she was learning, Susie showed her the material she had brought home. Together they read statements explaining that the church's purpose is to unite the world as one. The materials said that each person is able to develop a oneness with the "eternal," and every form of life is divine. They stressed the goodness of human nature, and stated that salvation is a matter of character development, joined with faith in God and with good works. The group's ethics are derived from the teachings of Jesus, whom they regard as a human being no more divine than any other.

This group's understanding of Christ is:

The main weakness, if any, of this teaching is:

Number 2: During a speech class at school, Sarah was surprised when a fellow student, Greg, chose to give his speech on the topic of self-sufficiency. He said that each person is in charge of his or her own destiny, with no help from outside, supernatural forces. Sarah heard later that Greg had been studying the writings of various philosophers and had become convinced that there is no God.

Greg's understanding of Christ is:

The main weakness, if any, of his philosophy is:

Number 3: Christmas was just around the corner. Richard stopped by Dave's house (a friend from the swim team) and noticed that they did not have a Christmas tree. Richard casually asked if Dave's family always waited until the last minute to buy a tree. Dave explained that his family does not celebrate Christmas or Easter because these celebrations have pagan roots. This led to a conversation about other things in which Dave made the comment that his church believes that Jesus is the first and highest creation of God.

Dave's understanding of Christ is:

The main weakness, if any, of this teaching is:

Number 4: Jim and Tom were comparing notes on their churches one day during lunch hour. Jim explained that his church believes that the god of this planet (one of many gods in the universe) was once a human being, and that human beings can become exalted to the status of gods. Jesus is also a god. His death on the cross atoned for the sins of Adam, but may not be sufficient to cover some sins of some people.

This group's understanding of Christ is:

The main weakness, if any, of this teaching is:

Number 5: Sue and Lynn got into a discussion about Jesus one day after their English class studied a short story in which the characters discussed religion. Lynn said that her parents taught her that Jesus was a great leader, a moral example, a teacher to be admired—but was merely human.

Lynn's parents' understanding of Christ is:

The main weakness, if any, of this teaching is:

Number 6: Jack invited Rick to come to Sunday School and church with him. Afterwards they talked for a while. Rick said he appreciated being invited to Jack's church, but that he really didn't believe that Jesus ever existed. "He's just a story some people made up—a myth," insisted Rick.

Rick's understanding of Christ is:

The main weakness, if any, of this belief is:

Number 7: Craig was apprehensive when his parents decided to house a foreign exchange student from India. When the student arrived he seemed like a pretty nice guy, although his customs were very different and his speech was a little difficult to understand. When Craig asked him about his religious background he said, "I believe that God was once on earth in human form. While He was on earth He taught us how we should live. In my next life I will go to live with Him."

The Indian student's understanding of Christ is:

The main weakness, if any, of this belief is:

The Handy Dandy Lie Detector

Your Handy Dandy Lie Detector is a convenient reference guide that will quickly show you some of the foolish beliefs of human religions contrasted with the wisdom and truth of the Bible.

Cut it out, stick it together, and keep it in your Bible for future use.

Page 1

Cut out this area

GOD

JESUS CHRIST

THE HOLY SPIRIT

SIN

SALVATION

What they say:

The Handy Dandy Lie Detector

What the BIBLE says:

God is one being who exists as three eternal persons. (Isa. 43:10; 44:6-8; 1 Cor. 8:6; Matt. 28:19; John 1:1 with Rev. 19:11-16)

Jesus Christ is God come down from heaven as man. He was resurrected from the dead. (1 Tim. 2:5; John 1:14)

The Holy Spirit is eternally God. (Acts 5:3,4; Acts 13:2; 1 Cor. 3:16; John 14:26; John 16:7—17:11)

All human beings have sinned and continue to sin. (Gen. 3:16,19; Rom. 3:23; 5:12-18; 6:23)

Salvation is only by means of Jesus Christ and His sacrifice; salvation is entirely by grace, not works. (John 1:29; 3:16,17; 6:29; 14:6; Acts 4:10-12; Eph. 2:8-10)

Page 2

Handy dandy Instructions:

1. If necessary, paste thin card stock to the back of Page 1 and Page 2.

2. Cut out both dials and assemble as shown. If you have a hardcover Bible, you may wish to stick the tack into the inside cover. Otherwise use a piece of cardboard or wood.

3. By spinning the top dial, you can readily compare the Bible's truths to the world's lies. Pretty snazzy, eh?

Mormonism

God is a man. You have to learn to be gods yourselves.
. . . The same as all gods have done before you.

Denies the virgin birth of Jesus.
He was conceived by Adam-God.

A Spirit Person, a Spirit Man,
He can be in only one place
at one time.

There is no original sin. It is possible to transgress a law without sin—as Adam and Eve did.

Saved by obedience to the laws of the church.

Christian Science

The Father, Son, and Holy Spirit represent principles or forces, rather than being distinct Persons.

Jesus was not born of virgin birth.
He is a son of God not His equal.
He is the "higher self" of every person.

Divine Science.
The development of love,
life and truth.

Matter and evil
(including all inharmony, sin,
disease and death) are unreal.

Man is already saved.

Jehovah's Witnesses

Satan is the originator of the idea of the trinity. The Father is greater and older than the Son.

Jesus is a creation of God and not divine in His own right. Before He came to earth He was in heaven as the angel Michael.

Not a separate personality but God's active force by which He accomplishes His purpose.

There are two kinds of sin: inherited, which does not incur death; and willful, which brings a sentence of everlasting destruction.

You must love, proclaim and remain true to Jehovah's sovereignty at all costs to escape Armageddon.

Eckankar

All who help mankind in this world and who seek peace and social reform are deceived. Reformers are doomed to a lower distorted world.

Only the living Eck Master can bring this grace to those who seek it.

Gives life to all.

The voice of Sugmad.

One of the many Eck masters along with Krishna, Vishnu, Zeus, Buddha.

Sugmad (God) is present in all life.

Unification Church ("Moonies")

God's essential positivity and negativity are attributes of his character: male and female respectively.

Jesus failed. Rev. Moon saves us physically.

The Holy Spirit is female.
Since the Spirit is the true mother, one cannot become the bride of Christ without "her."

Lucifer felt a decrease of love and tempted Eve to submit to him, this was the motivation of the fall.

God had to send Rev. Moon, since Jesus was crucified.

Rosicrucians

We came from the one Omnipotent Spirit as unconscious spirits.

The highest initiate of the Sun period.

Reincarnated many times before occupying the body of Christ.

The law saves.

Man must attain spiritual enlightenment.

Dealing with False Teaching

Winter #6

What Do You Say?

Read the statements below and decide whether you
agree or disagree with each one.

1. A false teaching is not the same as a difference in interpretation.

2. If a church is truly a Christian church, it will not have any false teachings.

3. A church can be correct in many of its beliefs and still be false in some.

4. A sincere Christian can have an incorrect understanding of a Bible passage.

The Biblical Brilliance Quiz

Read 1 John 2:24-27; John 16:12-15; Acts 17:11; 2 Timothy 3:16,17; Hebrews 4:12; Hebrews 10:24,25. Then complete the statements below by selecting the correct word(s) to fill in the blanks.

1. The people John wrote to in 1 John had probably "heard from the beginning"

   that _____.
   a. nice people wash their hands before dinner
   b. Jesus was the Son of God
   c. Jesus was one of God's children just as they were

2. The Holy Spirit teaches believers _____
   a. how to get ahead in life
   b. how to "tune-in" to the cosmos
   c. truth

3. The Bereans were more noble than the Thessalonians because _____
   a. they received more blessings from God
   b. they didn't eat meat
   c. they received the gospel eagerly and compared it to Scripture

4. Christians today should _____ like the Bereans.
   a. be suspicious of Paul
   b. study Scripture
   c. be noble

5. Scripture comes from _____
   a. wise teachers
   b. a bunch of guys who died 1,900 years ago
   c. God

6. Scripture is good for _____.
   a. impressing others with your good memory
   b. teaching, rebuking and training
   c. recording ancient customs and poetry

7. One way Christians can continue to grow is by _____
   a. giving each other vitamins as gifts
   b. not developing bad habits
   c. sharing with and encouraging one another regularly

8. Based on the Scriptures you have just read and on your own ideas and experiences, list ideas for ways believers can prepare themselves to recognize and deal with false teachings.

Encounter in Samaria

Examine the incident recorded in John 4:1-26. Notice how Jesus treated the woman and how He dealt with her religious questions. Then write a modern-day incident similar to the biblical one, in which a Christian young person is talking to a person who is involved with an organization that promotes an unbiblical teaching about Christ. **The Christian should respond to the other person with the same kind of courtesy and care that Jesus showed to the Samaritan woman.**

Think Defensively, Act Lovingly

When confronted with a religious teaching you're not sure about, you need to check it out. You need to be prepared to defend yourself against it if it is false. And at the same time you need to be gracious toward the person who is presenting it to you. (Remember, many of the people in cults are unknowingly misled and are desperately trying to find God. They are not necessarily foaming-at-the-mouth mad dog agitators.) The following pointers will help you when you encounter cults.

---

1. **Know what you believe.**

   You need to know what the Bible says. You find out by reading *and studying* it.

2. **Don't make any quick decisions.**

   Situations can be manipulated to make just about anything look right at the moment. Don't make choices based on emotions; make them based on your intellect, which involves your study of the Word with the help of the Holy Spirit.

3. **Seek the wisdom of others.**

   Ask for advice and insights from spiritually mature people.

4. **Check out the facts.**

   God's truth can stand up to investigation. Check out what you hear with what the Word of God says.

5. **Don't be fooled by those who distort the Bible.**

   Anyone can twist the meaning of Scriptures. That's why it's important to have a good grasp of the Word of God.

6. **Remember that God loves the person.**

   Jesus died for all of us, even the person who is trying to sell you on a false doctrine. Be kind and courteous.

7. **Keep your cool.**

   Even if a person frustrates you with his or her insistence on certain teachings that are obviously unbiblical, don't become angry or hostile. Just keep pointing to the truth in God's Word. Let the Holy Spirit work in the person's heart.

"Every spirit that acknowledges that Jesus Christ has come in the flesh is from God, but every spirit that does not acknowledge Jesus is not from God" (1 John 4:2,3, NIV).

"Who is the liar? It is the man who denies that Jesus is the Christ" (1 John 2:22, NIV).

Walking in God's Light #6

Plan of Action _____

Use this sheet to plan how you will approach and talk to someone you know who is involved in a cult or other form of false teaching. You might wish to write your plan in dialogue form, supplying the words you think your friend will say. Or you might wish to write only your side of the dialogue, planning what you could say to express clearly the biblical teachings about Christ. Remember to stick to the essentials and not get sidetracked on less important issues.

Cult this person is in:

Scriptures I will use:

What these Scriptures mean:

How I will get together with the person:

Something I could do to demonstrate the love of Christ to the person:

R Is for Relationship

Whose God?

So you think you're a history whiz, huh? Let's see! Listed below are the legendary gods of various cultures. Match the name of the deity with the description in the right hand column.

Janus_____

Bacchus_____

Osiris_____

Molech_____

Pele_____

Thor_____

Buck_____

a. A Scandinavian god who possessed great strength. He was supposed to have gotten his jollies by beating up all the demon-type gods.

b. The Egyptian god of the underworld; a funerary god.

c. The Roman god of the door from whom we get the name of one of the months. He was thought to be one of the many gods who resided in homes.

d. A small paper deity worshiped in the western hemisphere in the twentieth century.

e. The Greek god of wine.

f. A god worshiped by the Ammonites. He was appeased by the sacrifice of children on his fiery arms.

g. The Hawaiian goddess of the volcano. She literally blew her top when she was displeased.

Fact Finder _____

"And now, dear children, continue in him, so that when he appears we may be confident and unashamed before him at his coming.

"If you know that he is righteous, you know that everyone who does what is right has been born of him.

"How great is the love the Father has lavished on us, that we should be called children of God! And that is what we are! The reason the world does not know us is that it did not know him. Dear friends, now we are children of God, and what we will be has not yet been made known. But we know that when he appears, we shall be like him, for we shall see him as he is. Everyone who has this hope in him purifies himself, just as he is pure.

"Everyone who sins breaks the law; in fact, sin is lawlessness. But you know that he appeared so that he might take away our sins. And in him is no sin. No one who lives in him keeps on sinning. No one who continues to sin has either seen him or known him.

"Dear children, do not let anyone lead you astray. He who does what is right is righteous, just as he is righteous. He who does what is sinful is of the devil, because the devil has been sinning from the beginning. The reason the Son of God appeared was to destroy the devil's work. No one who is born of God will continue to sin, because God's seed remains in him; he cannot go on sinning, because he has been born of God. This is how we know who the children of God are and who the children of the devil are: Anyone who does not do what is right is not a child of God; neither is anyone who does not love his brother."

1 John 2:28—3:10 *(NIV)*

One Fine Day in a Traffic Jam

(Based on a True Incident)

GRRR! LOUSY TRAFFIC! LOUSY TRAFFIC LIGHTS! I'M GONNA BE LATE FOR SURE!

BEEP WHAT IS THAT FOOL BEHIND ME DOING? CAN'T HE FIGURE OUT THAT I CAN'T GO ANYWHERE IN THIS MESS?

BEEP BEEP ARGHH! WHAT A JERK! I'M IN JUST AS MUCH A HURRY AS HE IS.

BEEEEP THAT DOES IT! ONE MORE TIME AND I'M GONNA GIVE THAT x&*#!& A PIECE OF MY MIND!

BEEP &*%$-@!&(+&!!! @& !? &&3

OK, WHAT ON EARTH ARE YOU BLOWING YOUR STINKING HORN AT ME FOR ?!? ...

And then . . .

The Last Frame

. . . Draw what you think happened next.

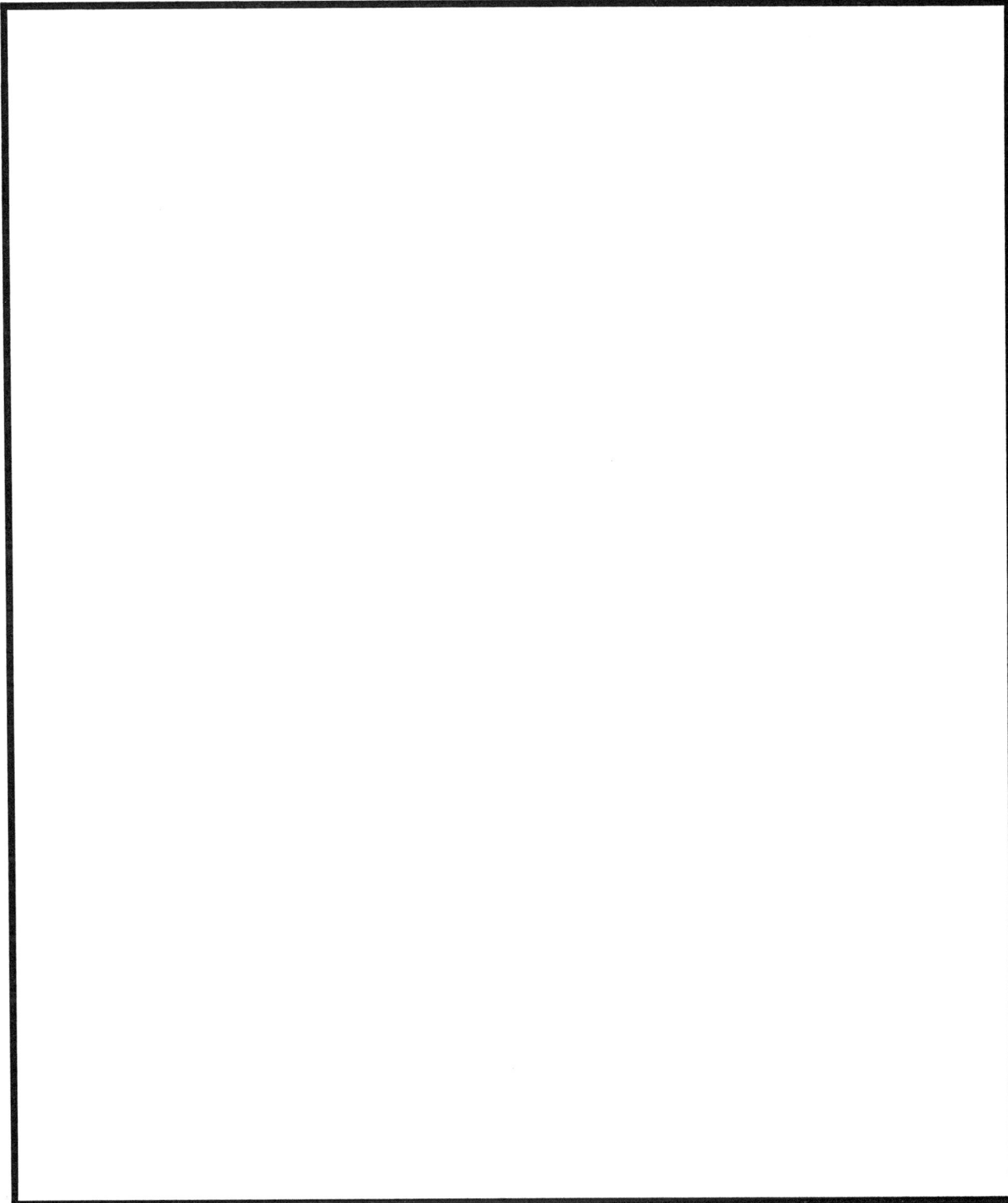

The Last Frame

What really happened:

What Can a Poor Kid Do?

Read **Matthew 25:34-46; Luke 14:12-14 and James 1:17.** Make a list of the examples of people in need that are given or implied in the Scripture. Next, try to describe the situation in your community which most closely parallels the biblical example.

Finally try to give a good example of what a person your age could do to help correct the situation or show caring in the situation.

Biblical Examples	A Parallel in My Community	What Could Be Done to Help

Personalize . . .

If <u>anyone</u> has material possessions
(your name)

and <u>sees his brother in need</u> but
(someone in need)

<u>has no pity</u> on him, how can the
(something you can do to meet his or her needs)

love of God be in him?

1 John 3:17

Rewrite this verse
and personalize it.

Get God's Assurance

Winter #9

Walking in God's Light

Tips on What to Do

1. **Investigate, study, explore. Truth can stand investigation. Research until the doubt dies.**

2. **Make sure of your commitment. Some people use doubts as excuses for not having to live the way God wants them to.**

3. **Trust God's promises, not your own emotions.**

4. **Reinforce yourself with the assurance that "Everything is possible for him who believes" (Mark 9:23; see also Phil. 4:13). Depend on God to help develop your skills and your character.**

5. **Look for signs of His love. It's even OK to be emotional in your search. The writers of some of the Psalms cried and pleaded for God to reveal Himself to them. Just be careful that you aren't so caught up in your own problems and emotions that you miss the indications of God's love when they come!**

6. **Put your faith and trust in God. Don't look back at what happened in the past. Fix your focus on God and keep walking with Him.**

I'm Not Sure

Read the case study assigned to you. Then determine what the person should do, based on the Scripture you have studied in 1 John, to develop assurance of his or her salvation.

Steve

Steve accepted Christ several years ago, but recently he has begun to question whether he really has eternal life. His grandfather died not long ago, and Steve was very upset. He missed his grandfather so much that he questioned God's goodness and love. Now he wonders if that time of doubt means that he is not saved.

Lisa

Lisa works at a hamburger place after school. Some of the other people who work there believe that Jesus was a man who was temporarily filled with God's Son, but was not actually God in the flesh. Lisa isn't sure what to make of this teaching or how it stacks up against the Bible. It is confusing her so much that she is no longer sure of her own relationship with God.

Don

Don is a person almost everybody likes. He's willing to go out of his way to help others, especially those in some sort of need. He received Christ several years ago, and his kindness has been increasing ever since. But Don is very sensitive to sin. He has become terribly aware of his own sinful nature, and has begun to wonder how he can possibly be God's child.

Theresa

Theresa has been going to church all her life. Some of her earliest memories involve her parents telling her how much Jesus loves her. When she was a small child she decided that she loved Jesus and wanted Him to be part of her life. Now that she is older, though, that childhood decision seems rather dim and remote. She just isn't sure any more if she really belongs to God or not.

Jack

Jack has a teacher who makes fun of Christian beliefs. Even though Jack has received Christ and loves the Lord, he is beginning to wonder about some of the events in the Bible that his teacher ridicules, such as the resurrection of Christ.

Frankly . . . I Doubt It!

John wrote his Epistle to Christians who were having some doubts about their relationship with God and some struggles about doctrine because they had been influenced by false teachers. Other people of God down through the years have also struggled with doubts. In our age, unfortunately, some Christians have made people with honest doubts feel very unwelcome. (An honest doubt is one which we will actively try to resolve; it's not something we are using as an excuse to avoid God.)

Fortunately, God is able to use people in spite of their apprehensions about themselves and even their questions about Him.

Read **1 John 3:19—4:6.** Then read at least one of the additional passages listed below. For each passage, fill in the chart.

Additional passages: **Exodus 3:11—4:13,20; Judges 6:1-18; Matthew 14:22-33; John 20:24-29.**

Who Was Having a Problem with Doubt?	What Was the Doubt About?	What Was the Solution to the Doubt?

Write a paragraph giving an example of how the kind of doubt in the passage(s) you have read might show up in a group like yours.

What Would You Do About It?

For each category described below, write some ideas about what you could do to resolve doubts in that area.

1. **Doubt about the historical reality of some events in Scripture (such as the resurrection of Christ, the Flood, or the origin of the Bible).**

2. **Doubt about personal salvation.**

3. **Doubt about your ability to do what God has asked of you.**

4. **Doubt about God's love, care, presence and protection.**

Review Your Assurance Policy

Do you need God's assurance? If yes, complete this section.

Assurance of Salvation

Evaluate your life for the last three months by marking the chart with a 1, 2, or 3 for each area.

1 = never   2 = sometimes   3 = usually

	three months ago	two months ago	last month
I treated my family with consideration.			
I went out of my way to help other people.			
I treated my friends well even when they didn't do so to me.			
I believed that Jesus is God in the flesh.			

If you don't see any improvement in your capacity to show selfless love or in your convictions about Christ, note any struggles and improvements in attitude that only God knows about.

Do you have God's assurance? If yes, complete this section.

Thank you Father, because . . .

Do you need to commit yourself to God? Talk to Him about it in prayer. (You can do this inside your head, or write a prayer on a piece of paper.)

Are you unsure about God or about what you want to do? Maybe talking it over with your teacher or pastor will help. Don't be afraid to say, "I don't understand."

I Tend to Have Doubts . . .

. . . in the area of:

Next time I have these doubts, I will take the following steps to resolve them:

Even if I've never had a doubt in my life; I can make some plans for handling doubts if they ever come. I plan to:

Buy into God's Kind of Love

Winter #10

Walking in God's Light

Take Apart Love

Dear friends, let us love one another, for love comes from God. **1.**	We love because he first loved us. **8.**
Everyone who loves has been born of God and knows God. **2.**	If anyone says, "I love God," yet hates his brother, he is a liar. **9.**
Whoever does not love does not know God, because God is love. **3.**	For anyone who does not love his brother, whom he has seen, cannot love God, whom he has not seen. **10.**
This is how God showed his love among us: He sent his one and only Son into the world that we might live through him. **4.**	And he has given us this command: Whoever loves God must also love his brother. **11.**
This is love: not that we loved God, but that he loved us and sent his Son as an atoning sacrifice for our sins. **5.**	
Dear friends, since God so loved us, we also ought to love one another. **6.**	
No one has ever seen God; but if we love each other, God lives in us and his love is made complete in us. **7.**	

1 John 4:7-12, 19-21, *NIV*

For Instance

Sometimes we can read a whole passage of very deep thoughts without very much of it sinking in. Some parts of 1 John are like that.

Try taking a verse from 1 John 4:7-12 or 19-21 and giving it roots by describing a "for instance" from everyday life.

Here's an example taken from 1 John 4:6, which says, "We are from God, and whoever knows God listens to us":

For instance, if a group of us are in a discussion at lunch time and some spiritual idea comes up, those who are Christians or who are open to God will not shut out what is being said. Those not interested in God may not listen, and might even get up and leave.

Brain Busters

The problem with love is that some people feel that they have not received their fair share. Look at the ideas below and come up with a good answer for at least one of them.

1. If God is love, He can't send people to hell!

2. God cannot be a God of love and allow people (especially believers) to suffer.

3. A loving God will not be strict with His children.

4. Why would a loving God make a lot of rules to spoil our enjoyment of life?

5. A God of love would not permit all the hunger, illness, and other suffering we have in the world today.

Determine
God's
L.Q.*

Read 1 John 4:7-12, 19-21 and answer at least one set of questions.

*Love Quotient

God and love (verses 7-10)

1. What is the source of love, according to verse 7?

2. What do you think John meant when he said that God is love (verse 8)?

3. How do you define God's kind of love? (For further help, see 1 Corinthians 13:4-8.)

Christ's sacrifice (verses 9,10)

1. What do you think John meant by "his one and only Son" in verse 9?

2. Describe God's probable feelings about sending His Son. (See Isaiah 42:1.)

3. Why did John include "not that we loved God" in verse 10?

Loving others with God's love (verses 11,12,19-21)

1. Compare the reason why most people love others with John's reason for loving other people (verses 11, 19). What difference does it make?

2. "If we love each other, God lives in us and his love is made complete in us" (v. 12, *NIV*). What does that mean? What does that have to do with no one having seen God?

3. John said that people who claim to love God, yet hate their brothers, are liars (see verse 20). Why is this so?

Because He Loves Me . . .

**In the space below write some ideas about ways
you could respond to God's love for you.**

Live-in Help

The letter of 1 John talks about believers living in God and God living in us. Read 1 John 4:13-18. Then create a job description that shows what a Christian needs to do as "live-in help," living for Christ. Also list the benefits of this job.

The person who lives in God needs to do the following:

The benefits of this position include the following:

Devotional

By:

Read:

Some thoughts on this passage:

A question to consider:

Something to Ponder

Sometimes we can get more out of our Bible study if we focus our attention on a series of questions and use paper and pencil to note our ideas. The questions listed here will help you do this. You may wish to use them in your personal Bible study at home. For now, read 1 John 4:13-18 and answer one or more of the questions.

What does this tell me about God?

What does this tell me about myself?

What promise does this give me?

What instruction do I find here?

What part of this Scripture do I want to try to remember throughout the day?

Resolve the _____ Riddle
WINTER #12

Walking in God's Light

Pick from the Pile . . .

. . . The best word to describe the idea conveyed by *all* the pictures.

Kindness   Spirituality

Faithfulness

Self-discipline

Love

Stewardship

Obedience   Service

Forgiveness

Trustworthiness

Responsibility

Yeah, I guess I could spare a little more...

Hidden
Highlights

Read 1 John 5:1-12. Some key words from this Scripture passage are hidden in the word puzzle below. Circle the words (look across, up and down and diagonally).

```
K   W   K   G   I   V   E   N   L   M   N   L   B   Q   G   B   C
O   D   E   S   R   E   I   E   V   E   R   Y   O   N   E   M   T
L   D   S   T   I   O   N   C   P   M   P   F   R   V   Q   H   E
G   R   J   P   L   J   S   H   T   O   E   F   N   Y   E   Q   S
E   R   H   Y   I   I   Z   R   C   O   M   M   A   N   D   S   T
U   G   E   T   F   R   A   I   R   V   R   D   H   I   W   Z   I
E   S   A   A   E   P   I   S   F   E   C   Y   T   O   T   A   M
P   O   R   G   T   W   A   T   E   R   W   O   R   L   D   H   O
D   C   T   V   H   E   R   E   J   C   G   E   U   S   V   R   N
W   G   H   D   S   A   R   B   L   O   O   D   T   O   N   L   Y
A   V   K   R   I   J   B   Q   T   M   D   A   H   N   G   I   S
U   B   E   L   I   E   V   E   S   E   T   E   R   N   A   L   T
```

List the reasons highlighted in these verses for obeying Christ:

Good Ol' First Church

The high school crew at First Church (Podunk, U.S.A.) is an obedient lot. But they could be a dud of a youth group if they obeyed for the wrong reasons. (In fact, they could be downright dangerous if they obeyed God for the wrong reasons.) Fill in the thought balloons in the first set of pictures as if these people were being obedient because of fear, peer pressure, guilt, or other not-so-good motivations. Then fill in the thought balloons of the second set of pictures showing the same group being obedient because they love God.

Bite
the
Bullet

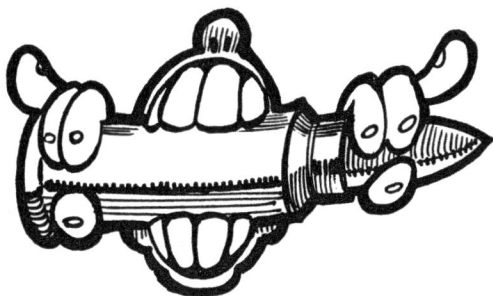

1. Name an area of your life in which you need to initiate more obedience.

2. How could love and/or faith make it more enjoyable to obey?

Undigested Reader Department

The Abbreviated 1 John

Together with a friend, read over 1 John. In your own
words abbreviate the book to fit on this page by pulling
out the main thoughts and ideas from the book and
stating them simply.

KEY VERSES

Deal with Sinful Tendencies

1. "We proclaim to you what we have seen and heard so that you may have fellowship with us. And our fellowship is with the Father and his Son, Jesus Christ. We write this to make our joy complete." (1 John 1:3,4)

2. "If we confess our sins, he is faithful and just and will forgive us our sins and purify us from all unrighteousness." (1 John 1:9)

3. "My dear children, I write this to you so that you will not sin (continually); . . . But if anyone obeys his word, God's love is truly made complete in him." (1 John 2:1a, 5a)

4. "Do not love the world or anything in the world. If anyone loves the world, the love of the Father is not in him." (1 John 2:15)

Major in Central Issues

5. "Who is the liar? It is the man who denies that Jesus is the Christ. Such a man is the antichrist—he denies the Father and the Son." (1 John 2:22)

6. "Now the Bereans were of more noble character than the Thessalonians, for they received the message with great eagerness and examined the Scriptures every day to see if what Paul said was true." (Acts 17:11)

7. "How great is the love the Father has lavished on us, that we should be called children of God! And that is what we are!" (1 John 3:1)

8. "If anyone has material possessions and sees his brother in need but has no pity on him, how can the love of God be in him?" (1 John 3:17)

Cultivate Godly Characteristics

9. "The one who is in you is greater than the one who is in the world." (1 John 4:4)

10. "Dear friends, since God so loved us, we also ought to love one another." (1 John 4:11)

11. "And so we know and rely on the love God has for us. God is love. Whoever lives in love lives in God, and God in him." (1 John 4:16)

12. "This is love for God: to obey his commands. And his commands are not burdensome, for everyone born of God overcomes the world." (1 John 5:3,4)

Maturity

13. "We know also that the Son of God has come and has given us understanding, so that we may know him who is true. And we are in him who is true—even in his Son Jesus Christ." (1 John 5:20)

All Scriptures quoted in this page are from *NIV*.

Design-It-Yourself Section!

The following pages contain all sorts of fun artwork. Cut 'em out, paste 'em up, and there you have it! A beautiful handbill, poster, or mailer like this one:

(Only bigger!)

On the inside rear cover you will find a grid pattern you can use in a number of ways:

- Use it for an eye-catching background like our mailer above.

- Use it to design your own crossword puzzles or other word games.

- Put a photocopy of it on a light box as shown. Use the lines to help you make your pasted up art straight. Much easier than using a ruler and T-square!

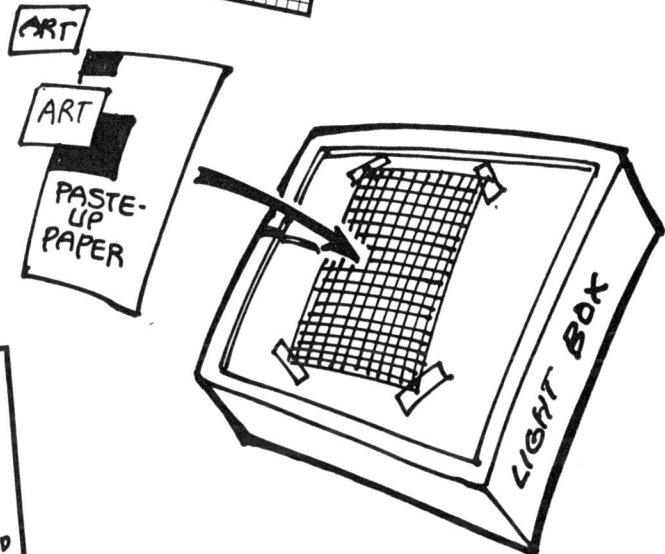

We've included a page full of "comment cards" which are very useful in youth work. Photocopy onto cardstock, or have a local printer run them off for you. Make them available at each meeting.

You'll also find a handy form for making a calendar mail-out. Fill it up with all the great activities you have planned, and encourage your youth group members to hang their copies up at home.

Be sure to look for additional "Design-It-Yourself" sections in other Light Force youth courses!

New Year's event

NEW YEAR'S MOVIE NITE!

Merry Christmas!

Valentine's day

KA-THUK!

KA-THUK!

Merry Christmas!

Announcement pointers and banners

Calendar form

SUNDAY	MONDAY	TUESDAY	WEDNESDAY	THURSDAY	FRIDAY	SATURDAY

Comment Card

Name _____

Address _____

Zip _____ Phone _____

School _____

Grade _____ Birthdate _____

Age _____

Check any or all.

☐ I'd like to become a Christian

☐ I'd like to talk to someone

☐ I'd like prayer for _____

☐ Please put me on your mailing list

☐ Other: _____

_____

_____

Comment Card

Name _____

Address _____

Zip _____ Phone _____

School _____

Grade _____ Birthdate _____

Age _____

Check any or all.

☐ I'd like to become a Christian

☐ I'd like to talk to someone

☐ I'd like prayer for _____

☐ Please put me on your mailing list

☐ Other: _____

_____

_____

Comment Card

Name _____

Address _____

Zip _____ Phone _____

School _____

Grade _____ Birthdate _____

Age _____

Check any or all.

☐ I'd like to become a Christian

☐ I'd like to talk to someone

☐ I'd like prayer for _____

☐ Please put me on your mailing list

☐ Other: _____

_____

_____

Comment Card

Name _____

Address _____

Zip _____ Phone _____

School _____

Grade _____ Birthdate _____

Age _____

Check any or all.

☐ I'd like to become a Christian

☐ I'd like to talk to someone

☐ I'd like prayer for _____

☐ Please put me on your mailing list

☐ Other: _____

_____

_____